Pasta
Classica

NOVA
ITALIÆ
DELINEATIO

Julia della Croce's Pasta Classica

125 authentic Italian recipes

CHRONICLE BOOKS • SAN FRANCISCO

Printed in Singapore by Toppan Printing Co. (s) Pte. Ltd.

Library of Congress Cataloging-in-Publication Data
della Croce, Julia.
  Pasta classica.

  Includes index.
  1. Cookery (Macaroni)   2. Cookery, Italian.   I. Title.
TX809.M17D45 1987   641.8'22   87-13515
ISBN 0-87701-414-0

ISBN 0-8118-0248-5 (pbk).

Book: Linda Herman + Company
Composition: G & S Typesetters, Inc.

Distributed in Canada by
Raincoast Books
112 East 3rd Avenue
Vancouver, B.C.
V5T 1C8

10 9 8 7 6 5 4 3 2 1

Chronicle Books
275 Fifth St.
San Francisco, CA
94103

For my mother,
Giustina Ghisu della Croce,
and her mother before her,
Giulia Esu Ghisu

TABLE OF CONTENTS

Acknowledgments

The writing of this book was to a great extent made possible by the help, kindness, and generosity of many people. My husband, Bob Stien, in encouraging my complete devotion to this project, as well as his enthusiasm for Italy, its people and its food, was a great source of joy, strength, and inspiration. Flavia Destefanis led me to discoveries about the authentic Italian kitchen that I would have otherwise never known. I cannot imagine this project without her intelligence, knowledge, and assistance. Eva Agnesi and the Museo Storico degli Spaghetti in Pontedassio (Imperia) provided me with much of the extraordinary artwork that graces this book, and I am deeply grateful. Paolo Destefanis went far beyond the photographer's assignment in helping me to acquire artwork.

Much of the original inspiration for this book came from my family. From snail-hunting forays in Pompeii to boat rides in search of sea urchin and other edible mollusks off the coast of Cagliari, my childhood memories have lingered deliciously and formed my pride in and passion for Italian food. But mostly, credit should go to my mother, an extraordinary and incorruptible Italian cook, who taught me so much of what I know. During the two years it took to complete this book, she spent many long hours in my kitchen helping to create and test recipes.

Last, to Nancy Q. Keefe, without whom none of this would have ever begun, and my editor, Bill LeBlond, I express my deepest gratitude.

Pasta Classica

INTRODUCTION

Pasta is the creation of the professional housewife. Under economic pressure, and by exploiting local ingredients for sauces, the various typical kinds of pasta were born. Every housewife used to prepare almost daily the same dish. It had to be perfect, but it also had to be better than her neighbor's, as if it were part of her own beauty.

—Professor Peter Kubelka
Pastario

Sellers of Cooked Macaroni, *by Nappa, Litògrafo Migliorata Editore, early 19th century.*

2

This is a book for home cooks and pasta lovers, a celebration of the best Italian pasta cookery. It is a compendium of recipes that date back to the Renaissance, when Italy developed a revolutionary form of cooking, a style that relied on diverse fresh ingredients instead of spices for flavor. I've included both classic and original preparations in the best Italian tradition. There are also some modern dishes that make use of new culinary ideas while adhering to the long-held Italian notions of simplicity and harmony in cooking.

As kitchen putterer, professional cook, culinary writer, and restaurant critic, I have enjoyed cooking and eating pasta. Of the many international forms that pasta takes, none, to me, are so delightful as those of the Italians. In short, the intention of this book is to entice you to take a culinary journey with me, fork in hand, through the irresistible world of Italian pasta, a world sadly misunderstood outside Italy. It will be a beautiful journey with clear, bright colors—the opulent red of tomatoes, the precious gold of saffron, the vibrant greens of basil, parsley, rosemary, and spinach—heady smells, and beguiling flavors.

I have gathered the recipes for this book from Italian sources, by studying, watching, listening, and tasting. Mostly, though, they reflect what I have learned from my mother, whose skill and good taste in culinary matters never cease to amaze me. A number of them are variations on classic Italian ways of preparing pasta. Some are heirlooms, some my own adaptations. Others were given to me by professional chefs and home cooks whose kitchens I have found culinary strongholds. Still others are favorites that I remember with special clearness from the homes, restaurants, and *trattorie* I have eaten in during time spent in Italy. Recipes of historical interest are included only if they are easy to follow and if they produce creations that modern people would enjoy. All of the dishes recall the flavors, perfumes, and hues of pasta's natural homeland.

Probably few Americans grew up eating as many different forms of pasta as I did. My mother, thank heaven, did not come from the same school as many American Italians who too often trade exuberant home cooking for bland convenience, or who have never had the opportunity to learn the rich culinary tradition of their ancestors. My mother was fresh from Italy, so to speak, having met and married my father there after the last war. When she came here, she brought only her most treasured possessions, and packets of fragrant saffron and lovely recipes dating from her Sardinian child-

The Macaroni Eater, *by G. Dura,*
Litògrafo Gatti & Dura, 19th century.

hood and her adolescence in Rome.

It was not only that she loved to cook. It was her quiet passion. It was her poetry. In the way of other great Italian cooks I have known (home and professional cooks alike), she just *knew* what went with what. She never departed from the quintessential Italian sense of harmony of flavors and reverence for fresh ingredients. She was always an adventurous cook, trying to work with things she'd never seen before, such as American squashes, indigenous seafoods and game, and other native and foreign foods previously unfamiliar to her.

I can remember only two cookbooks in the house where I grew up. One was a 1954 edition of *The Family Circle Cake and Cookie Cookbook,* with a photograph of a pink layer cake on the cover. I think my mother bought it to learn what she could about American cooking, though I don't think she ever used it. When she used a cookbook at all, it was her 1946 edition of Ada Boni's *Il Talismano della Felicità* ("The Talisman of Happiness"), containing some two thousand recipes from as far back as the Renaissance. It now sits on my oak credenza, yellowed and crumbling, alluring and wonderful. Although I never understood those Italian measures (what was an *ettogrammo?*), I understood the words: *fettuccine primaverili, maccheroni Principe di Napoli, rigatoni con gli uccellini.* The prescriptions calling for fresh basil, tender artichokes, little birds, baby lamb still form beautiful images in my mind of what Italian cooking truly is.

My mother stocked our cupboard with fresh garlic, saffron, rosemary and other aromatics, pine nuts, imported dried mushrooms called *porcini,* and sharp black olives. We always had fresh lemons and good olive oil on hand. But in characteristic Italian fashion, the fresh seasonal flavors of carefully, even reverently cooked foods were at the heart of her table.

We ate plenty of lamb and veal as well as beef and chicken. The many innards (politely called "variety meats" by the A & P) that my mother bought, both for economy and because we loved them, inevitably caused the grocery cashiers in Rockland County, New York, to wrinkle their noses in disgust as they bagged kidney, tripe, heart, brain, and sweetbreads. We always had fresh vegetables, even watercress foraged from a stream in a nearby wood no doubt long gone. My mother made *gnocchi* at home, and we ate pasta in endless variations that depended on what was in the market, in our little garden, or in her fancy. I think of her tomato and *orzo* soup with special delight, of the just-cut noodles that were served with the savory drippings of Sunday's roast, or of the *maccheroni* with broccoli and anchovies that was the all-time family favorite. When she prepared these dishes, even the children stuffed their tiny bellies with at least two helpings, and after that, scrapped for the bits that were left at the bottom of the bowl.

The Italians eat farinaceous foods other than pasta. On my mother's native island of Sardinia, which was once trespassed by the nomadic Saracens, bread and a type of couscous are staples. In other parts of Italy, *polenta* (cornmeal) or rice predominates. But in the last century, even in the north, where it was little known before the war except for the homemade variety, it is pasta that is ubiquitous, and that so engenders our loyalty.

Pasta and the Italians

We really don't know where pasta got its start. In almost every nation where there is wheat, there is pasta in some form or other—Chinese *mein,* Japanese *udon,* French *nouilles,* Polish *pierogi,* German *spaetzle,* Siberian *pel'meni.* But the Italians have, from the beginning, claimed pasta as their own, and the rest of the world defers. The reason is pure and simple. In the words of Italian poet Filippo-Tommaso Marinetti, pasta "is the Italian gastronomic religion."

It is a food to which are ascribed potent and poetic qualities, perhaps because it has abated starvation in the poor southern regions of Italy for centuries. Its gentle composition invites communion with all manner of sauces and spicings, and numerous affectionate names. For the Italians can't seem to resist the impulse to christen all the little ribbons, strings, and lovely shapes with superlatives and diminutives. I would like to think that some passionate eater of long ago, who loved pasta as much as I do, gave it the name it has today, which has stuck to it as naturally as sauce to a noodle. For the word *maccheroni* is thought to have derived from *ma, che carini!* which literally means, "My! What little dears!" There are *lumache,* "snails"; *amorini,* "little loves"; *ziti,* "bridegrooms"; and even *tirabaci,* "kiss catchers." These are flour-and-water artifacts of Italian life, and can be anointed with countless artful sauces.

In Italy, there are three hundred names for one hundred pasta shapes. The seemingly endless variations of *maccheroni* reflect the expansive nature of the Italian people, their love of variety and their love of show. It is not enough to make pasta bows (*farfalle*); there must also be little bows (*farfallette*) and much bigger bows (*farfalloni*). There are not only small reeds (*cannelle*), but also very small reeds, large reeds, large smooth reeds, and large grooved reeds. There are clowns' hats and priests' hats, trouts' eyes, wolves' eyes, and sparrows' tongues.

A pulcinella at the Roman Carnival, by Bartolomeo Pinelli, 1821.

5

Eating spaghetti outdoors, by an unknown artist, 19th century.

All this imagery is not so surprising when you think of the Italians—the prodigious animation in their every activity, their flair for the dramatic and the artistic, their *gusto* for life. The air of Italy is always filled with many voices, all speaking at once. The government changes on the average of once a year. From Tiepolo ceilings to sleek Ferraris, from making love to making pasta, Italians joyfully combine necessity with style. With their voluptuous dispositions, they produce masterpieces of art and cuisine that the whole world loves.

Few people outside Italy realize how dramatically pasta dishes vary from region to region. The reasons for this are based in history as well as temperament. For in spite of unification in 1861 (nearly a century *after* the United States became a nation), Italy's nineteen regions, divided by geography and by centuries of political turmoil, remain individual entities, each with a distinct culture and cuisine. Every region—indeed every town—has its own special and "superior" version of some dish or other.

In a cliffside restaurant in Sorrento, you can order *spaghetti alle vongole,* delicious pasta specked with the smooth little greenish-shelled clams that burrow in the beds of the Mediterranean Sea. In Sicily, which was dominated by the Saracens for almost two centuries, you might find raisins in your pasta dish, an ingredient reminiscent of the Levant. In the mountainous, inland region near the Swiss border, you are likely to encounter the local *fontina* cheese in such dishes as the Piedmontese specialty of egg noodles with *fonduta,* "fondue."

Generally speaking, pasta in the south has traditionally been made with coarse flour made from durum wheat, called semolina, and water. In the richer north, noodles are made with white flour and eggs and characteristically sauced with butter, cream sauces, and other luxuries such as meat and the revered truffle.

La Vera Cucina Italiana
The True Italian Kitchen

To understand the nature of the authentic Italian pasta kitchen, it is necessary to know something about Italy's history. The biggest influences on Italian cooking came from the Etruscans, the Greeks, and the Saracens, and from the Crusaders bringing foods and spices and ideas about eating back from the East. Once seminated, culinary customs were rooted in the peasant class. For this reason, traditional Italian cooking is called *la cucina casalinga,* "home-style cooking."

Civilization in Italy started with the Etruscans, those ancient, peaceful people who had the good sense to come to this beautiful land before anyone else did. No historian has ever figured out where they came from, when exactly they came, or why. They built underground cities in which to hide from the Romans, but finally, setting a precedent that continued for centuries of Italian history, the Etruscans let the invaders in. Ever since, up until Mussolini let in the Nazis, the Italians have tolerated, welcomed, and even wooed foreigners. It is hard to say why, and since even the Italians can't say, we will leave speculation aside. The fact is that they did, and because they did, Italian cuisine is an intoxicating amalgam of foreign influences and native ingredients.

The Greeks contributed their love of seafood, but left behind more philosophy than recipes. They had great things to say about the wisdom of moderation and good sense in eating. As the world knows, it was a lesson never learned by the otherwise derivative Romans, who preferred spice and pomp with their food. According to Reay Tannahill (*Food in History*), "[Rich] Romans certainly appear to have had a rooted dislike for natural, unadulterated flavors and customarily gave meat, fish and vegetables an entirely new complexion with sauces consisting of at least a dozen strong ingredients."

The Saracens as well as the migrating Jews, whose presence is at least as old as the Romans, had a genius for stove-top cooking, a technique popular with people on the move. This method still characterizes most of Italy's cooking. There are many Italian recipes that originated with the Hebrews, whose oppression by the Romans is well-known. The Saracens introduced numerous foods— buckwheat, spinach, nuts, spices, and aromatics—that continue to play a role in the cuisine. From the Americas came the tomato, peppers, squashes, potatoes, turkey, and chocolate.

Unlike France, where gastronomy was codified into a highly technical art, cooking in Italy remained informal. Despite the indulgences of the very rich, it kept its peasant aspects. For all the diverse cultures and localized tradition within its geographical boundaries, the Italian landscape and climate offered similar raw materials. Cheeses, sausages, hams, and breads have been made throughout the country for centuries, although they differ from region to region. These basic ingredients, as well as oil from what Aldous Huxley so aptly called the "numinous" olive tree, are common to all Italian cuisine.

The sea nearly surrounds Italy, assuring an extensive network of port trade that saved the Italians from insularity. Thus, despite chronic internal feuding and a fractured political system—a sur-

The Saracens introduced numerous foods to Italy, among them the pistachio. From A Curious Herbal *by Elizabeth Blackwell, London, 1737–39.*

7

vival of the Middle Ages that put town against town, city against city—Italy maintained solid connections with the outside world. The port cities were greatly influenced by other cultures and civilizations. Even throughout the Renaissance, when political relations between the city-states were often tense and sometimes hostile, diplomatic and cultural exchanges continued.

The mother cuisine, as we now know it, is one of harmonious, savory flavors in juxtaposition. Each ingredient stands on its own, unlike French cuisine where each element is blended with others to contribute to a final integrated taste. The shocking tastes associated with northern European dishes are absent, except for some Roman and Venetian sweet-and-sour specialties. There is not the distracting sweetness and the masked spiciness of many foods of the East. Italian cooking has evolved into a pleasant blend of its origins. It is at once gentle and virile, for while its soul is sensual and complex, its preparation is fresh and direct.

So at the same time that Italy is full of diversity, it is also united by a way of cooking that, through its peasant roots, retains a historical and natural connection to the land.

Pasta and the Americans

It is ironic that the dreary standardization of Italian cooking in America was brought on by none other than the Italian immigrants themselves. The staples of their home regions—for the most part, Naples, Sicily, Calabria, and Abruzzi—were the prolific tomato, the rich oil of the tenacious olive tree, and dried pasta. Although a great variety of dishes appears on the native Italian's family table, the formula of tomato sauce and "Parmesan" cheese was fast, profitable, and suited to the unsophisticated American palate. What a sad day for pasta.

Fortunately, America today is in the midst of a gastronomic revolution. The contemporary American palate is less restrained than it once was in its consideration of unfamiliar foods and flavors. Foods once considered strictly ethnic and strange—squid, strong cheeses, chewy *prosciutto,* and sausage of different kinds—have become commonplace, even outside Italian neighborhoods.

Pasta innovations have burst in a spectrum of unorthodox flavors and colors, sauced with everything from caviar to kiwi fruit. It has become fashionable to make pasta in new and complicated ways. Some are good and some are not. The authentic cuisine is so transformed by the addition of every imaginable spice and herb, novelty food and sauce, that the basic ingredients are sometimes scarcely

Italian immigrants waiting to embark for America from the port of Naples, 1910.

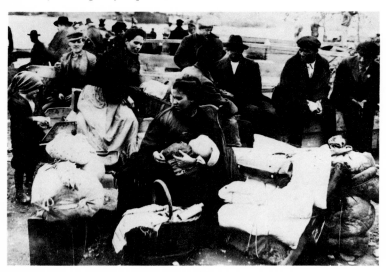

recognizable. The classic Italian school decries the travesty made on what is considered authentic preparation of pasta. An added flavor such as mushroom is meant to go in the sauce, not in the dough. Undaunted, the new school, led by the proponents of what might be called novelty cuisine, crank out pasta in an assortment to rival ice cream producers' propensity to deliver dozens of flavors. Among the creations are red tomato pasta (albeit a classic), purple beet pasta (also with its roots in the classic cuisine), and the more shocking avocado, asparagus, *pesto,* broccoli, mushroom, and curry noodles, combined with such unlikely sauces as raspberry vinegar and walnut-oil dressing. Whereas before we were faced with advice in cooking columns and recipe books to make pasta sauces with such things as Miracle Whip and ketchup, now we are faced with an exotic array of discordant accompaniments.

The Italians make an eloquent case for respecting age-old dicta about pasta. While there is plenty of room for invention of the right sort, the idea is that improvisation in cooking, as in art, should be guided by an understanding of composition and balance, by a point of view that takes experience into account. Thus, spontaneity should result in harmonious, not discordant dishes.

La Nuova Cucina Italiana
The New Italian Kitchen

For a time, even Italian cooks flirted with *nouvelle cuisine.* The result was a frenchified form of cooking unofficially labeled *la nuova cucina,* "the new [Italian] kitchen." At heart, the fad was a challenge to traditional ideas of Italian cooking. It preached streamlining the classic cuisine, and in the spirit of all things modern, minimal portions. One witness to the new movement reported that a chic Milan restaurant served an arrangement of three pieces of macaroni placed between asparagus tips, a presentation better suited to sushi. But pasta? Ingredients never heard of before in Italian cooking were given a fling—avocados, vodka, smoked-fish stuffing for ravioli, walnut oil. Some ideas such as blending sweet with savory flavors harkened back to the Renaissance, to the Middle Ages, and to Rome before that.

Although *la nuova cucina* has left a certain impression on the kitchens of grand hotels and fashionable restaurants, it has gone the way of all fads. I believe that the home kitchen remains the place to find the best Italian cooking.

The underlying mission of this book is to set forth, against a cul-

A French chef spinning sugar. Unlike French cuisine, which evolved into a highly technical art, Italian cooking, with its peasant roots, remained informal.

"... *inde domum me ad porri et ciceris refero, laganique catium.* (... [then] I take myself home to a bowl of leeks, chickpeas, and *lasagne*.)

—Horace

tural and historical background, guidelines for cooking pasta in the Italian manner. In essence, this means using the freshest and best foods obtainable, retaining their character throughout the cooking, and bringing together ingredients that have an affinity with each other. This message is not new. I am merely giving the old ways a new forum. The subtlety, variety, and exuberance of classic Italian cuisine were little known in this country before now. The happy irony is that the simplicity that is the essential attribute of authentic pasta cookery is in perfect harmony with the current American love of natural, healthful food.

THE STORY OF PASTA

The Origins of Pasta

The origins of pasta in Italy are unclear. At least the age-old myth that Marco Polo discovered pasta in China and brought it to Italy has been discredited. The world now generally concurs that pasta eating in Italy began much earlier.

Even before the Romans arrived in Italy, the resident Etruscans had kitchen tools for making and cooking pasta. A bas-relief in an Etruscan tomb at Cerveteri, thirty miles north of Rome, shows all the utensils for making pasta: a jug for drawing water, knives, a rolling pin, a large pastry board with a raised edge for keeping the water close by when mixing it with flour, and a fluted-edged pastry wheel for cutting. These are the same tools that are used today in many Italian kitchens for making fresh pasta.

Along with Etruscan sovereignty, the predilection for pasta was passed on to the Romans. The Romans made *gnocchi,* a type of pasta dumpling, and other types of fresh pasta, including wide, flat ribbons called *laganum,* precursor of our *lasagne.* In one of his satires, Horace reproves his friend, a wealthy man, for not being able to stroll freely the streets of Tivoli without his servants at his heels. He instead goes where he pleases, taking pleasure in a simple life. "I wander through the streets . . . or often in the forum I stop at a fortune teller's. Then I take myself home to a bowl of leeks, chickpeas, and *lasagne*."

One of the earliest references to pasta appears in *De re coquinaria* ("On Cooking"), a recipe book first compiled in the first century by a Roman noble and gourmet, Marcus Apicius. The original manuscript was lost, but during the Middle Ages copies were made supposedly based on notes that Apicius himself had written. In the fifteenth century, when there was a renewed interest in the classical kitchen, facsimilies of *De re coquinaria* appeared in Italy and Germany. The dishes prescribed include dumplings made with flour and chopped meat, and a *pasticcio* made with alternating layers of *laganum* (*lasagne*) and meat.

The Romans held Sicily, cultivating large parts of it for the wheat from which bread and pasta were made, until the Arabs conquered it. The Arabs made pasta in many forms, and they still do. But they are credited with being the first to hollow it out in the center so that it would dry quickly. According to Al-Idrisi, the Arab geographer commissioned by King Roger II of Sicily in the early twelfth century to write a book about his explorations of the is-

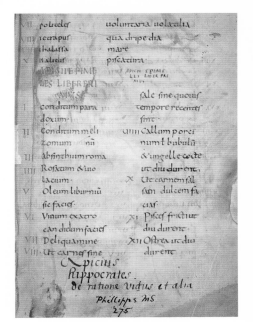

Title page from De re coquinaria, *the oldest known cookbook.*

Marco Polo tastes spaghetti at the court of the Kubla Khan.

The city of Syracuse (Sicily). The Romans cultivated large parts of Sicily for wheat from which bread and pasta were made.

land, Sicilians made a type of pasta called *itriyah* (the Persian word for "string"). It was fashioned around a knitting needle to make it hollow. It evolved into *tria* and then *trii,* a kind of spaghetti still used in Sicily and some other parts of southern Italy. The antique *tria* (meaning "little strings") were served with sweet sauces often based on honey and cinnamon, ingredients that remain prominent in Sicilian cooking.

The evolution of pasta is not easy to unravel, but it does appear that while the Romans and the Etruscans before them had been making fresh pasta for centuries, the Arabs, Persians, and nomadic barbarians from the East relied on dried pasta. In the twentieth century, the Italian futurists, aiming to reform Italian eating habits, tried to argue that the continued use of dried pasta was evidence that Italians had failed to shed the barbarian influences of the past. One Dacovio Saraceno, quoted in Marinetti's revolutionary 1932 manifesto on food, *La Cucina Futurista,* wrote that Theodoric of Ravenna, who reigned from 493 to 526, learned about *macarono* through his contact with the barbarians. He passed the recipe on to his cook, Ratufo, so that it could be made for him. A scullery maid, who fell in love with one of the palace guards, passed the royal secret on to him, and *macarono* soon became wildly popular among the people. They "boiled it with onions, garlic, and turnips, and licked their fingers and their faces."

There is scarce word of artful cuisine during the Middle Ages. General eating habits in Europe then were rather grim. Written history says that a black cloud descended upon the land: a combination of barbarian savagery and Christian asceticism. Pleasure and merrymaking of the earthly variety vanished. Or did it? Most people subsisted on gruel, and hunted, fished, and foraged, as they had always done. But the rich and privileged ate well, as *they* had always done. In ecclesiastical quarters the gastronomic flame still flickered. The sisters and brothers continued to roll out pasta, cooking it mostly as an ingredient in stews. No doubt pasta and other earthly pleasures were enjoyed more than medieval humans admitted to in the confessional box.

Thirteen years before Marco Polo returned from China, a will dated 1279, bestowing a *bariscella piena de macaronis* ("a basketful of macaroni"), was recorded in the city archives of his hometown of Genoa. It was written by a certain Ponzio Bastone, a military man and sailor. (The archives also contain an earlier document, written in 1244, that mentions *pasta lissa,* "flat noodles.") By some accounts, Bastone's will indicates the great worth of pasta. But in fact, at this time it was already a common staple aboard ships from the Orient to the West, for dried pasta was a solution to the problems of conserving grain at sea. From the thirteenth to the sixteenth centuries it was the sailor's sustenance as he went from port to port in the Mediterranean basin. It was cooked with lard and salt, and vegetables were added when they were to be had.

Indeed, dried pasta (*pasta secca*) seems to have a history all of its own. According to Italian food writer Vincenzo Buonassisi, it may have originally been invented by the Arabs as a way of preserving wheat for their lengthy caravans through the desert. The records of the Museo Storico degli Spaghetti (The Museum of the History of Spaghetti) in Pontedassio show that Marco Polo dined on Chinese pasta at the court of Kubla Khan and did in fact bring some form of dried pasta back from Java. In his journal Polo writes, "they have flour from the breadfruit tree . . . and with it they make bread . . . and *lasagne* that are very good."

As was pointed out earlier in the discussion of *tria,* it is clear that the Saracens introduced dried pasta to Sicily. A number of classic and quintessentially Sicilian pasta dishes made with other ingredients of Arab import persist on the island to this day. Among them are many pasta and eggplant specialties, spaghetti with bread crumbs and raisins, and pasta with sardines flavored with raisins and wild fennel.

Pasta secca may have taken a firm hold in Italy once the trade routes were revived between Asia and the Mediterranean at the end of the first millenium A.D. The Roman trade routes had been disrupted by the disintegration of the Roman Empire and subsequent barbarian invasions. The populations of the Mediterranean fled into the countrysides during the early Middle Ages, and a primitive and feudal rural economic system replaced the commercial Roman economy that had been able to support a thriving international trade. During the latter part of the Middle Ages, however, more cohesive political units developed throughout Europe, and a growing economy based on revenue began to replace the barter system that had prevailed in early feudal times. The spice trade, which had been of great importance to the Romans and had a lasting influence on Italian cooking, had continued only feebly after the demise of the empire. But with the discovery of new trade routes to the East Indies and an improving economic picture, trade and commerce were revived for the first time since the Roman Age. The ancient Arab dried-pasta tradition became established through the trade and commerce to which the wealthy had access. Historian Reay Tannahill points out that in the thirteenth and fourteenth centuries, many well-to-do Italian households had domestic servants from the

Marco Polo. In his journal, he wrote, "[The Chinese] have flour from the breadfruit tree . . . and with it they make . . . lasagne *that are very good."*

Timballo di maccheroni alla Lombardo, *an old recipe from Lombardy.*

One Renaissance recipe calls for pasta to be combined with sugar, chocolate, and sweetened poached oranges for dessert.

East, particularly Chinese Mongolian slaves to whom noodle dishes were familiar.

During the Renaissance, the history of modern cooking began, with Italy, then Europe's most developed nation, leading the way. The cuisines of the Florentines and the Venetians, two of the most powerful Italian states, were renowned. Pasta was made in many forms, often cooked with sugar and spices, as this excerpt from Bartolomeo Sacchi's 1475 work *De Honesta Voluptate ac Valetudine* ("Of Honest Pleasure and Well-Being") illustrates:

> *The flour should be well sifted, mixed with water and prepared extended on a table. It should be rolled with an oblong polished piece of wood such as bakers use for this purpose. Then it should be drawn out and cut up to the length of a little finger, or a ribbon. It should be cooked in a fatty broth, kept on a boil. . . . When cooked, it should be transferred to a vessel and served with cheese, butter, sugar, and aromatic sweet spices.*

In the Italian city-states, the papal sumptuary laws prohibited the serving of more than three courses at a banquet (and no more than forty guests at one time) in order to impose moderation on the wealthy. To get around these restrictions, the *timballo* was invented as a second course. It was a huge pie containing *ravioli,* macaroni, chickens and game, sausages, eggs found inside the chickens, truffles, and ham, distributed between layers of pastry alternating with dates and almonds. This extravagant creation was crowned with a lid of sculptured pastry, cooked in the open hearth, and served before a meat course. Another way of eating pasta was as a dessert in a type of *pasticcio* with chocolate and sweetened poached oranges, pears, and other fruits stuffed between layers of fresh noodles. In *Maccaronee,* a farcical work written by sixteenth-century Mantovan poet and *letterato* Merlin Cocai, reference is made to *piadoni,* a sweet-filled *ravioli* made in Brescia, and sweet *tortelli* found in Genoa. It was not until the tomato became an accepted food in the late seventeenth century that pasta dishes generally took on savory rather than sweet and spicy characteristics.

It was also during the Renaissance that pasta eating became popular among the people. By the fifteenth century, pasta was made commercially in many parts of Italy. Eventually, the pasta makers (*vermicellai*) formed guilds and standards for proper pasta making were established. *Vermicellai* fought with bakers to prevent them from competing for the pasta market as its popularity increased. The pasta wars brought in the pope, who tried futilely to bring the bakers under the regulation of the *vermicellai* guilds, and later, under another papacy, made illegal pasta making punishable by a fine and three lashings of the whip. The controversy lasted for three centuries. A 1641 papal decree finally put an end to the battle, according to Anna Del Conte's *Portrait of Pasta,* by declaring that there had to be at least twenty-five yards between pasta shops in Italy.

These same centuries found the city-states in endless competition or war, a situation that had plagued their economies since the Middle Ages. As a result, pasta developed unique characteristics of shape and styles of cooking in different regions and towns. People invented endless ways to make pasta, relying on what was at hand or in season. A firmly rooted peasant cooking tradition (*la cucina casalinga*) developed based on local customs, geography, and resources. Christian fast-day restrictions brought about a host of meatless fillings for fresh pasta, such as pumpkin-filled *tortellini* in Mantua, and Ravenna's *cappelletti di magro* (fast-day *cappelletti*), made with a fish, cheese, and herb stuffing. Although today such preparations as *ravioli* and *cappelletti* stuffed with chard or spinach are national dishes, their origins are regional (as are almost all Italian dishes).

Iconoclasts, Reformers, and Fascists Wage War on Pasta

As pasta rose to ascendancy on the Italian scene, scholars, scientists, men of power, and even governments warned against its malignant properties. One of the first such iconoclasts, Doctor Giovanni da Vigo, wrote an article four hundred years ago defaming, by reason of its threat to health, that beloved Italian gastronomic passion. In the fifteenth century, the religious fanatic Girolamo Savonarola condemned such worldly pleasures as good eating as obstacles to everlasting salvation. In an attempt to wrench the Italians from their luxurious pasta habit, the Florentine monk shouted from the pulpit, "It's not enough for you to eat your pasta fried. No! You think you have to add garlic to it, and when you eat *ravioli,* it's not enough to boil it in a pot and eat it in its juice, you have to fry it in another pan and cover it with cheese!" It would be out of character for the Italians to accept self-denial as a regular diet. They eventually fried Savonarola himself—at the stake.

In the early twentieth century, when issues of supermen and wartime preoccupied Europeans, it was conjectured that the meatless pasta diet of the poor south had bred an effete population. Danzig-born Arthur Schopenhauer, renowned for his philosophy of pessi-

A pasta-seller in Naples, holding a flyswatter, by an unknown 19th-century artist.

Left: *In the 1930s, the Italian futurist party charged, "spaghetti is no food for fighters," calling for Mussolini to ban its consumption throughout Italy.*
Right: *Girolamo Savonarola, a 15th-century Florentine monk, preached against the luxurious Italian pasta habit. He was hanged and burned as a heretic in 1498.*

mism, had published antispaghetti views during the nineteenth century. The Italian fascists renewed the antipasta propaganda. Amidst furious public protest, including telegrams from America lobbying for pasta, Mussolini considered banning its consumption throughout Italy.

In the 1930s, Marinetti, the Italian futurist poet and social reformer, embarked on a well-publicized crusade to change the Italian diet, specifically the centuries-old "addiction" to pasta. "It is necessary, once and for all, to annihilate pasta. . . . *Pastasciutta,* however grateful to the palate, is an obsolete food; it is heavy, brutalizing, and gross; its nutritive qualities are deceptive; it induces sloth, skepticism, and pessimism." There was speculation that heavy pasta eaters were slow and placid, while meat eaters were aggressive and purposeful. In a country on the threshold of war, Marinetti's charge, "Spaghetti is no food for fighters!" did not fall on deaf ears. From the quarters of government, medicine, science, and academia, the guardians of power and public conscience wondered if in embracing pasta as a national food, the Italians had not also forfeited their predatory and virile instincts, and dimmed their intellectual capacities.

Food of the Famished

But among the people there was reverence for pasta, and even a superstition, widely held among the starving masses of southern Italy, that pasta was a food containing magical properties. In the seventeenth, eighteenth, and nineteenth centuries, it was already the national main course of southern Italy, particularly of Naples, the poorest of all the provinces. During the industrial revolution, which made cheap, dried pasta more widely available than ever before, Naples became the center of commercial pasta manufacturing. From the early 1700s until 1930, when Mussolini influenced the move of the industry to north-central Italy, pasta was the symbol of the city. The hot southern Mediterranean sun and the breezes from the sea produced the perfect environment for drying pasta. A street culture developed around the cooking, selling, and eating of dried pasta. Charcoal fires surrounded by makeshift wooden stalls were to be seen everywhere, offering a pot of boiling, salted water full of macaroni. A mound of grated cheese waited to be piled on top of it, and the pasta was eaten just that way, with fingers.

In the beginning of the nineteenth century, a national patriotic fervor swept Italy, partially in reaction to centuries of often-oppressive foreign domination by the Spanish, French, and Austrians and partially in response to revolutionary movements in other parts of Europe and in Latin America. The idea of a free and united Italy became part of the literature, politics, and popular thought of the century, cutting across all social classes. Until this point, the country had been a collection of sovereign regions, each governed by home rule, each very distinct in its traditions and often disparate in its interests.

Among the most important figures of the era was Giuseppe Garibaldi, adventurer, patriot, and fearless military leader, who was largely responsible for liberating Milan, Sicily, and Naples. With his Expedition of a Thousand, volunteers from all parts of Italy, he set out to liberate the entire south from the despotic Spanish. Garibaldi's men secured dramatic victories against astonishing odds as they made their way to Sicily, then across the sea to Naples and the southern mainland. His bold military feats inspired patriotism in a population demoralized by past defeats and humiliations. Soldiers returning to their homes in the north brought more than a taste for liberty to their countrymen, however. Along with a united Italy, the fight for unification no doubt eventually established pasta as a national, rather than a regional dish.

Pasta Progress

For hundreds of years, the making of commercial pasta was a primitive affair. While at home it was mixed and kneaded by hand, in the factories it was mixed by foot and hung out to dry on long racks. As late as the nineteenth century, commercial pasta operations were outfitted with huge troughs filled with dough, which was kneaded by barefoot workers trodding to the rhythm of mandolin music. The king of Naples, Ferdinand II (1830–59), tried to modernize by hiring a famous engineer to design a new, more hygienic system. (The result was a mechanical man with bronze feet.) My mother still talks about the donkey-driven grinding wheels that turned wheat into flour for pasta and bread in Sardinia, where she grew up. A similar device was used in the first pasta factory in the United States, located in Brooklyn, where horses were har-

Top: *A 19th-century pasta factory in Amalfi, by P. Scoppetta. In the early manufacture of pasta, men and children were employed to knead pasta by foot, and to power primitive machinery.* Bottom: *Giuseppe Garibaldi led Italy to liberation from foreign rule in the mid-19th century.*

Torchio for making spaghetti,
17th century.

Hand mill used in the commercial
manufacture of pasta, 19th century.

nessed to a kneading device.

The giant southern Italian pasta industry that developed in the eighteenth and nineteenth centuries was founded on the discovery that hard durum-wheat flour (semolina) made a dough superior to that made with standard bread flour. Semolina pasta did not become brittle when dried, and held up under packaging, shipping, storing, and ultimately, during boiling. Since, as has been said, the coastal climate was the perfect environment for drying pasta once it was made, factories mushroomed along the seaboard, where Russian ships carrying the durum grain could easily unload.

While other nations created parliaments and empires, often poking their noses where they did not belong, Italian creativity manifested itself in the artistry of the Renaissance. It is a trait of the Italian character to transform necessity into art, introducing a touch of the sublime into everyday life. Nowhere is this ability more evident than in the art of eating. Thus, in a country where the mundane aspires to the exquisite (from a doorknob to a pair of shoes), it is not surprising that the small, intricate shapes that emerge from a simple dough of flour and water have become a beloved food the world over.

1 PASTA BASICS

. . . if Italian cookbooks do not wish to deceive their readers, they should start out with these words: Recipe (procure) the best of ingredients, as fresh as they can be found, and within the bounds of skill, preserve their identity in the preparation. Thus forewarned, the reader could . . . attain not only the true cooking of Italy—la vera cucina Italiana—but a deep understanding of Italy and the Italians.

—Luigi Barzini, introduction to *The Cooking of Italy*

Agnesi pasta label, c. 1920.

A view of Brescia (Lombardy). Emilia-Romagna, famed for its pasta fresca, *is bordered on the north by Lombardy.*

Pasta Secca versus *Pasta Fresca*

An important distinction is made by the Italians between *pasta secca* and *pasta fresca.* The first is the commercial machine-made variety, including the different types of spaghetti and macaroni. It is made of semolina flour. Delicate homemade pasta is made with ordinary white flour. Dried pasta has traditionally been a product of the south of Italy, while in the north, fresh pasta is more usual. These are not hard and fast rules, but general distinctions based on historical differences in cooking and eating tradition. Fresh green pasta contains spinach. Other popular varieties may include beet or tomato, or corn, whole-wheat, or buckwheat flour. Fresh pasta usually contains eggs and is also known as *sfoglia.*

With the increasing interest in authentic Italian cooking, many American cooks assume that fresh pasta means superior pasta. This is simply not true. The two are treated very differently in cooking; sauces that go with one do not necessarily go with the other. Fresh pasta, when made properly, is more delicate because it is very thin and includes eggs. The semolina from which dried pasta is made makes it more chewy. Chapters 6 and 7 on fresh noodles, and dried pasta, respectively, give suggestions for the kinds of sauces that go best with each type.

The northern Italians, particularly the Emilians, take great pride in their *pasta fresca.* Emilia-Romagna is a verdant, opulent, and ebullient land, bordered on the east by the Adriatic, on the west by the cheese-producing provinces of Parma and Reggio, on the south by the Tuscan hills, and on the north by the fecund valley of the Po River. It is not accidental that the capital city is nicknamed Bologna, or "the fat." Pasta has become more important in the north since World War II, for Italy has become less parochial and the popularity of dried pasta has spread northward. In Emilia, the making of *pasta fresca* is an ancient art. Things haven't changed much there since the late Waverly Root, in 1971, wrote in *The Food of Italy:*

> *[The Bolognese] maintain that no machine can duplicate the hard hand labor of skilled women pasta makers, who knead and roll their dough interminably until their haunches are bathed in sweat, which, it is locally agreed, is the sign that the pasta is ready.*

The Emilians believe that handmaking pasta with a wooden rolling pin produces a superior dough which, because it has a porous texture rather than the polished and elastic one produced by the steel rollers of a pasta machine, accepts sauces more easily.

The Tuscans, on the other hand, do not generally make such a to-do about hand rolling pasta. They prefer a softer dough which is achieved by adding oil to the eggs.

Knowing Quality Pasta

In the first edition (1987) of this book, I wrote that only imported Italian dried pasta was worth buying. But in recent years there has been some improvement in American-made dried pasta. The reason for the traditional superiority in flavor and texture of Italian brands lies in the know-how acquired through centuries of manufacturing pasta. Also, by Italian law, dried pasta must be made solely from the endosperm or heart of *durum* (Latin for hard) wheat. Hard wheat flour, or semolina (*semola* in Italian), which is obtained in the first stage of the milling process, contains less starch, is higher in protein, and is more digestible than farina and refined white flour, which are subsequent by-products. Dried pasta that contains soft wheat flour, as some American brands do, does not remain firm after cooking, even when cooked *al dente*. Cooked properly, good quality dried pasta of 100% semolina remains firm and somewhat chewy from the pot to the table, and it is more tasty than pasta blended with soft flour, since it contains the pure nutty essence of the heart of the wheat. However, not all pastas made of 100% semolina are equal. The Italians blend different semolina flours in order to achieve the perfect balance of color, flavor, and texture. They believe that the best dried pasta is made with Italian *sèmola,* which doesn't break down in cooking, blended with Canadian or North Dakota semolina, which produces pasta with great texture and expandibility. American manufacturers rely mostly on domestic wheat.

Dried pasta is made without eggs (spaghetti and macaroni), and with eggs (*pasta all'uova,* egg noodles such as *tagliatelle, pappardelle,* and *fettuccine*). In the factory, semolina and water (and eggs in the case of egg pasta) are combined to form a paste which is extruded through dies to form the various shapes. For centuries in Italy, manufacturers have used bronze dies, which produces pasta with a rougher surface than the smooth, shiny pasta that results from the newer teflon dies that American and many Italian manufacturers now use. A rougher surface is preferable, because the porous quality of rough dough absorbs sauce better than the polished surface of pasta extruded through teflon dies. There still are some brands

The Golden Rules of Perfect Pasta

Never overcook pasta.

Never overdrain pasta. Except when saucing with thin or brothy sauces such as fresh tomato or seafood, pasta needs to be moist to combine well with sauce.

Never oversauce pasta. Perfectly prepared pasta has no extra sauce over it or at the bottom of the bowl. It is evenly moistened throughout with just the right amount.

Never muddle the taste of a dish by using aromatics or flavorings with opposing properties or in large quantities.

Whenever possible, use ingredients that are authentic in order to achieve the true flavors of genuine Italian cooking.

Use the best quality, freshest ingredients you can find. They will affect completely the flavor and the aesthetics of what you cook.

Spaghetti making, etc. in Naples in the 1800s.

produced with bronze dies—you can tell by the dull, rough surface of the pasta.

When buying dried pasta, look for the following characteristics: The pasta should be golden with faint brownish speckles, and it should not pale during cooking. It should have a translucent quality to it when held up to light. When it cooks, it should fill the room with a nutty perfume. Dried egg noodles don't have the translucent quality of good non-egg dried pasta, but the best dried egg noodles have a rough texture like that of home-made pasta. The taste of dried pasta is as important as the sauce that goes on it: pasta should taste wheaty. Finally, the water in which it cooks should not be excessively cloudy and there should be no sediment on the bottom of the pot.

Do not, I implore, be mislead into thinking that the so-called "fresh pasta" sold at a premium in American markets is better than good dried pasta. True fresh pasta should be made the same day it is eaten, just like fresh bread. Most commercial "fresh" pasta has none of the virtues of authentic, delicate, home-made pasta, nor the delicious flavor and lovely chewy texture of good factory-produced dried pasta; it is bland and gummy, far too thick (fresh pasta should be very thin and delicate), and often has an unpleasant waxy texture. I see no reason to resort to it when excellent dried pasta, including dried egg pasta, is available.

Pasta Shapes and Sizes

Although at least three hundred types of pasta have been invented by the Italians, the industrialization of the dried pasta industry made it impractical to produce them all in the factory process. Now, probably no more than fifty or sixty shapes are made commercially. There has been controversy in America over Italian dogma that makes it imperative to match pasta shapes and sizes to certain sauces. While Italian eating tradition puts every pasta in its proper place, Americans are characteristically laissez-faire about the matter. James Beard, for example, once told me that he felt such strictures were unnecessary for Americans who do not share the tradition; they can be inventive and spontaneous with pasta recipes. Italians, in contrast, feel that there is a long and fine history behind pasta eating in their country, from which, over the centuries, tried and true guidelines have evolved. (Although, in characteristic fashion, Italians sometimes argue among themselves about the rules.) See chapter 7 for further explanation about matching sauces to various pasta shapes.

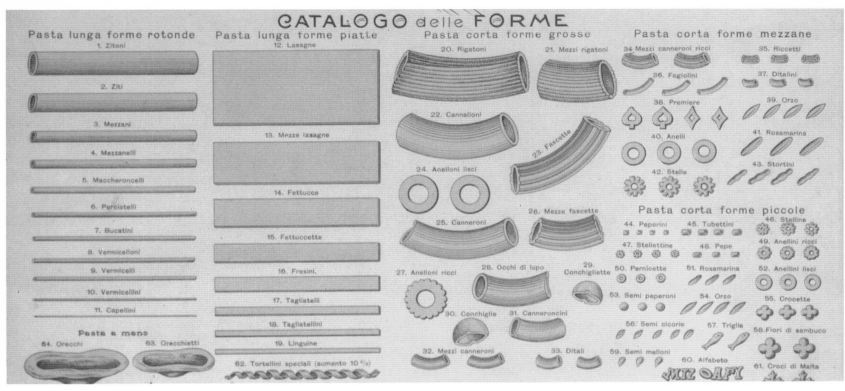

Italian pasta poster, 19th century.

Cooking Dried Pasta

[For] boiled macaroni, cook [it] in boiling salted water twenty minutes or until soft, drain in strainer, pour over it cold water to prevent pieces from adhering; add cream, (or tomato sauce), reheat, and season with salt.

— Fannie Merritt Farmer, *The Boston Cooking School Cook Book,* 1923

I suspect that, except for Italian Americans, people in this country, through no fault of their own, have taken seriously such shocking advice about cooking pasta, even up until this day. *Larousse Gastronomique,* published in 1961 with an introduction by Escoffier, is, in French culinary matters, a recognized authority. But about cooking macaroni it says:

Boil [it] very fast for 16 to 20 minutes (9–12 minutes for spaghetti), according to the thickness of the macaroni. Remove the saucepan from the stove. Cover it and leave the pasta to swell in the water for a few minutes.

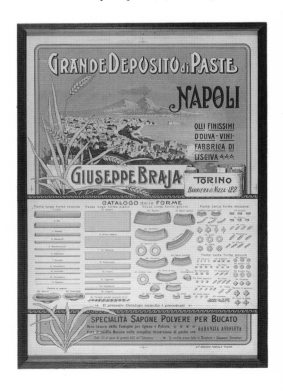

Makes Glorious Dishes

ARMOUR'S MACARONI

SCIENTIFICALLY MADE AT BATTLE CREEK, MICH.
MANUFACTURED AND GUARANTEED BY THE
ARMOUR GRAIN COMPANY
CHICAGO

Just Try One Package!

Then You'll Continue to use Armour's Macaroni as do Millions of Other Careful Buyers

Armour's Macaroni establishes a new standard of excellence—that same superiority which has made thousands—yes, millions—change to Armour's Oats.

Meaty, white, tender in quality, Armour's Macaroni is perfect for your delicious butter sauce, cheese or tomato. This is Armour's exclusive product—wholesome and appetizing.

Cut in short lengths and uniformly thin-walled, Armour's Macaroni cooks quickly and economically. It is wonderfully convenient to handle—a fact much appreciated once it is tried.

If the cost is a little more, consider that you enjoy a product scientifically manufactured; a product from a modern, sunlit plant in Battle Creek, Michigan, where every process insures purity and delicious quality.

Ask for Armour's Macaroni, Spaghetti or Noodles. Your grocer should have them.

Manufactured by
Armour Grain Company, Chicago

Makers of Armour's Guaranteed Cereals—Oats, Corn Flakes, Macaroni, Spaghetti, Noodles, Pancake Flour

EASY TO MEASURE

CONVENIENT TO HANDLE

AVOIDS AWKWARD EATING

Early 20th-century American advertisement for pasta.

A meal that offers nothing to bite does not satiate. For this reason, in very poor regions, pasta, which often constitutes the main dish, tends to be harder.

—Professor Peter Kubelka
Pastario

It goes on to instruct that for macaroni with cream sauce, or macaroni *à l'italienne,* and other recipes calling for sauce to be put over pasta, the macaroni should be thoroughly drained, put back into the saucepan, and returned to the fire until all the moisture in it is evaporated!

To Italians, such counsel is absolute heresy. Cooking pasta even half a minute past its perfect state of doneness can completely ruin it, turning what should be a gentle, toothy texture into mush. It should not remain in the water, but be drained instantly. Equally important, pasta should never be overdrained. It should still be wet when it is turned into a heated and buttered bowl. Draining pasta this way helps the sauce to go further; in effect, it lubricates the pasta, which allows for smooth and easy distribution of the sauce. This is one of the most important things to keep in mind in cooking pasta, and something of which many people are unaware. If pasta is overdrained, it has a tendency to stick together and also to absorb an enormous quantity of sauce. The pasta, not the sauce, is meant to be the dominant taste experienced. It is easy to cook perfect pasta following these rules:

1. Use at least four quarts of water (five is plenty) to cook one pound of pasta. For over a pound of pasta, increase the amount of water proportionately. The water should be at a rolling boil before the pasta is dropped in.

2. Add the salt, which should be about one and a half tablespoons to a pound of pasta, at the same time the pasta is added. If the salt boils alone with the water, an unpleasant odor is formed that affects the taste of the pasta. The quantity of salt can be more if preferred, but should not be much less. Undersalted pasta is tasteless, no matter how flavorful the sauce.

3. There are two schools of thought about whether to break spaghetti in half before putting it in boiling water. One says that spaghetti and other long pasta were meant to be the length they are and that to break them is to destroy their character. The other school says that since breaking spaghetti does not alter its flavor, and lets it cook uniformly by submerging it all in the water at the same time, it should be snapped in half. This is a matter of preference for aesthetic over pragmatic solutions.

4. Stir the pasta with a wooden fork as soon as it is dropped into the boiling water, to prevent it from sticking together. Cover the

pot until the boil returns and then remove the lid. Stir now and then to make sure that the pasta cooks evenly. Have a colander (or pasta paddle, if using one) ready for draining it.

5. Because of variation in pasta shapes, thicknesses, and ingredients, as well as outside variables, it is impossible to give an absolute cooking time. The best way to test for *al dente* (tender but firm) consistency is to fish a strand from the pot and taste it. Package instructions often advise cooking pasta too long, so test it at least five minutes before suggested. If you have any doubt, err on the side of undercooking. (Don't forget that pasta continues to cook as long as it is hot.) If you are going to cook it further in the oven, boil it for less time. You can add a cup of cold water to the pasta water as soon as it has been turned off to prevent further cooking, but if you are quick to drain it, there is no need to do this.

6. Have a heated bowl containing about two tablespoons of melted butter ready to receive the drained pasta. The butter helps to prevent pasta from sticking together and to carry rather than soak up the sauce. When you are draining pasta in a colander, always save some of the hot cooking water, in case you should unintentionally overdrain it. Dried pasta should actually be dripping wet when tossed with butter and sauce; fresh pasta less so, but it should still be very moist. Very quickly transfer the pasta to the bowl and toss it with the butter. Some brands of pasta absorb water more than others. If your pasta turns out too dry, you can add some of the hot water to restore it to its proper moist consistency. Concentrated sauces such as *pesto* should be mixed with a little of the hot pasta water to help distribute them through the pasta. Immediately toss the pasta with the sauce.

Because fresh pasta is still a soft dough, it is cooked for far less time than dried pasta is. See chapter 2 for instructions on cooking fresh pasta.

An Exception to the Classic Rule for Cooking Pasta

With all that said, Italians have invented other ways to cook pasta that produce excellent results. One such method in which most of the cooking takes place away from the immediate source of heat, was pioneered by the Agnesi firm, among Italy's largest commercial producers and exporters of dried pasta. A benefit of this tech-

Spaghetti vendors and eaters, a typical Neapolitan street scene at the turn of the century.

Top: Macaroni Sellers of Naples,
by Bartolomeo Pinelli, c. 1817.
Bottom: *Neapolitans eating macaroni,*
19th century.

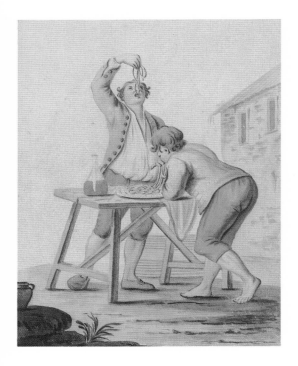

nique is that more of the nutrients are retained, some of which are drained off when pasta is cooked in the traditional way. In fact, with the Agnesi method, the water in which the pasta has cooked does not become cloudy the way it does when pasta is boiled in the conventional manner. Here is the Agnesi method:

1. Boil the usual amount of water for cooking pasta in a large pot. When it comes to a rapid boil, add the salt and the pasta at the same time. Stir thoroughly.

2. Cover the pot and bring the water to a boil again over the highest possible flame. When it boils, remove the lid and boil rapidly again for another two minutes.

3. Turn off the heat and stir again thoroughly. Put a kitchen towel, double thickness, over the pot and replace the lid tightly over the cloth. With the heat still off, time the pasta as many minutes as you would normally cook dried pasta.

4. Drain the pasta in the usual manner (see previous section, *Cooking Pasta*), being sure not to overdrain it. Add sauce.

Cooking pasta by this method has the advantage of producing firm pasta even if you have left it a minute too long in the water, whereas in the traditional method pasta becomes instantly mushy if cooked beyond its proper time.

Reheating Pasta

Before the advent of the microwave, I would have said that it was difficult to reheat pasta successfully. Because the microwave heats only the water molecules of food, it warms pasta without drying it out. Cover and set "high" for about one minute (depending on the microwave and the quantity of pasta). A very acceptable dish of leftover pasta will result. To reheat leftover pasta without a microwave, wrap and seal it well in foil and put it in a preheated 350-degree oven for fifteen to twenty minutes until it is hot.

Serving Pasta

Except for *lasagne, pasticci,* and certain other main-course pasta dishes, pasta is almost always eaten as a first course, preceding a meat or fish entrée. This is very different from the way Americans eat pasta, which is most often as the centerpiece of a meal, alongside salad or vegetables, and bread. The first course is where the Italians have really shown their culinary genius, particularly with homemade pasta dishes—egg noodles, stuffed pasta such as *ravioli, tortellini, cannelloni,* and so on. An Italian meal is composed of many diverse flavors and textures, each course in harmony with the other and with no one element making up an overwhelming part of the eating experience. First-course servings of pasta are usually four ounces (uncooked weight) per person—a substantial portion by American standards.

It is important to consider what will be served as a second course if you are serving pasta first. A pasta served with a cream sauce, for example, should not precede a main course that also includes a rich cream sauce. Herbs or aromatics used in flavoring a pasta sauce should not be repeated in the meal. Complementary flavors and textures should be juxtaposed from one course to the next.

As to what kinds of cheeses to serve with pasta, see the section on cheeses later in this chapter. Despite the ubiquity of *parmigiano* in Italian cooking, not every dish requires it. In fact, quite a number of sauces would be ruined by it. This is true of seafood dishes, which, containing their own highly aromatic characters, would be muddled or foiled by the addition of cheese. When cheese is used, it should be freshly grated, either in a food processor or a cheese mill. I think that the fine side of a regular grater makes *parmigiano* much too fine and the coarse side much too coarse. But if a standard *grattugia* ("grater") is all you have, it will do. The pregrated, prepackaged "Parmesan-style" cheeses sold in many American markets are impostors. I do not know what sly things are in those bottles and cans, and I don't think I want to. They should not be considered, for they are anathema to fine cooking, however simple to use.

In an Italian meal, bread is served with the main course, not at the beginning of the meal. But there is nothing wrong with offering bread with pasta. Use a good Italian, French, or even sourdough-type bread. It should not be rye, whose flavor would be too distracting with the other flavors present. It should not be sliced white or sweet bread of any sort, of which Americans are inordinately fond, nor contain raisins, and so on.

There is no better drink with pasta than wine. There are no set rules for when white or red should accompany pasta, except for those dictated by common sense. A wine should not overwhelm the dish. A strong-bodied red could drown out *spaghettini* with white clam sauce. Conversely, a light white wine will not rise to a virile dish such as spaghetti with olives.

A mangiamaccheroni, *by Percival Seaman, 1843.*

27

Pasta Etiquette

Spaghetti can be eaten successfully if you inhale it like a vacuum cleaner.

—Sophia Loren

Some Italian almanacs tell when to eat what kinds of pasta with what kinds of sauces—according to the stars, the moon, and the planets. Neapolitan writer Giuseppe Marotta has a different formula: "Adapt your dish of spaghetti to circumstances and your state of mind." It is also good to consider what is seasonal and fresh in the market, a more down-to-earth approach probably followed by most Italian cooks.

The proper way to eat pasta is with a fork—not with the help of a tablespoon unless the sauce is very thin, such as is the case with some seafood sauces. The idea is to twirl a moderate amount at a time around the tines, using the curve of the plate as the pivoting point. According to Italian rules of etiquette, *pastasciutta,* that is, pasta and sauce, should be served on flat dinner plates. There is not much more than meets the eye in pasta twirling, and it takes only a little bit of practice. If it is too easy to twirl, it might be over-cooked; pasta that is properly cooked, that is, tender but firm, is harder to twirl because it retains its own unruly shape better. I have seen people go to extraordinary lengths to maintain their decorum while struggling with spaghetti: cutting it up with a knife and fork (a heretical activity, by Italian accounts) or eating only a few strands at a time to maintain the appearance of delicacy (a sure way to end up with a plate of cold pasta).

During the eighteenth and nineteenth centuries, the impoverished masses ate spaghetti with their hands. But when the four-pronged fork was invented by Gennaro Spadaccini, a chamberlain at the Bourbon court of Naples, pasta became a food fit for royalty as well, for they could now eat it without loss of dignity. Beyond using a fork, pasta etiquette is not something Italians worry much about today. I have heard the notion from some Italians that you can tell something about a person's character from his or her way of twirling spaghetti—whether he is warm or stiff, generous or not; whether she is ambitious or lazy, honest or not; and so on. I suspect there is something to this, for it is common sense that a man is not only what he eats, but how he eats it.

Beggar eating macaroni, 19th century. Artist unknown.

Special Kitchen Equipment for Making, Cooking, and Saucing Pasta

FOR MIXING PASTA:

A **very large pastry board,** at least two feet by three feet, or a large, clean work surface of wood or marble. Cutting pasta on a formica countertop will scratch the surface.

A **dough scraper** or sturdy spatula for scraping bits of dried dough off the work surface.

FOR ROLLING PASTA:

Your large pastry board or work surface is also your mixing and rolling space when making pasta.

If you are making pasta completely by hand instead of using a pasta machine, you must have a long, smooth, well-sanded **rolling pin** (thirty-two inches long and one and one-half inches in diameter).

A **pasta machine.** There are basically two types of pasta machines available, the extrusion variety and the roller variety. The extrusion machine pushes the dough through a disk with holes in it, which forms the different pasta shapes. But it skips the important step of rolling, which gives pasta good texture. Extrusion machines require the use of cake flour instead of hard-wheat flour, because only this finer flour passes easily through the dies that cut the pasta shapes. Cake flour makes an inferior tasting (and less nutritious) pasta. Cleaning the extrusion machine after use takes considerable time, so in the end, the old-fashioned roller machine takes no more time to use.

Satisfactory manual roller-type machines can be bought for under twenty dollars. Most of them have the same problem: they do not work well on the last notch, which produces the thinnest pasta dough. Because the machines are cheaply made, the rollers that press the dough are often not properly aligned, causing the dough to shirr and producing an uneven and often torn sheet of pasta. Higher quality manual roller machines, at about twice the cost, are worth the extra expense. They do a better job of even rolling, produce wider strips of pasta, and have more sophisticated mechanisms for controlling noodle thicknesses.

The electric machine with plastic rollers in place of polished-steel ones produces a more porous sheet of dough than the manual machine, closer in texture to hand-rolled pasta, but it does not break

Top: *A macaroni seller in Naples,*
by James Godby, 1805.
Bottom: *Fluted-edged pastry wheel*
and straight-edged pastry wheel.

down the gluten sufficiently during the rolling process. The electrical mechanisms on some of the roller-type pasta machines have proved unreliable. Unless you are making pasta in very large quantities, I don't think there is anything to be gained by using an electric machine or electrical attachment to convert a manual machine.

FOR CUTTING AND DRYING PASTA:
A **fluted-edged pastry wheel** and a **straight-edged pastry wheel** (also known as a pizza cutter) for cutting pasta.

A round **cookie cutter,** approximately three inches in diameter, for *tortelli, cappellacci,* and similar-sized stuffed pastas, and a two-inch one for smaller varieties, such as *tortellini.*

A *pasta drying rack* is useful to hang noodles on once they are cut.

Other types of specialized equipment for cutting pasta and making *ravioli* are available, but the Italian kitchen is not so concerned with such paraphernalia. Start out with simple devices first, then go on to some of the more sophisticated tools, if you like. Personally, I prefer working with nothing more than a pastry wheel and a fluted-edged cookie cutter for cutting pasta by hand.

FOR COOKING PASTA AND SAUCES:
A **skimmer** or **slotted spoon** for *gnocchi* and stuffed pasta forms that must be lifted out of boiling water individually. When such types of pasta are drained into a colander, they can easily break open. It is useful to have a **flat skimmer** as well as a deep **spoon-type skimmer** for retrieving different shapes of stuffed pasta.

A long-handled **wooden** *fork* for stirring pasta and lifting strands out of the pot to test for doneness, and a **pasta paddle,** a large, flat wooden spoon with several prongs that rise perpendicular to the bowl. A variation on the paddle is the pasta lift, which is made of stainless steel and resembles a comb. The paddle is for lifting spaghetti and noodles out of the boiling water, rather than pouring the contents into a colander. I like to use a paddle because it is the quickest way of removing pasta from the pot and there is no chance of overdraining. If I am cooking several types of pasta in boiling water, I can reuse the same water instead of waiting for another pot to boil.

A sturdy **colander** with handles and feet and enough holes so that the pasta drains quickly. Some of the cheap, plastic types have very small holes that don't let water run out quickly enough.

A good-quality set of **cookware** that heats evenly and has heavy bottoms. The pasta cooker, a three-piece unit that includes a bottom pan, a deep, perforated insert, and a lid, is not good for cooking macaroni or spaghetti because the water never drains fast enough; the pasta just languishes in the bottom of the perforated pan, overcooking, until the water finally trickles out. But this pot is useful when cooking more than one batch. The insert can be lifted out, the contents drained into a colander, and the boiling water reused.

For sauces and general cooking, I like to use nickel-lined copper pots and pans. They conduct heat evenly and retain it well. This cookware is expensive, however, and needs to be polished in order to remain both heat efficient and attractive. Terra-cotta is the favorite of Italian cooks, especially for sauces that require long, slow cooking. But it is difficult to find in America, requires some care, and is probably impractical for most American cooks. Enameled cast iron is an excellent and even conductor of heat, and has the advantages of being easy to clean and ovenproof. Aluminum and cast iron react with the acidity in tomatoes and create an unpleasant taste. Stick to the recommended pans, stainless steel, or other coated types of cookware.

A **flame tamer,** a hollow steel disk about an inch tall, to diffuse heat on a burner when very slow, even cooking is necessary, such as with cream sauces.

Mezzaluna ("half-moon"), a crescent-shaped steel or carbon-steel blade with a wooden knob at each end, is what Italians generally use for chopping vegetables and herbs. It is rocked back and forth quickly on a cutting board for very efficient chopping. It is far more effective than the little spring-type plastic choppers that are popular, and takes less effort than using a conventional knife. I have made visitors in my kitchen into instant converts, anxious to extol the virtues of this simple but wonderful tool. At one time, the *mezzaluna* was hard to come by here; now it is common in cookware shops.

A **food mill** for puréeing tomatoes and other vegetables. Get one with assorted disks (there should be three, each with different-sized extrusion holes). A food processor is not a good tool for puréeing

Top: Family of Fishermen, *by G. Dura, 19th century.*
Bottom: Mezzaluna.

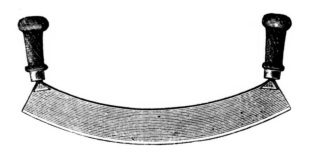

tomatoes for sauce; unlike the food mill, it doesn't restrain the seeds.

A regular box or flat metal **grater** for making bread crumbs and grating certain vegetables (carrots, celery, onions).

A **pepper mill** for grinding black and white peppercorns.

The Italian Cupboard

HERBS, SPICES, AND FLAVORINGS

Italian cooking, despite the widespread stereotype, relies very little on the use of herbs and spices. The first lessons in cooking my mother gave me were these: Use ingredients that are impeccable in their freshness and flavor, combine them with compatible ingredients to bring out their character and create contrasting textures and colors, and add herbs and spices with discretion. The Italians are lavish in their use of raw materials in cooking, which is different from the French, whose cooking is based on the parsimonious employment of every part of their ingredients and a greater reliance on added flavorings.

Spices from the East Indies, India, and Ceylon made their way through Egypt and the Middle East to the ports of Genoa and Venice in Roman times. Up until the seventeenth century, the food of the wealthy was, as a result, highly spiced and extravagantly prepared. But it was also often poorly prepared, for arbitrary and excessive use of spices and flavorings resulted in veiled and muddled flavors.

During the Renaissance, the Italians, beginning with the Florentines, returned to simpler notions of cuisine. A more natural form of cooking that stressed fresh ingredients and few aromatics and spices evolved. Essentially, the peasant kitchen, which had remained localized and traditional until that time, prevailed. Today, the herbs and flavorings used in Italian cooking are only subtle, pleasant reminders of their excessive patrician origins.

Fresh herbs lend a more delicate, clear aroma and taste than do dry ones, so it is best to stick with them when you can. Certain herbs retain their scent and flavor better when dried than others, such as rosemary, thyme, marjoram, bay, and oregano. Some herbs, parsley among them, are useless except when fresh. But all herbs should be used with care, keeping in mind that they are meant to complement, never replace, the flavor of food. And herbs in combination produce a new flavor and bouquet different from each of

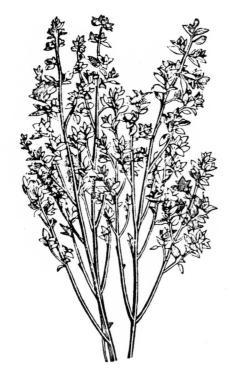

Basil

the original ingredients. Dried herbs should be kept in a tightly sealed glass jar.

Basil, in Italian, *basilico:* This sweet, fragrant herb is known for its affinity with tomatoes in Italian cooking. I grew up with basil growing in the family garden and flowing out of large terra-cotta pots on the windowsill. Along with fig trees, red wine made by my grandfather, and artichokes stewing with garlic, peas, and parsley, basil figures in my earliest memories of Italian food. It is the traditional herb of Genoese cooking and the primary ingredient in *pesto,* the famous sauce eaten with pasta (and in soups and with meat and fish) that originated in the Liguria region. The aromatic plants populate the gardens and windowsills of country and city households alike. To this day, my mother, when she comes to visit, will more often than not bring me a bouquet of garden basil or even a jar of fresh-made *pesto.*

Dried basil is not a good substitute; fresh basil has become more common in American markets, however, especially in the summertime. For use in sauces (but not for *pesto,* for which only the fresh herb should be used), basil leaves can be frozen for winter use.

Bay leaves or laurel, in Italian, *alloro:* Bay is the leaf of the laurel tree. It is a very strong herb that should be used carefully (rarely more than one leaf in a soup, sauce, or stew). Bean-and-pasta combinations are particularly complemented by its addition. A bay leaf is sometimes used to flavor the stuffing for *tortellini, tortelloni,* or other filled forms when pork is an ingredient, for it marries well with the meat. The leaf is always removed after the pork is sautéed, before it is ground for the stuffing.

Celery, in Italian, *sedano:* Though celery is a vegetable, to be sure, it is included here because of its importance in some pasta sauces. It adds body to certain tomato-based sauces such as *pomarola,* and soups. The leaves of the celery impart the most intense flavor; they are sometimes chopped up along with the stalk and sautéed in the *soffritto,* which is the first step in the making of the sauce. Dried celery should never be substituted for fresh.

Fennel, in Italian, *finocchio:* The whole fennel plant (Florentine fennel) resembles a squat, bulbous celery and has a flavor reminiscent of anise. The leaves are fine and dill-like in appearance, and can be used for flavoring much in the same way dill is employed. The bulb is often eaten raw, sprinkled with olive oil and pepper and salt, as

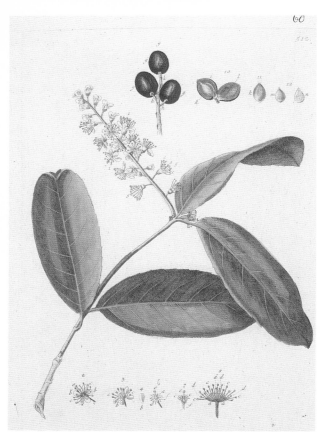

Bay leaves. From A Curious Herbal, *by Elizabeth Blackwell, London, 1737–39.*

an appetizer or even after the meal in place of fruit. *Pasta e finocchiella,* (chapter 9), a Calabrian specialty, mixes fennel and macaroni in a very nice way. The seed of the fennel is frequently used in the Italian sausages so beloved by Italian Americans.

Garlic, in Italian, *aglio:* If we were to be led by our noses, we would never look for garlic in a flower patch, although in fact garlic is a member of the lily family. If I could believe all I have read about the medicinal and restorative powers of it, I would eat nothing else. Among the remarkable claims, beginning with those of Plato and continuing to the present day, are that garlic restores virility; helps cure bronchitis and asthma; prevents tuberculosis, diphtheria, typhus, leprosy, and gangrene; reduces blood pressure; prevents worms; and cleans infected wounds. I can testify, despite my own skepticism, that a friend of mine cured her dog of mange by feeding it large doses of garlic for a year.

Garlic was first cultivated in ancient times by the Egyptians and later by the Greeks and Romans, and was used extensively throughout southern Europe and the Middle East. We in America are so influenced by southern Italian culture, that it is assumed garlic dominates Italian cooking. This is untrue. Garlic is used very little in northern Italian cooking; even in the south, it is less obtrusive than in Italian-American cooking. Still, the flavor of garlic is the soul of many Italian dishes. It has a particular affinity with dried-pasta dishes. Even the American palate, which began as a facsimile of the restrained British one, has an affection for what was once considered a vile taste:

> *There are two Italies; one composed of the green earth and transparent sea and the mighty ruins of ancient times; and aerial mountains, and the warm and radiant atmosphere which is interfused through all things. The other consists of the Italians of the present day, their works and their ways. The one is the most sublime and lovely contemplation that can be conceived by the imagination of man; the other the most degraded, disgusting, and odious—What do think? Young women of rank actually eat—you will never guess what—garlick. Our poor friend Lord Byron is quite corrupted by living among these people.*
>
> —Percy Bysshe Shelley, letter to Leigh Hunt in London, from Naples, December 20, 1818

Powdered dried garlic, dessicated garlic bits, and garlic salt are not substitutes for fresh garlic cloves. Neither is bottled chopped garlic preserved in oil (usually soy oil, which has no culinary merit). I have found the taste of the garlic to be rank and unpleasant when preserved this way. The little bit of green (the sprout) that is found in the center of an older clove of garlic should be removed, for it will impart a bitter flavor. It is best to chop garlic with a sharp chopping knife or a *mezzaluna,* not a garlic press, which only releases the juice and a little of the pulp. When making soups, add an unpeeled clove of garlic rather than a naked clove, which can impart too powerful a flavor.

Marjoram, in Italian, *maggiorana:* The wild marjoram that grows all over the arid southern Mediterranean landscape is stronger than sweet marjoram, which is cultivated and with which we are most familiar. Both varieties are used for flavoring soups and stews, more commonly in southern than northern Italian cooking. Sweet marjoram's flavor is similar to that of oregano, though less sharp. I prefer fresh marjoram to dried, though marjoram is an herb that can be dried successfully.

Mint, in Italian, *menta:* The Romans were fond of mint, and carried it all over the empire. They are still fond of it and use it in soups, vegetables, salads, with bean dishes and fish, and, most commonly of all, with tripe. In Sardinia, where mint grows wild everywhere, it turns up in dishes such as *maccheroni* with tomato-and-beef sauce flavored with mint and red wine, and seasons a *ravioli* filling of mashed potato and sheep's cheese, a specialty of the island.

Mint has mysterious combinations of opposing properties. Powerful but delicate, penetrating but soothing, it is the opposite of an herb such as sage, which is ponderous and bitter. Some Italian cooks I know like to replace basil with mint in their tomato sauce from time to time. Unlike basil, which can be put in by the cupful, or used entirely on its own as in *pesto,* mint must be used parsimoniously. Two or three tablespoons on a sauce for six people is enough. Dried mint is not so successful, but it is passable if fresh can't be found. Mint leaves can be successfully frozen for winter use.

Nutmeg, in Italian, *noce moscata:* One can't say too many good things about nutmeg. Without it, there would be mostly sad fillings inside wonderful *tortellini, cappelletti,* and the many other beguiling pasta specialties of northern Italy. It is also an essential flavoring in *salsa besciamella* (béchamel), an important element of

Top: *Percy Bysshe Shelley.*
Bottom: *Lord Byron. Italy has eternally enchanted artists, writers, and poets. Shelley, who wrote some of his greatest verse there, and Byron, were among them.*

many noodle and baked pasta dishes. It is better to buy nutmeg in nut form and grate it fresh every time you need it; the extra labor results in a clearer flavor.

Oregano, in Italian, *origano:* Similar in flavor to marjoram but stronger, this is an herb I rarely use in pasta cookery. It has been overused by Americans, who generally regard it as the herb most characteristic of Italian cuisine. American soldiers who grew fond of Neapolitan pizza during the war caused a ready market for oregano when the pizza mania was imported here. This assertive herb overwhelms pasta sauce unless it is added judiciously. It is sometimes used in southern Italian cooking, but rarely in northern.

Parsley, in Italian, *prezzemolo:* Food historians say that parsley is native to Sardinia. Despite what must have been tranquil beginnings for the bold little herb, it developed a sadly malevolent reputation in food lore. After it was brought to England, it was believed that the seed, which germinated slowly, went down to the devil and came up again nine times before a single tenuous sprout saw the light of day. Some people believed that a sprig picked simultaneously with the mention of an enemy's name would cause the unfortunate's death within forty-eight hours. Wild tales for a harmless herb that enjoys little more distinction than as garnish for pork chops and the like.

Parsley is very important in Italian cooking. Its mild, grassy taste is irreplaceable. Unfortunately, it is sometimes difficult to get the flat-leafed Italian variety here, which is really the only variety suitable for cooking. The curly type is good for ornamental purposes, but has comparatively little taste. Dried parsley is of no use; it retains none of the character of the fresh and is even bitter. Fresh parsley is almost always available, and in a pinch, the curly-leafed variety can be used.

Once parsley is washed and dried thoroughly, the stems, which have a lot of flavor, should be separated from the leaves and saved for soups or stocks. Unless a recipe says otherwise, use just the leaves when chopped parsley is called for. Chop the leaves by hand with a chopping knife or a *mezzaluna;* a food processor bruises them and makes them mushy. (Note: Chewing raw parsley freshens the breath.)

Pepper, in Italian, *pepe:* The pepper plant sends out a vine with flowers that bear the pepper fruit, small berries that are green when they are immature, red when fully ripe, and black when dried.

Mint. From Hortus Eystettensis, *illustrated by Wolfgang Kilien and others, 1613.*

When black pepper is soaked and hulled, a slightly milder white pepper berry is produced.

Various types of pepper are used in Italian cooking. Black pepper is most common. White pepper is used to blend with white sauces. The red pepper berry (not to be confused with red pepper flakes) is rarely seen in the Italian kitchen, but green peppercorns, which have a quiet but pleasantly pervasive presence, are sometimes used. The red pepper flakes popular in many southern Italian dishes, particularly in tomato sauces for pasta, come from dried whole red peppers (*peperoncino*).

There is no substitute for freshly ground pepper. The preground variety is a mere memory of the real thing, for the pepper has lost its strength and clearness. Green peppercorns are used in both dried and pickled forms. Dried, they are ground in a mortar and pestle before use. The variety in brine is usually added whole. Red pepper flakes can be formed by crushing whole dried peppers (what a pleasant sight to see bunches of these long, thin peppers hanging, like crimson curls, from their gnarled stems in the markets), or you can purchase pepper flakes.

Rosemary, in Italian, *rosmarino:* This is a favorite herb of the Italians, especially for flavoring veal, pork, and lamb, as well as chicken. It is too strong to be used without special attention. Crush it in your hand before adding it to the pot so that the flavor is released from the leaves. A pinch in a chicken-liver sauce for spaghetti or fresh noodles is lovely.

Rosemary retains its character well when dried, but it can't be kept too long; it starts to get brown and lose its potency after six months on the shelf. A good way to preserve fresh rosemary is to pack it in a jar between layers of coarse salt. Do not wash it first or mold will form; wash it just before using. Preserved this way, rosemary retains its color, much of its original fiber, and a great deal of flavor for up to two years. If rosemary leaves are called for, do not substitute powdered rosemary.

Saffron, in Italian, *zafferano:* The Phoenicians had a great love for saffron, and I can't help but suppose that it rubbed off on the Sardinians, whose island they visited during the ninth century in search of trade. Saffron is still much loved in Sardinia, where my mother was born and spent her childhood. Ever since I was a small girl, I have never heard my mother speak of saffron without letting out an only faintly audible, but unmistakable sigh simultaneous with the word, so that it sounded something like "zsahhhhffron." It was

Red Pepper. From Hortus Eystettensis, *illustrated by Wolfgang Kilien and others, 1613.*

a tone of voice I usually only ever heard when she said prayers with us children before we went to bed. So I got the idea from a very young age that there was something precious, even holy about the strange little fire-colored threads that came in miniature glass vials or, sometimes, in pretty little red-and-white packets. It is a lovely thing to think that the "threads" are the stigmas of crocus flowers. There are only three in each flower, which blooms and is picked by hand in the autumn. It takes eighty-five thousand crocuses to supply the stigmas for one pound of true saffron, which accounts for its dearness.

When buying saffron, be sure you're getting the real thing and not a substitute containing turmeric, a mixture sometimes passed off as saffron. One envelope of powdered saffron contains .005 ounce (about one-sixteenth teaspoon). If you are using the filaments rather than the powder, you will have to use a small or large pinch as a measure, or rough measuring spoon equivalents. Heat filaments on a dish in the oven or on the stove for a minute. The heat releases the oils in the filaments. Powdered saffron doesn't need to be heated before being used.

Sage, in Italian, *salvia:* The very strong, musty character of sage goes well in pork, sausage, and game dishes. It is used sparingly in pasta cookery. But in the Piedmont, far in the north of Italy, it is sometimes added to a simple sauce of melted butter and cheese for potato *gnocchi.*

Salt, in Italian, *sale:* There is a new taste for low-salt eating in America. As a result, many Americans may find traditional Italian cooking a little salty. Throughout this book, I have suggested "salt to taste," sometimes giving guidelines where I feel sure less salt would detract from the dish. Coarse salt (such as our kosher salt) has better flavor and is used instead of fine salt in many Italian kitchens. The natural-foods movement has led us to believe that sea salt is more healthful than ordinary table salt, but this is not true. In terms of nutritional value, they are identical. The taste of sea salt in food is superior to that of ordinary table salt, however.

When making broths, stocks, soups, or sauces that will be refrigerated or frozen for some time before using, leave the salt out and add it at the time of use. Salt imparts a slight sour taste to liquids over a period of time.

Saffron Crocus. Hand-colored stipple engraving by Pierre-Joseph Redouté.

Essential Provisions

These classic Italian ingredients are available from Italian grocers and food specialty shops. Resort to American substitutes only when the authentic item is not available.

Anchovies, in Italian, *acciughe:* Salted anchovies packed in pure olive oil are the only kind that should be used in Italian cooking. Eaten on their own, they have an extremely salty taste. When heated, they disintegrate and blend in wonderful ways with other ingredients. Once a can is opened, the anchovies can be kept in the refrigerator for several weeks, but their saltiness will become more pronounced. Store the anchovies in a tightly closed glass jar. Anchovy paste is more convenient, particularly when a recipe calls for only a few anchovies, but the flavor is different. Do not substitute anchovy paste unless indicated in the recipe.

Artichokes, in Italian, *carciofi:* Use only very fresh, preferably young artichokes that don't weigh more than about seven ounces each. Sometimes, lovely baby artichokes, weighing about one ounce each, can be found in American markets. Large, old ones are woody and tough. Soaking artichokes softens the leaves permitting you to spread them more easily for stuffing. Artichokes can be cleaned one to two hours before they are cooked, as long as they are immersed in water with lemon juice or vinegar (two tablespoons to a quart of cool water).

Bread crumbs, in Italian, *pane grattugiato:* Canned bread crumbs, especially those marked "Italian bread crumbs," either plain or seasoned with dried parsley, onion, monosodium glutamate, and other ingredients heretical to fine cooking, should not be used when bread crumbs are called for. Hard bread can be easily pulverized in a food processor or blender, or by using a hand grater. Do not preseason crumbs. Use sturdy (not airy) Italian or white so-called peasant bread containing no sugar. Keep crumbs in a

Sage. Hand-colored stipple engraving by Pierre-Joseph Redouté.

Top: *Artichoke. From* Hortus Eystettensis, *illustrated by Wolfgang Kilien and others, 1613.*
Bottom: *Eggplant. From* Hortus Eystettensis, *illustrated by Wolfgang Kilien and others, 1613.*

closed glass jar or container in the pantry. Bread absorbs moisture, so it is important to keep crumbs in a dry place—not in the refrigerator. Toast the crumbs before using, to prevent them from absorbing oil too easily.

Broth (synonymous with stock), in Italian, *brodo:* For recipes and additional information on broths, see chapter 4. When making fresh broths ahead of using them, do not add salt. Salt will sour stocks, soups, and sauces made in advance. Add it at the point that you plan to use them. Although bouillon cubes do not take the place of good stock, they are widely used in Italian cooking to add flavor to soups, stews, sauces, *risotti,* and the like. I have found Knorr bouillon cubes to be among the best brands, for both chicken and beef flavor. Stay away from the loose bouillon in jars, sold by the same companies that also make stock cubes. Vegetable bouillon has a very artificial taste and should not be used in place of fresh vegetable stock, which is so easily made from celery leaves, carrots, onion, and parsley. Fish stock, for which there is also a recipe in chapter 4, should always be made fresh.

Butter, in Italian, *burro:* Sweet (unsalted) butter should be used when butter is called for. Its flavor and aftertaste is far superior to salted butter, though it is more perishable. Salt is added to butter to preserve it. This can mean that the salted butter on the market shelves is far less fresh than the unsalted butter. Butter takes on the flavors and odors of other foods it comes into contact with, so always be sure to keep it in a closed glass or plastic container or butter dish, especially when storing it in the refrigerator. Keep only as much butter in the refrigerator as you need for ready use and freeze the rest.

Capers, in Italian, *capperi:* Capers (*capparis spinosa*) grow wild in the Mediterranean region, North Africa, and India. The tiny pickled green buds we are accustomed to seeing submerged in brine in small elegant jars are actually flower buds of the caper plant. They are picked by hand before sunrise while still tightly closed. Nasturtium buds are often passed off as capers, but they don't have the proper firm texture or peppery taste. The finest capers have tulip-shaped buds and are very small and solid.

The Italians often use capers in sauces for boiled meats, in veal and fish cookery, and in olive oil–based pasta sauces.

Eggplants, in Italian, *melanzane:* Use the deep-purple type in Italian

40

cooking. When you are shopping for an eggplant, look at the bottom for a small "navel," which indicates the male vegetable. Female eggplants have larger "navels" and larger seeds, which make the vegetable very bitter. (I am only glad that such sorrow inflicted upon the fair female sex is restricted to the vegetable kingdom.) It took me years to figure out why some eggplants were so bitter, even after salting them to leach the bitterness from the seeds.

Eggs, in Italian, *uova:* Luigi Barzini went on to explain to Mimi Sheraton the advantage of keeping chickens for fresh eggs: "When you have a soft-boiled egg at my house, you know it left the hen less than one hour ago and when you open such an egg, it smells like a gardenia." Fresh eggs from free-range chickens are startlingly different in flavor from the usual store-bought eggs. The latter come from chickens raised in cages on a diet of chemicals designed to fatten them. The yolk of a freshly-laid egg is bright orange and sits erect in the firm puddle of white that surrounds it. Eggs from free-range chickens are also more nutritious and result in superior homemade pasta.

Flour, in Italian, *farina:* Commercial dried pasta is made with semolina, a coarse golden flour made from high-protein durum wheat. Semolina is sometimes used in the south of Italy for *pasta fresca* (see recipe in chapter 2), while unbleached bread flour is used to make the more delicate fresh pasta of the north. Stored in a tightly closed container, white flour will keep almost indefinitely in a cool, dry cupboard, preferably on the lowermost shelf (though not on the floor, where it might be subject to more changes in temperature and to humidity). Whole-wheat and buckwheat flours have a much shorter shelf life and should be kept in the refrigerator.

Mushrooms, in Italian, *funghi:* When cultivated mushrooms are called for, use only fresh mushrooms. These are not, however, interchangeable with either fresh or dried wild mushrooms. Chanterelles, oyster mushrooms, morels, and other wild mushrooms are becoming somewhat more common in large city markets and specialty grocers, but for the most part they remain difficult to find.

Some recipes in this book call for *porcini* (known as *cèpes* in France), mushrooms that grow wild in Italy, occasionally reaching enormous size. (The *porcini* I have eaten in Italy are so large, they are served as a main course, sautéed in olive oil with garlic and fresh parsley, each cap the size of a steak.) There is tremendous excitement surrounding the hunt for the valuable and elusive *porcini*

Top: *Chanterelle.* Middle: *Morel.*
Bottom: Porcino.

Making Olive Oil, *By Johannes Stradanus, from* Nova Reperta *("New Discoveries"), c. 1580.*

Olives. By Henri Louis Duhamel du Monceau, from Traité des Arbres Fruitiers, *c. 1801.*

when they appear in autumn and spring. They are greatly prized and very expensive to buy, even in their native areas. Immensely flavorful, with a rich, woodsy aroma that is positively intoxicating, *porcini* are dried and packaged and easily found in American markets. They still retain much of their wonderful flavor (drying, in fact, concentrates it). Be careful that what you buy is the fleshy and predominantly light-colored part of the mushroom, not the dark, gnarled pieces, which are not as good. Dried *porcini* are very expensive, but it only takes a very small amount to impart a powerful flavor.

To use dried mushrooms, soak them in warm water for thirty minutes. Rinse in clear water only if they are sandy and squeeze dry. Chop or prepare them in the manner directed in the recipe. Strain the water in which they have soaked through a paper towel or clean cloth to remove any grit and save it for use in sauces or stocks.

Cultivated mushrooms have their place in Italian cooking, although the white varieties commonly available in this country are very bland. They cannot stand on their own in a mushroom sauce, and should be combined with dried *porcini* if used for this purpose. Fresh mushrooms lose their texture if they are washed, so it is best just to dust them with a towel or a mushroom brush. If they are sandy and gritty, wash them quickly in cold water (don't soak them) and dry them immediately and thoroughly.

Olive oil, in Italian, *olio di oliva:* Olive oil is at its best when it is very young. The taste and aroma of just-pressed olive oil is exquisite. If you are in Italy during olive-pressing time in December, find your way to a *fattoria* where it is done. It is well worth the effort to get a taste of the first day's pressed oil, dribbled onto a slab of country bread. Only the best olives are selected for oil that is labeled "extra virgin." They are handpicked and, soon after, crushed between huge circular stone presses. The most pungent, fruity-flavored oil is released in the first pressing.

"Extra virgin olive oil," *spremuto a freddo* (cold pressed), or *prima spremitura* (first pressed) are terms to look for when you want to buy this highest-grade oil. It is sometimes passed through cheesecloth to obtain clarity. I prefer the stronger flavor and aroma of the cloudy, fruity, unfiltered first-pressed oil for most types of cooking, and the clear virgin oil for cooking delicate dishes such as fish and sweetbreads, and for making salad dressing. But both have a rich green-gold color that is unmistakable when compared to the pale gold color of lesser grades, which are the products of subsequent pressings. It is these lighter oils that are generally used in this country, for they accommodate a predilection for blander flavors. Virgin olive oil is easily bought in most markets. It should not be used for frying, for it is too rich tasting as well as too expensive. For the best results, use virgin olive oil when it is called for in this book.

The best way to keep olive oil is to cap it tightly and store it in a cool place. Do not refrigerate it and do not store it near a direct source of heat. Also, do not top already stored oil with fresh oil from a new bottle. Buy olive oil in small quantities, because it becomes rancid as it ages. By following these measures, the oil will keep up to two years or more.

One of the best things about this ubiquitous oil of the whole Mediterranean is that it is healthful as well as delicious, for it contains no cholesterol and is a pure oil. In fact, recent studies show that because of its properties as a monounsaturate, it will lower excessive levels of cholesterol in the blood.

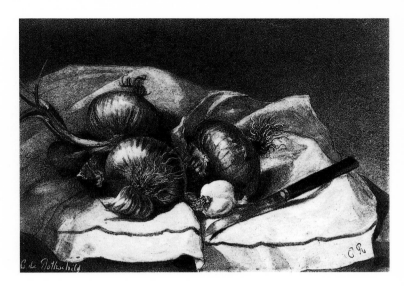

Onions and garlic, 19th century. By Charlotte Nathaniel de Rothschild.

Olives, in Italian, *olive:* Black and green olives both come from the same fruit, the green being younger than the black. It is a poetic and epic food, this olive, one that many Americans have yet to experience in its unspoiled, vigorous, pungent, and oily greatness. Americans have proverbially dropped olives into their martinis, while the Italians, the French, and the peoples of the Middle East have made them into entire meals. I speak not of the cocktail olive, nor of the canned olive, which is only a ghost of its original self, preserved in water and all its flavor leached out. . . .

Niçoise or *Gaeta* olives are my favorites for the recipes in this book calling for black olives, especially for the *olivada* sauce (a kind of olive *pesto*) for spaghetti that can be found in chapter 7. *Ponentine* and then *Kalamata* are second and third choices. The green olive I like to use most in pasta sauces is the *piccholine,* a small, firm, pungent but not sour olive. See the recipe for Spaghetti with Sundried Tomato Pesto, also in chapter 7, in which these small olives are mixed with the tomatoes. The strong and sharp, yet full, fleshy taste of olives makes a happy marriage with dried-pasta dishes.

Onions, in Italian, *cipolle:* There are three main types of onions used in Italian cooking—yellow, white, and red. Yellow onions are stronger than the other two. Recipes that call for white or red onions require a more subtle onion flavor, white onions being the mildest. Shallots are delicate, but more pungent than white and red onions.

Signor Telesforo Fini in front of his salumeria *in Modena (Emilia-Romagna), Italy, 1912. The Fini firm now exports its pasta and cured meats around the world.*

Pancetta: There is no American equivalent for *pancetta,* an unsmoked Italian bacon that is cured with salt and mild spices in a rolled form. Many specialty shops carry it. Its subtle flavor is inimitable, and where it is called for, it is preferable to go to the trouble of finding it. If you cannot locate it, substitute American bacon, blanched for one minute. Blanching removes some of the smoked taste from bacon without actually cooking it.

Prosciutto: Prosciutto is a general term for ham, which includes both *prosciutto crudo,* (raw ham), and *prosciutto cotto,* (cooked boiled ham much like ours). The most famous and remarkable is the *prosciutto crudo* made in Parma in the region of Emilia-Romagna. Salted and air-cured with extraordinary skill, authentic *prosciutto di Parma* has no equal. It was banned by the F.D.A. for twenty-two years but has been available in the United States since 1989. This precious product is best uncooked, sliced very thin, and eaten without melon, figs, or any other embellishment. Other imported and domestic *prosciutti* are less expensive and are perhaps more sensible for use in pasta sauces. When buying any *prosciutto crudo,* look for a pleasant pink color. Avoid it if it is dark in hue. It should be dry but not dried out and tough. The best *prosciutto crudo* is naturally sweet and not excessively salty. The tasty border of fat surrounding the slice of *prosciutto* is essential to the *prosciutto* experience, whether eating it raw or using it in cooking. When used in cooking, *prosciutto* should be sliced as thin as American bacon. *Prosciutto* is best eaten within several hours after slicing, or up to a day after purchase.

Mortadella: This popular sausage resembles a very large boloney with little white circles of fat throughout. This is a specialty of Bologna, from whence came the name of the American meat that otherwise bears little resemblance to the original. *Mortadella* is made from very finely minced high-quality pork (one of the essential differences from American boloney, which is made of pork scraps). Whole peppercorns and other spices are added before the mixture is put into a huge sausage casing. *Mortadella* of fine quality is buttery tender, subtle but immensely flavorful, and goes into the fillings of the *tortellini* and other such stuffed pasta for which the Emilians are renowned (see chapter 5). We can buy good *mortadella* here. It has no substitute, but is not very difficult to find (all Italian delicatessens I have ever been in carry it).

Salame: As with *prosciutto,* there are many different kinds of *salame* made in Italy. Italians are as adamant about the superiority of the *salame* made in their respective regions as they are about other aspects of their localized cuisine. Genoa *salame* is very common here, as well as other imports from Tuscany, Piedmont, and Sicily. *Soppressata* is a very flavorful, meaty *salame* from southern Italy suggested for some of the recipes in this book. I have found *salame* sold under the Citterio label consistently good. Used in pasta dishes, *salame* is not cooked for long, but briefly heated or put in at the end.

Salt pork, in Italian, *strutto:* This is very different from bacon, as it is salted rather than smoked. Although the slabs of salt pork we buy in supermarkets resemble bacon slabs, their taste is completely different. Substituting one for the other would alter completely the character of a recipe. Keep salt pork in the freezer and cut off small pieces as you need them.

Antique equipment for making salame.

Tomato paste, in Italian, *pasta di pomodoro:* Use this densely flavored ingredient parsimoniously. Too much of the concentrated taste of tomato paste can ruin a sauce. To avoid opening a can, which almost always contains more than you need, buy tomato paste in tubes so that you can use a tablespoon at a time. Test different brands, for some are much sweeter than others. Don't be tempted to use an entire can when you only need two tablespoons.

Tomatoes, in Italian, *pomodori:* The commercially grown tomatoes we get may look flawless, but are hard and tasteless, for they are bred for shipping rather than flavor. Uniform in size and containing few seeds, these poor specimens are picked very green, which allows them to be shipped as trouble-free as baseballs. Then, denied their proper right to puberty, they are forced into the red blushes of maturity with a burst of ethylene gas.

We owe the adventuring Spaniards for their interest in the tomato plant, which they found in Mexico and South America. Raw tomatoes were long considered poisonous. Early recipe books advised cooking them for three hours to make them safe to eat. The Italians were actually the first Europeans to recognize the culinary potential of tomatoes. The incorporation of tomatoes into southern Italian cuisine dates back to the mid-eighteenth century. These early tomatoes were quite different from the fruit as we know it today. They were yellow (hence the name "golden apple"), small, and oval—more like plum tomatoes, but ribbed lengthwise like a pumpkin.

The tomatoes used in modern Italian cooking are the sweet, soft, fleshy "plum" variety that are difficult to grow in colder climates.

I have tried growing them in my New York garden from seeds brought back from Italy, but they are a mere shadow of Italian plum tomatoes. They need a long, dry growing season in a very hot climate. Cherry tomatoes can be substituted, for they are sweet, though they take some patience to peel and seed. If you can grow your own, plant Roma or San Marzano variety plum tomatoes, both are firm and sweet and more suitable for sauces than the "giant" breeds so popular here. Home-grown vine-ripened tomatoes have no equal in simple pasta sauces.

Tomatoes, canned: There are canned tomatoes that retain much of the goodness of vine-ripened tomatoes. Montini and Redpack brands seem to be the sweetest and the most fleshy and flavorful. Rienzi is a runner-up. I have found most other brands, including imported Italian ones, acidic, dull, and sometimes thin rather than fleshy. Buy tomatoes packed in purée rather than juice for making sauce. If you are using tomatoes in juice, add tomato paste or your sauce will be too thin. One six-ounce can of paste added to a twenty-eight ounce can of tomatoes in juice will give the sauce the correct body. Canned tomatoes are improved by removing their bitter seeds. Do not substitute tomato sauce or canned tomato purée when whole canned tomatoes are specified.

Tomatoes, frozen: Freezing home-grown tomatoes preserves their flavor far better than home canning. You will find that you can make excellent tomato sauce off-season with sweet, ripe fresh-frozen tomatoes. First blanch them in rapidly boiling water for thirty seconds, remove them from the water, and slip off the skins. Then cut a conical-shaped hole on the top to remove the tough flesh surrounding the stem. Halve the tomatoes and lift out and discard the seeds.

It is a good idea to separate the tomatoes into five-cup portions in freezer containers or plastic bags. Freezing tomatoes leaches out a tremendous amount of their water, so that five cups of frozen tomatoes will yield only about two and one-half cups when thawed, the quantity necessary to make sauce for a pound of pasta. Put a basil leaf in with each container or bag and tightly close. If using a bag, be sure to press out all the air before sealing it.

Thaw the tomatoes before cooking them. This will insure a fresher tomato taste because you will need to expose them to heat for a shorter period of time. Discard some of the water that has leached out during thawing. Depending on your climate, you may find your tomatoes excessively watery. Compensate for this by

Tomatoes. From Hortus Eystettensis, *illustrated by Wolfgang Kilien and others, 1613.*

adding two to four tablespoons of tomato paste to each two and one-half cups of thawed tomatoes.

Tomatoes, sun-dried, in Italian, *pomodori secchi:* Needless to say, sun-dried tomatoes have become trendy in America, often used in ways that make little culinary sense. Actually, they are little known in most parts of Italy except for Liguria and the deep south (Sardinia in particular), where tomatoes are harvested at the end of the summer and dried in the sun for winter use. They are then packed in salt and sometimes formed into big loaves. Pieces are sliced off the loaves when needed for cooking or just for spreading on bread.

Dried tomatoes are the precursors of tomato paste. They can be chopped up and sautéed with olive oil and garlic or onion for sauce, or added to meat- or vegetable-based sauces for a richer taste. (See the recipe for Spaghetti with Sun-dried Tomato *Pesto* in chapter 7.) To reconstitute sun-dried tomatoes that are not preserved in oil, cover them with boiling water for fifteen minutes. Drain and pat thoroughly dry. Lay them out on a cookie sheet and place in a preheated 250-degree oven for ten minutes. Remove from the oven, pack into a jar, and cover with olive oil. Add a few peppercorns and peeled cloves of garlic to the jar and tightly seal. Preserved this way, dried tomatoes will keep for a long time in the refrigerator.

Tuna. By Marcus Elieser Bloch, from Ictyologie ou Histoire des Poissons, *c. 1782.*

Tuna, in Italian, *tonno sott'olio:* Canned tuna is a useful thing to have around when it comes to pasta cookery, for it can be made into a sauce with tomatoes or used in other ways, such as tossed with warm *maccheroni* and a good-quality mayonnaise for a delicious summer dish. The best tuna to use is Italian tuna packed in olive oil, what is called light-meat tuna. It is from the belly of the fish, the most tender and flavorful part. Americans are accustomed to eating the white meat of the tuna, which is much drier (especially if it is packed in spring water instead of oil). For pasta sauce, the light-meat tuna is necessary. You can substitute some American brands of "light" tuna for Italian tuna, but stay away from brands that are fishy and more brown than pink.

Wine, in Italian, *vino:* Unfortunately, the majority of Italian wines exported here are not those that should be taken seriously if one is to experience what Italy has to offer. Not that such wines as the Lambruscos, Chiantis, and Soaves—among the most popular—didn't originally have character, Italian wine expert Victor Hazan once told me, "but they [have now become] bland and undistinguished."

Piedmont, the mountainous region in northern Italy bordered by France to the west and Switzerland to the north, produces some of Italy's most distinguished wines. The river Po claims Piedmont as its source, and there also flows the Tanaro. It is on the slopes of the hills that ruffle the river valleys that the Nebbiolo grape grows, which is transformed into two of Italy's most imposing wines, Barolo and Barbaresco. Tuscany also produces some of Italy's most noteworthy wines, among them Vino Nobile di Montepulciano and Brunello di Montalcino.

There are many fine Italian wines that don't have the reputations or the status of the "greats." Because a number of these excellent wines are bottled by family vineyards in relatively small quantities, they are kept for local consumption. In addition to the renowned labels mentioned here, there are additional notable Italian wines available in our country, and the Italians have ambitious plans for increasing the variety and quantity of their exports.

Wine is an important element in Italian cooking. There are numerous recipes in this book that call for white or red wine, or fortified wines such as vermouth and sherry. When using wine in cooking, it is important to use good wine, that is, wine that you would enjoy drinking, not so-called cooking wine. If all you have is an unopened bottle of good wine, by all means open it for that half cup the recipe calls for. After all, you can drink the remainder with your dinner. If recorked, an opened bottle of wine can be used for cooking for up to a week. (White wine should be stored in the refrigerator once opened.) Fortified wines keep well for months if they are not exposed to extremes of heat and cold or fluctuating temperature. Neither the taste of the wine itself nor the sensation of alcohol should ever be present in a dish once it is finished cooking. In cooking, use wine in conservative quantities and "evaporate" it completely by simmering it with other ingredients.

Cheeses

HARD CHEESES
Parmigiano: Parmigiano-reggiano is the most famous and the most precious of Italian cheeses. The Emilians say it has been produced in their region for at least two thousand years. It was known to Taillevent, born in 1326, the author of the oldest French cookbook.

Great care is taken in the making of this cheese. It must be aged for at least two years before it can be eaten. Connoisseurs insist that it should be at least three years old, when it is called *stravecchio,* or

Sheep. By Baron Cuvier and Geoffrey St. Hilaire, from Histoire Naturelles des Mammiferes, *Paris, 1818–42.*

even four, when it is called *stravecchione*. A rule of thumb offered by the *parmigiano* producers in the Enza valley is that it must be two years old for eating, three years old for *pastasciutta,* and four years old for *tortellini.* The unpasteurized cow's milk used for *parmigiano-reggiano* is particularly rich and sweet. The aging is a completely natural process in which no antifermatives are used. The air of the five provinces in which it is produced is essential to the success of this cheese, as is the craft of those making it. Naturally, the results are an inimitable product that is expensive, even in Italy.

Parmigiano-reggiano is only one of the cheeses of the overall category called *grana padano,* produced in the same five-province region. The less noble, but still fine *grana* is a sensible substitute for *parmigiano-reggiano.* Because *grana* is produced in larger quantities outside the designated provinces, aged less, and processed without as much ceremony, it is much cheaper to buy.

The best *parmigiano* is a rich, yellow color, firm yet moist in texture, with no holes. Always ask to sample some before you buy it. I have been charged for the best and been sold dry, salty, crumbly cheese that had deteriorated from not having been stored properly. *Grana* is sharper and less subtle and complex in taste. The markings on the rind tell you whether a cheese is *parmigiano-reggiano* or *grana.* Be sure to look for them, for it is not uncommon to see *grana* sold for its more precious relation, for an equally more precious price.

To keep these cheeses, wrap them in lightly dampened paper, then in a damp towel or cheesecloth and store in the refrigerator. It is best to grate cheese just before you are ready to use it, or it will dry out and lose flavor. Freshly grated cheese can be frozen for later use, although it is best fresh. Never use the pregrated bottled or canned cheeses called "Parmesan" or "Italian-style grating cheese." These are not *parmigiano* and have little merit for use in the kitchen at all, as far as I can tell. Sometimes, however, authentic *parmigiano* is called Parmesan, which is confusing unless you ask just exactly what is being sold.

Pecorino: This term refers to cheese made from sheep's milk. *Pecorino*-type cheeses are produced in all stages of maturity, from soft to hard, mild to very strong. What is exported here is the harder *romano* and *sardo pecorino* cheeses characteristic of Rome and Sardinia. These are saltier, sharper, and less rounded than *parmigiano-reggiano* or *grana* and should not be substituted for them. They are used with certain pasta sauces that are very tangy, or can be mixed with *parmigiano* to cut the sweetness of *pesto. Pepato* is a

The Innkeeper, *by Ducleré, 19th century.*

Top: *Knife for cutting hard cheeses.*
Bottom: Cheese Seller at the Market in
Bologna, *by G. M. Mitelli, 17th century.*

type of *pecorino* that is riddled with whole black peppercorns. It is used much as *romano* or *sardo* would be, in pasta dishes with racy characters or simply sprinkled over a dish of pasta with butter.

Other Hard Cheeses

Asiago: The Veneto region is home to this firm cheese made from partly skimmed cow's milk. When aged, it is a "poor person's *parmigiano*," not complex or distinguished, but all the same quite good and inexpensive. An *asiago* is also produced in the United States.

Cacio cavallo ("cheese astride a horse"): Christened as such because it resembles two little saddlebags, this strong, hard cheese resembles *provolone* to some extent. In the same way, it is a little too domineering with most pasta sauces. But it is good with pasta alone, along with pepper and a lump of butter.

Provolone: Ranging from a sweet and soft cheese (*dolce*) to strong and hard (*piccante*) varieties, *provolone* originated in southern Italy, though its production has now expanded to the Po Valley. The sweet variety is best for pasta.

Ricotta salata ("salted *ricotta*"): This is a very rustic cheese, made by salting fresh *ricotta* (see below) and allowing it to solidify. It is good grated over pasta that has been tossed with simple tomato sauces.

SOFT CHEESES
Fontina: A soft cheese made in Piedmont, *fontina* is used in pasta dishes of that region. It is also one of the four cheeses used in the many versions of the popular pasta *ai quattro formaggi* ("with four cheeses").

Gorgonzola: This blue-veined, rich, creamy cheese is made from cow's milk. Young *Gorgonzola* is creamy and sweet. As it ages, it becomes very strong. For pasta sauces, the sweet one is best. A *Gorgonzola* and cream sauce is typically served with *penne* or *gnocchi,* but makes a happy marriage with other types of *maccheroni* and fresh pasta. *Roquefort* and other strong-flavored blue-veined cheeses should not be substituted for *Gorgonzola.*

Mascarpone (also, *mascherpone*): A fresh Italian cream cheese (though not technically a cheese because it contains no rennet) produced from double cream, *mascarpone* should be consumed as soon as possible after it is made. It is a naturally sweet cheese that is often eaten with fruit, mixed with sugar and brandy, made into desserts, or used in pasta sauces. In general, cream cheese in the United States is thicker and not as soft, and commercial brands contain a substance that makes them gummy. Some cheese shops sell fresh cream cheese, which is a better substitute.

Mozzarella: True *mozzarella* is a fresh, soft cheese that suffers if it is not eaten on the same day it is made. Authentic *mozzarella* is made from the milk of water buffaloes, which even in Italy is increasingly rare. Many Italian food shops and delicatessens here make their own *mozzarella* daily. The creamy-white braids and fists of cheese can be seen bathing in large stainless-steel pans or in huge glass jars on the counter, most often offered in salted and salt-free varieties. These cheeses are made from cow's milk, as is most *mozzarella* cheese today. Salt-free *mozzarella,* an Italian-American phenomenon, is virtually tasteless. Authentic Italian *mozzarella* is always salted. The rubbery, plastic-wrapped *mozzarella* sold in the dairy sections of supermarkets is not a good substitute for fresh *mozzarella.* A bland cheese, *mozzarella* nonetheless has an unqualified charm and acts to pull together the flavors of a pasta casserole in a very pleasant way. It is used mostly in southern Italian cooking. Italian Americans are very fond of it, most probably because of its Campanian (Neapolitan) origin, from whence many Italian-American immigrants came.

Ricotta: This fresh cheese made from whey is used frequently for pasta fillings, sauces, and pastry fillings. Our *ricotta* is creamier and more watery than the Italian variety, so it must be drained first when used in pasta fillings.

The Ricotta Eaters, *by Vincenzo Campi (1525–91).*

2 MAKING FRESH PASTA

La Pasta Fatta in Casa

Beautiful and white
As you emerge in groups
Out of the machine
If on a cloth
You are made to lie
You look to me like the milky way.

Zounds!
Great Desire,
Master of this earthly life,
I waste away,
I faint from the wish
To taste you,
O maccheroni!

—Filippo Sgruttendio,
from *Le Laude de Li Maccarune*
("Praise to Macaroni"), Naples, 1646

The Art of the Pasta Maker, *c. 1767.*

Pasta fresca ("fresh pasta"), *pasta fatta in casa* ("pasta made at home"), *pasta fatta a mano* ("pasta made by hand"), *sfoglia* (literally, "sheets" of pasta), and *pasta all'uovo* ("egg pasta") all mean a similar thing: lovely fresh Italian pasta made at home. To those who find a great pleasure in eating the lightest and freshest pasta possible, I recommend this ancient, peaceful activity, which is not so complicated as many may think.

Years ago, when I lived in Edinburgh, an Italian woman, well in her nineties, lived down the street from me. Whereas it was my work then to visit old people who came within the jurisdiction of a certain district of the city's Social Work Department, I visited her out of pleasure, not out of duty, for a more spry and happy human I rarely saw. She emitted a kind of cellular cheer and contentment foreign to most modern people. Every day she made fresh pasta for herself and her unmarried son who lived with her. (They had, alas for him, that curious and ancient mother-son bond that so puzzles us post-Freudian folk.) She piled flour and salt onto a huge board. Then she made a well in the center of the flour and added oil and eggs, mixing and kneading until she had a tidy little bun of dough. She rolled it out skillfully and with great and surprising strength, and then cut the large, thin sheets into ribbons and other shapes with a sharp knife. It took perhaps an hour every day, and she did it as punctually as the sun rose every morning.

At the time, I thought this was an odd and wonderful thing, for my own mother, wonderful Italian cook though she is, had always reserved this ritual for special occasions. I suspect her lapse in this area of Italian cooking had to do with my father's preference for the more rustic dried-pasta dishes of the southern Italian kitchen. He worried that she would be "ruined" by America. There were no fancy threads in her closet and no convenience foods in her pantry— or any other such indications that she was becoming "modern." He wanted her to be a simple, old-fashioned wife and a simple, uncomplicated cook. In Tolstoi-like fashion, he had a romantic notion about the peasant classes. I suspect he meant it, for although he went as far as studying at New York University at night and became a cub reporter for several major New York City newspapers in the 1930s, he gave up that career to be a stonemason. I suppose he thought fresh pasta was a concession to the refined cooking of my mother's upbringing in a relatively wealthy family. My father, despite his birth in Italy, still had what my mother called "the pasta and tomato sauce mentality," by which she meant that he didn't

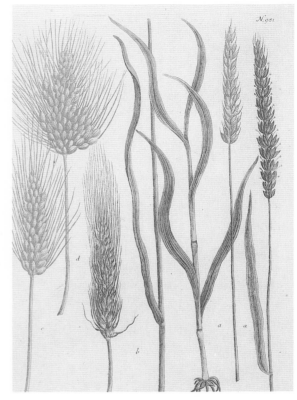

Wheat, 18th century.

know anything about real Italian cooking. She certainly managed to sneak everything else she liked onto the family menu, but making pasta was not one of her daily activities.

Ironically, living in Britain is what made me the most aware of fresh pasta—how good it is and how easy it is to make. My mother has assumed the role of ruler of the roost in her old age, as Italian custom would have it, and now she makes fresh pasta often (though not every day).

Making Fresh Pasta: Some Pointers

ABOUT THE DOUGH:
• If you are inexperienced at making pasta, don't try it on a rainy day. Humidity makes the dough harder to roll.

• Don't make pasta near a heat source, such as a radiator, fireplace, or oven that is turned on. Pasta dough must be kept soft and pliable in order to knead, roll, and cut it easily. A hot, dry environment will dry it out quickly.

• If you are making spinach or beet pasta, it is best to use fresh spinach or beets, never canned or frozen. Spinach should be *thoroughly* washed to rid it of sand and all the stems removed. Boil rather than steam the spinach, for sweeter flavor. Do not cut tops off beets before boiling, or they will bleed all their lovely color into the water. Press as much moisture as possible out of the vegetable before adding it to the dough or the dough will be too soft and unworkable. Finely chop or purée spinach or beet thoroughly to prevent ending up with a speckled rather than an evenly colored dough.

• When making tomato pasta, use only tomato paste to color the dough, not the more watery tomato sauce.

• Knead the pasta dough thoroughly and roll it sufficiently to give spinach, beet, or tomato paste uniform consistency and color.

• If the dough is hard and unworkable, wet your hands and continue to knead until it becomes pliable. If it is too soft, add small amounts of flour until it becomes elastic.

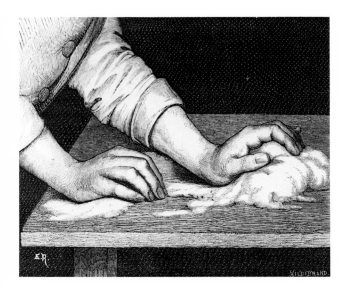

• The amount of flour that eggs absorb varies with the weather, the quality of the flour, and the size and freshness of the eggs. A very fresh egg contains more water and therefore absorbs more flour. It is important to draw in the flour gradually, in case the dough, due to any of these variables, does not absorb all the flour called for in the recipe. A dough that contains too much flour is too stiff to work with easily, and will result in a pasta with tough texture when cooked.

• As you work, always keep your pasta board or work surface free of dry dough particles.

ABOUT THE PASTA MACHINE:
Please read the general notes about pasta machines in chapter 1. I prefer the roller-type pasta machines. Here are some things to remember before you begin:

• Before using a new machine or one that has not been used for some time, put a small piece of dough through the rollers several times to remove oil and dust that has collected inside.

• Never wash the machine or get water in it. Wipe it clean with a slightly damp sponge without using soap or detergent. To clean between the rollers, dust them with a clean, dry pastry brush.

• Always keep the machine covered between uses.

Making Fresh Pasta: Method

ASSEMBLE:
Ready all the ingredients in your recipe, a bag of flour (for dusting the board and the dough as you go along), a dough scraper or spatula (to keep the board or work surface clear and free of hardened dough particles), several clean dish towels, a sharp knife, a pastry wheel, and a drying rack or rig if you are planning to dry the pasta.

Please read my observations on flour and eggs in the Essential Provisions section of chapter 1.

Signora Ida Monaci making pasta in Montepulciano (Tuscany). Top: *Make a "well" in the center of the flour.* Bottom: *The object is to form a uniform, smooth, soft ball of dough.*

PROCEED:

1. Measure the dry ingredients—flour and salt—directly onto the pasta board or flat work surface. Make a "well" in the center of the flour. Put the wet ingredients—eggs, oil (and prepared spinach, tomato paste, or beet if using it)—in the center of the well.

2. Using a fork, beat the egg mixture to combine it, and gradually draw in the flour from the inside wall of the well. Always beat in the same direction, gently, to prevent air pockets from forming in the dough later. Do not let the egg mixture run out of the well. Protect the outside wall with the hand you are not using to beat, until the wet mixture is well enough integrated with the flour not to stream out. When the mixture is too stiff to use the fork any longer, scrape the dough from the fork into the well and continue forming the dough with your hands. Draw in the flour very gradually from the bottom of the well, again, to keep air out of the dough. When you have formed a very soft ball of dough, scoop up the flour left on the board and sift it. Discard all the dried bits of dough. Work the sifted flour into the dough as you knead. The object is to form a uniform, smooth, soft ball of dough. If there is too much flour to be absorbed to make a firm yet very pliable dough, don't use it all. The perfect consistency is soft but not wet or sticky in the least, responsive to being touched and worked with, and elastic. If the dough is too soft, add flour, a little at a time, until the right consistency is formed.

3. Scrape the board of dried particles of dough and clear off all but a light dusting of flour. Flatten the ball of dough, and using the heel of your hands, knead it from the middle of the disk outwards, folding it in half after you work it each time. Do this for about ten minutes, or until a smooth, even, elastic dough is formed. Be sure to knead the dough on both sides, working it through and through while keeping it a basically round shape. The kneading process is very important. Unlike pastry dough, pasta dough needs to be worked. Well-kneaded dough makes rolling and cutting easy and produces a noodle that is tender but firm. Do not, however, over-knead it or a less delicate noodle will result. Always cover the ball of dough with an inverted bowl or slightly damp towel when you are not working with it. Work quickly and do not let dough rest unnecessarily.

ROLLING AND CUTTING BY HAND:

1. Clear the work surface and dust it lightly with flour. Make sure

there is enough room to roll a large circle of dough easily. Divide your dough into two parts. Keep the part you are not using covered as described above in step 3. Flatten the dough with a regular rolling pin, rolling out a circle much as you would for a pie. When the disk of dough gets too large to be covered by the rolling pin, switch to the long pasta rolling pin described in chapter 2. Always using motions away from you, roll out the dough evenly, rotating the disk frequently as it gets thinner and thinner. Be sure your work surface is dusted with enough flour to prevent the dough from sticking; do not overflour it, though, or the dough will become too hard to roll out properly. Work quickly, pushing the rolling pin away from you, not into the work surface. Keep the circle as round as you can; it will be an indication that you are rolling the dough evenly. Be sure to roll the edges of the disk as well as the center; it is important that the dough be completely uniform in thickness. At this point, the thickness of the dough should be about one-sixteenth inch. Only a few fresh pasta recipes require the dough to be this thick. For most types of pasta, the dough must be rolled out extremely thin.

Always use motions away from you with the rolling pin. . . . Roll the dough out evenly, rotating the disk frequently as it gets thinner and thinner.

2. When the disk is too large and the dough too thin to rotate easily on the board, place the special pasta rolling pin on the far end of the disk. Curl the disk over it, being sure to center it in the middle of the pin. Make quick rolling motions starting with your two hands together in the center. As you roll the pin toward you, keep the dough curled around it, sliding your two hands outward and away from each other, then inward toward the center again, evenly and quickly. Again, work quickly to prevent the dough from drying out and becoming more difficult to stretch. Wrap the entire disk of dough around the rolling pin and unroll it onto its reverse side back onto the work surface. Repeat the same rolling procedure. The quick rolling of the pin and sliding motions of your hands will help keep the disk an even thickness and shape as it gets thinner and thinner. If it tears at any point, just "patch" it with a little dough from the edge, and a dab of water if it doesn't easily adhere. Dust lightly with flour and continue rolling until the patch is evened out. Roll the dough paper-thin, a thirty-second inch or less.

3. Immediately cut the pasta into noodles or cut and fill according to the requirements of your recipe. You can cut noodles quickly by rolling the circle of dough into a long "club" and cutting it into "rings," one-fourth inch to one inch wide, depending on the width of noodle you want. Be sure to cut all the rings exactly the same

width for an even batch of noodles. Shake the noodles loose and spread them out on clean cloths. While they are drying, roll out and cut the remaining section of dough. If you want noodles with a pretty fluted, or curly, edge, use your fluted-edged pastry cutter and cut them out carefully on the flat circle of dough. Make the width of each consistent.

ROLLING AND CUTTING USING THE PASTA MACHINE:

1. Set up your pasta machine so that everything on your work surface is within easy reach. Be sure the machine is thoroughly clean (see pointers on pasta machines at the beginning of this chapter).

2. Divide the dough into four parts (unless you are making more than two pounds of pasta, in which case plan on two parts per pound). With your hands or a standard rolling pin, flatten the piece you are working with and dust it lightly with flour. Set the machine at the widest possible setting for rolling. Feed the dough through the roller without pulling it or stretching it. Drape it over your hand with your thumb up in the air to avoid sticking your fingers through it. Fold it in thirds as you would a letter, overlapping the top third, and then the bottom third, over the middle third. (This will keep the piece of dough in a uniform rectangular shape, which is important as you roll it out thinner and longer through the machine.) Press it flat with your hands and fingertips to get all the air out and lightly flour one side only (the other side remains unfloured so that it will adhere to itself when you fold it in thirds again). Pass the dough through the first notch. Repeat the process of folding the dough into thirds and passing it through the rollers, six to eight times on the first notch, until the dough is evenly shaped. (The folding process accomplishes kneading of the dough.) Then set the rollers one notch past the previous one. Pass the dough through again, collecting it at the other end. Repeat the process of feeding it through the rollers using a higher notch each time, until you have the thickness you want for what you are making.

For all filled pasta, *cannelloni,* and *lasagne,* and for all noodles except *trenette* and *pasta alla chitarra,* set the machine for the thinnest possible dough (usually the highest number on the knob). The next to the last numeral will produce the slightly thicker noodles mentioned above. *Fettuccine,* which are meant to be just slightly thicker than *tagliatelle,* cannot be rolled thin enough on the next to last setting, but are slightly too thin on the last setting. It is best to roll them out on the last setting as for *tagliatelle.* The coarser-textured pasta made with buckwheat, whole-wheat, and cornmeal flour are best rolled very thin. Once dry, noodles that are too thick remain very hard, even when cooked. Since the numbers on pasta machines vary from make to make, it is best to experiment on your own machine until you find the notch that works best for the noodles you are making.

3. Roll out only one strip of dough at a time if you are making filled pasta, for the dough must be very soft to seal properly. If you find that the dough is not sealing properly, dip your finger in a little water or egg white and run it along the sealing edges. If you are making noodles, set each rolled-out strip of dough aside, uncovered, to dry slightly (about five minutes) before passing it through the machine's cutting attachments. This is to prevent the dough from sticking in the cutting attachment. If you get holes or tears in your pasta, fold it and pass it through the rollers again until it comes out smooth.

4. Insert the cutting attachment on the machine. Pass one strip at a time through the cutters and collect the noodles at the other end. If the dough sticks to the cutters, let the strips dry a little longer before cutting. Don't let them dry too much, or the edges will become brittle, making it difficult or impossible to feed the strips through the cutting attachments of the machine. Cut all the strips of dough in this way. You must work very quickly in order to prevent the dough from drying out. If you think it is drying out too much, place a damp towel over the strips while you work. If the edge of the strip is too brittle to pass through the rollers or cutter of the machine, trim them with a sharp knife and try passing the strip through the machine again.

5. Keep in mind that fillings for *tortellini* and other stuffed forms cannot be too wet, or they will soak through the pasta envelope (the recipes will direct you to drain *ricotta* before using, for example). Freshly filled pasta should not rest longer than about fifteen minutes at room temperature after filling, or an hour or two (depending on the moistness of the filling) in the refrigerator. *Ricotta* or vegetable fillings are more watery than most meat fillings. If left out too long, the pasta you stuff with these fillings will stick to the surface on which they are placed and the envelopes will tear when you try to lift them. If the fillings are not too moist, the envelopes can be left out for up to four hours or so before cooking. Otherwise, refrigerate or freeze them, spacing them well so that they do not stick together. (See the following section for information

Fold the dough into thirds as you would a letter, before feeding it into the rollers of the pasta machine.

Dip a finger or pastry brush in water or egg white and run it along the sealing edges.

59

Spaghetti making in Naples in the 1800s.

on preparing filled pasta for freezing.) Layer the stuffed envelopes only if you are going to freeze them, putting aluminum foil or waxed paper between each layer. If you plan to cook them right after making them, do not stack them; arrange them, well spaced, on trays.

Drying, Freezing, and Storing Pasta:

When you have cut the pasta, gently gather up the strands or ribbons with your hand. If you plan to cook them right away, shake the strands to separate them. Then spread them out on a clean towel to dry, or hang them on a drying rack for fifteen to twenty minutes, or until they acquire a thin skin. If you plan to refrigerate or freeze them, spread on a towel or hang on a rack in the same manner, fifteen to twenty minutes. "Flash-cook" them for fifteen seconds from the moment they are dropped into boiling, salted water to prevent them from sticking when they freeze. The water should not return to the boil. Be sure not to overcook or the noodles will be too soft after they are dropped in boiling, salted water for the second time. Drain immediately, immerse in a bowl of cold water to arrest cooking. Drain again. Transfer to airtight plastic bags, making sure to squeeze all the air out of the bags before freezing. As soon as frozen pasta is dropped into boiling water and stirred, it will separate easily. Cook until the pasta floats to the surface and drain immediately.

To refrigerate or freeze noodles for *lasagne* or *cannelloni,* cook first. Drain immediately and immerse in cold water to stop further cooking. Drain and pat dry on clean kitchen towels. Place in a large plastic container in layers with aluminum foil or waxed paper between the layers. Cover tightly. Refrigerate for up to five days, or freeze for up to two months. Use directly from the refrigerator, or thaw from the freezer and proceed to layer or stuff, according to the recipe.

If you are going to store the pasta dry, make sure it is thoroughly dry first to prevent mold. Allow it to dry, uncovered, on clean cotton kitchen towels, for at least twenty-four hours. Pasta racks are best for drying pasta evenly and quickly, but spreading noodles out on clean towels until they dry will work just fine. The drying time depends on the thickness of the pasta and the humidity of the air. Store dried pasta in a box (I find shoe boxes ideal for this) or tin to protect it from being crushed. Place paper towels between layers of pasta to prevent breakage. Homemade dried pasta loses its freshness after about a month. If you want to make a large batch at a time, you are better off freezing it. It can be dropped frozen into boiling, salted water and will respond like just-made pasta, except that it will take a few seconds longer to cook.

As with noodles, it is best to half-cook *ravioli* and other fresh filled pasta forms before freezing or refrigerating them, to prevent them from sticking together.

Cooking Fresh Pasta

Make your sauce in advance, because fresh pasta cooks in a wink. Drop the fresh pasta into plenty of rapidly boiling water at the same time as you add the salt. Follow the same guidelines for quantities specified for dried pasta in chapter 1. (Do not, as some misguided cookbooks say, add oil to the water. The oil that remains on the noodles will repel the sauce. If you cook pasta in plenty of water, it will not stick.) Stir and immediately cover. When the water comes to a second boil, remove the lid. Cook from five to fifteen seconds *from the moment the water has returned to a boil.* The time will depend on the thickness of the noodle (five seconds for all fine noodles, fifteen for thicker cuts, such as *trenette*), and on the type of dough. Spinach, tomato, and beet doughs take less time to cook because they are softer. Remove the noodles as soon as the water returns to a boil. Pasta doughs containing whole-wheat or buckwheat flour or cornmeal take a few seconds longer to cook. For fresh egg noodles, the total cooking time should not exceed one and a half minutes for most noodles, three to five minutes for filled pasta. (Fresh pasta is never cooked *al dente,* because it is tender to begin with; this is a term associated with dried pasta.) Drain the pasta immediately. It should still have some moisture, though not as much as dried pasta, which should actually remain dripping wet.

Boil filled pasta gently. If the boil is too vigorous, the pasta envelopes can break and the stuffing will be lost. Drop in several envelopes at a time to avoid breaking. If cooking filled pasta in broth, add all the envelopes at once and remove the broth with the pasta in it as soon as the pasta is cooked. Immediately ladle into individual bowls. For filled pasta that is to be served with butter or sauce, scoop the envelopes out of the water with a slotted spoon or other such device as soon as they are cooked, allowing just a little bit of the pasta water to remain with them to keep them moist. (Draining the envelopes in the colander will break them.) Transfer to a warm buttered bowl; when all the envelopes are cooked, add additional melted butter or whatever sauce you have prepared.

Agnesi firm booklet on corn pasta, c. 1940.

Pasta that has dried somewhat takes a little longer to cook. Taste to determine the correct moment to remove it. Thoroughly dried pasta and frozen pasta also take somewhat longer to cook. Cook for one minute after the water returns to a boil and then test.

Fresh Pasta Portions

2-cup flour recipe:

8 people for *ravioli* or other small filled pasta in soup
4–6 people for noodles with sauce
4–6 people for *ravioli* or other small filled pasta with sauce
6–8 people for *tortelloni* or *cannelloni*
6–8 servings of *lasagne* in a 14- by 9-inch baking dish
(about 10 very thin layers of pasta)

These guidelines are based on medium-sized first-course portions. They are only approximations, which will vary depending on desired portion sizes, quality and character of ingredients (e.g., fresher eggs absorb more flour because they retain more water), the richness of the sauce on the pasta, and so on.

Pasta all'Uovo I
Egg Pasta I

MAKES ABOUT 2 POUNDS

The egg pasta of central Italy contains oil and salt. That of the Emilians (Egg Pasta II) contains only flour and eggs. Adding oil makes a softer, more pliable dough that I think produces lighter pasta than the Emilian version.

4 cups unbleached white flour
5 extra-large eggs
¼ teaspoon salt
1 tablespoon olive or vegetable oil

Follow the steps presented in Making Fresh Pasta, this chapter. The amount of flour absorbed by the eggs varies. If you find that the dough is too soft, work in more flour as you knead the dough. Cut as you like.

Pasta all'Uovo II
Egg Pasta II

MAKES ABOUT 2 POUNDS

The classic recipe for *la sfoglia* "egg pasta," in the region that claims to make the best of egg pastas, Emilia-Romagna, is one-fourth pound (one cup) of unbleached white flour to one extra-large or jumbo egg. There is no oil or salt added to the dough. While this makes the dough a little harder to work with, the Emilians say that the formula makes lighter, more delicate pasta. They also claim that the absence of oil allows for better absorption of sauce.

4 cups unbleached white flour
4 jumbo eggs

Proceed as for Egg Pasta I, slightly beating the eggs before placing them in the "well" of flour. If the dough is too soft, work more flour in little by little until you have a pliable dough. Cut as you like.

Pasta Verde
Spinach Pasta

MAKES ABOUT 2 POUNDS

This pasta is simpler to work with than egg pasta because the addition of spinach makes the dough softer—easier to knead and roll. The dough also doesn't dry out as quickly as egg pasta, which makes it good for a beginner who may need extra time to practice cutting before the dough becomes too brittle to handle. Adding spinach makes a beautiful green pasta with only a subtle taste difference, but a softer and creamier texture.

½ pound spinach (cooks down to 3½ ounces, squeezed dry)
1 teaspoon salt, for cooking spinach

4 cups unbleached white flour
¼ teaspoon salt
4 extra-large eggs
2 teaspoons olive or vegetable oil

Remove all the stems and discolored and wilted leaves from the spinach. Wash leaves thoroughly, being sure to remove all traces of sand. Boil the spinach with 1 teaspoon salt in plenty of rapidly boiling water, covered, until it is tender (about 10 minutes). Stir the spinach several times while it boils. Drain it thoroughly, leaving it to drain further in a colander or sieve until it is cool. This will help to rid it of more water. When it is cool, squeeze it as dry as you can. Wring it in a dry, clean towel to absorb more of the moisture. Chop very fine by hand or, preferably, in a food processor or blender.

Proceed as for Egg Pasta I, adding the finely chopped spinach to the egg mixture (step 1) and mixing it in thoroughly. This softer dough is more likely to stick to the board and the machine, so you will find you use more flour for dusting the board and the dough as you go along. Cut as you like. Because the dough is softer, let it dry an additional 5–6 minutes before cooking it.

Pasta Gialla
Yellow (Saffron) Pasta

MAKES ABOUT 2 POUNDS

The golden color and subtle flavor of saffron in this pasta make it a most agreeable companion to creamy tomato sauces and delicate meat sauces such as those for *Pappardelle* with Veal Sauce and Spinach *Trenette* with Creamy Tomato-Sausage Sauce, both in chapter 6.

4 cups unbleached white flour
¼ teaspoon salt
5 extra-large eggs
1 tablespoon olive or vegetable oil
¼ teaspoon (4 envelopes) saffron powder, or ½ teaspoon saffron threads

Proceed as for Egg Pasta I, first incorporating the saffron powder into the eggs by beating lightly, always in the same direction, until it is completely dissolved into the liquid. Cut as you like.

Pasta di Mais
Corn Pasta

MAKES ABOUT 1 POUND

I like to serve this pasta with *stracotto*, a long-simmered meat sauce (chapter 3), or one of the game sauces I might make with *polenta* (an Italian cornmeal "mush"), such as those of rabbit or wild bird. The corn pasta sold in health-foods stores falls apart in boiling water because no wheat flour is added. My recipe is a mix of both flours, for the gluten in wheat flour is necessary to hold the cornmeal together. Make sure you use fresh, finely ground cornmeal for this recipe.

1 cup finely ground yellow cornmeal
1½ cups unbleached white flour
½ teaspoon salt
4 extra-large eggs
2 tablespoons olive or vegetable oil

Proceed as for Whole-Wheat Pasta. Cut into *tagliatelle*.

Note: In Italy, the leaves of the beet are boiled much like spinach, and eaten hot or cold with olive oil and vinegar sprinkled over them.

Pasta Rosa
Pink (Beet) Pasta

MAKES ABOUT 2 POUNDS

Italians also use beets to color pasta. Instead of the pale orange that tomato paste gives dough, beets make it a rather bright pink until it is cooked, when it fades to a creamy rose hue. Serve these noodles with butter or simple cream sauces. They are wonderful with green vegetable sauces, too (see the recipe in chapter 6 for My Mother's Beet *Tagliatelle* with Leeks).

Follow the next recipe for tomato pasta, but substitute 2 tablespoons cooked beet purée for the tomato paste. To arrive at the purée, start out with 1 large red beet or 2 or 3 small ones, which in either case will be more than you need. Scrub the beet(s) and remove the outer leaves, but leave the stem at the base to prevent the color from leeching out as the beet boils. Boil in plenty of water for about 1 hour or until tender. Older beets might take up to 2 hours. Drain and when cool, slip off the skin. Grate or mash the beet very fine, twice through a ricer or thoroughly by hand. Leave the beet purée in a sieve for 30–40 minutes, to drain off any liquid. Measure out exactly 2 level tablespoons. Proceed with the recipe.

Pasta Rossa
Red (Tomato) Pasta

MAKES ABOUT 2 POUNDS

Tomato pasta is simpler to work with than egg pasta for the same reason that spinach pasta is—the addition of tomato paste makes the dough creamier and softer. The tomato paste gives the pasta a light tomato taste and colors the dough a pleasant pale orange. The addition of the paste also produces a more tender noodle.

This pasta is a good match for white cream-based seafood sauces and simple cream sauces containing no nutmeg. Do not serve it with tomato sauces, but rather with those of contrasting colors and complementary flavors.

4 cups unbleached white flour
¼ teaspoon salt
5 extra-large eggs
1½ teaspoons olive or vegetable oil
2 tablespoons tomato paste

Proceed as for Egg Pasta I, adding the tomato paste to the egg mixture (step 1) and mixing it in thoroughly. As with spinach pasta, tomato pasta is more likely to stick to the board and to the machine. You will probably find you use more flour for dusting as you go along. Cut as you like. Because the dough is softer, let it dry an additional 5–6 minutes before cooking.

Pizzoccheri
Buckwheat Noodles

MAKES ABOUT 2 POUNDS

Buckwheat noodles are a specialty of Lombardy (see chapter 9, for the delicious dish made there that goes by the same name). Called *grano saraceno* ("Saracen grain") by the Italians, buckwheat is not a grain at all, but ground from the seed of a weed related to the rhubarb family. It seems to have originated in Africa or Asia, and been brought to Italy by the Saracens or the Crusaders. Ever since then, buckwheat has grown happily in the poor terrain and cool climate of the Lombard hills. It is full of nutrients, with a pleasant, nutty flavor. Because buckwheat has no gluten, wheat flour is added to it for making noodles.

1 cup buckwheat flour (available from natural-foods stores)
2½ cups unbleached white flour
½ teaspoon salt
5 extra-large eggs
2 tablespoons olive or vegetable oil
3 tablespoons warm milk

Proceed as for Whole-Wheat Pasta, combining the milk in the well with the eggs. Keep extra white flour on hand in case the dough gets too soft. Cut into *fettuccine,* then cut noodles in half on the diagonal, making a shorter ribbon.

Bigoli
Whole-Wheat Pasta

MAKES ABOUT 2 POUNDS

The use of whole-wheat flour in making pasta is not very common in Italian cooking, except in certain northern regions. Called *bigoli,* whole-wheat noodles, a specialty of Veneto, have a toothy, grainy texture and nutty flavor. They are served in various ways, including with cockscombs, with duck, and with anchovies. Try this pasta with nothing more than butter, grated cheese, and pepper, or with the sauce used for *Spaghettini* with Anchovies and Onions (chapter 7).

3 cups whole-wheat flour
1 cup unbleached white flour
¼ teaspoon salt
5 extra-large eggs
2 tablespoons olive or vegetable oil

Proceed as for Egg Pasta I, but knead the dough for 12–14 minutes instead of 10 minutes. Use a spaghetti-cutting attachment to make *bigoli* by machine. This dough can also be cut into *tagliatelle.*

Pasta al Cioccolato
Chocolate Pasta

MAKES ABOUT 2 POUNDS

Chocolate pasta may seem shocking, but in fact its use dates back to the Italian Renaissance. Because of the bitter nature of the pure chocolate used in the pasta dough, the sauces were as a rule sweet and might have included, for example, pine nuts, raisins, and sugar, as well as vegetables, meat, and spices. Such dishes were indulgences of the wealthy classes, for only they were privy to such delicacies as chocolate and spices imported from the Americas and the Orient.

I do not like the sweet and spicy sauces that are traditional with chocolate pasta, primarily because I simply dislike the juxtaposition of sweet and savory flavors.

The proportion of cocoa to flour in this recipe gives the pasta an unusual, subtle flavor that cannot be recognized as chocolate. It is delicious with mushroom and veal sauces (see the recipes in chapter 6 for *Fettuccine* with Dried Wild Mushrooms and *Pappardelle* with Veal Sauce).

4 cups unbleached white flour
5 extra-large eggs
¼ teaspoon salt
1 tablespoon olive or vegetable oil
3 tablespoons pure, unsweetened cocoa powder

Proceed as for Egg Pasta I, sprinkling the cocoa powder in with the flour before drawing in the wet ingredients. Cut as you like.

Pasta di Semolina
Semolina Pasta

MAKES ABOUT 2 POUNDS

Pasta made with semolina flour is higher in protein than pasta made with white flour. It has a firmer texture and goes well with all kinds of tomato sauces and meat sauces.

4 cups semolina flour
5 extra-large eggs
2 tablespoons warm water

Proceed as for Egg Pasta I, combining the water with the eggs in the "well." The dough is somewhat stiff, due to the grainy nature of semolina flour. If you find it difficult to work, lightly wet your hands with water and continue to knead. Cut as you like.

3 BASIC SAUCES

Salse, Sughi e Ragù

Sunday

As I entered the door, I smelled
the aroma of ragù.
So . . . Take care . . . Goodbye . . .
I am leaving . . . If I sit
I might not go . . .

I am sure it is macaroni
I heard cracking
As I entered the door.
Could it be?

A tomato skin is resting on your arm
like a blood stain . . . Permit me?
I will remove it!
How fine your skin feels . . .
like silk, slipping under my fingers . . .

You look especially beautiful this morning.
Your face reflects fire . . .
I am sure it's the macaroni . . .

I am going . . . Goodbye!
If I sit, I might not leave . . .
I might wait
'til you sit at the table,
to receive a ragù-flavored kiss!

—Rocco Galdieri, Naples, 1932

Two pulcinellas eating spaghetti, by
Michele Cammarone, Naples, late 19th
century.

I talian sauces are simple, natural, and sometimes even primitive. They are easy to make. If a cook can read and is willing temporarily to turn a deaf ear to all the gastronomic advice ever heard outside the borders of Italy on the subject of Italian sauces, 50 percent of the battle is licked. This includes what one might have been led to think from those spaghetti sauce commercials on television where a corpulent Italian *mamma* wardrobed in a polka-dotted house dress and frilly white apron is shown at the stove stirring a kettle of spaghetti sauce. She tells you she has been doing this for more hours than could be imagined, meanwhile putting mysterious and numerous spices in the brew to make it "authentic" and delicious. Another heretical raving on the subject of "spaghetti sauce" includes *never* washing the pot, thereby leaving a little bit of sauce from the last time always as a starter for the next time—something I do only when I make yogurt. Such a practice might land a commercial sauce company in jail, and I suspect that somewhere along the line a few home cooks following this dictum have wound up with a bellyache and wondered why.

I am fascinated to know where the modern notion derived to brew spaghetti sauce for hours to enhance its flavor. I suspect that it all started with the recipe for *ragù,* which is cooked for an unusually long time for its own special reasons. Or perhaps we should blame Madison Avenue. Out of a dogged desire to reform such misunderstanding about Italian cooking, I find myself keen to make clear my advice: Except for *ragù* (tomato-and-meat sauces), *stracotto* (literally, "long-simmered" [meat sauce]), or where otherwise indicated, cook tomato sauces very quickly.

The word sauce comes from the Latin, *salsus,* meaning "salted." Happily, the old Roman connection is only in the name. *Salse* take in the whole category of Italian sauces, from anchovy to *zemino* (tomato juice, olive oil, and parsley). Most sauces start out with a *battuto,* a sauté of oil or fat, chopped onion, garlic, celery, and carrot, which becomes a *soffritto* once it is cooked (celery adds body; carrot sweetens). Sauce that is used for pasta is usually called *sugo.* Corrado, the innovative eighteenth-century chef of the Neapolitan Bourbon court, is credited with being the first to feature tomatoes in sauce. Before that, they were only one of many ingredients in a recipe.

Specifically, *sughi di pomodoro* imply quickly cooked sauces usually of fresh, but also canned or frozen tomatoes. Whenever pos-

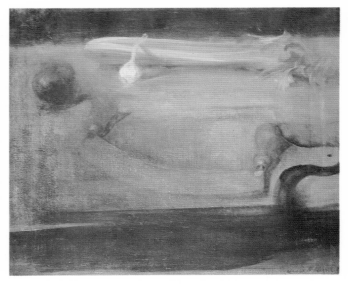

Vegetables for battuto, *with* mezzaluna, *by Mario Fallani, 1984.*

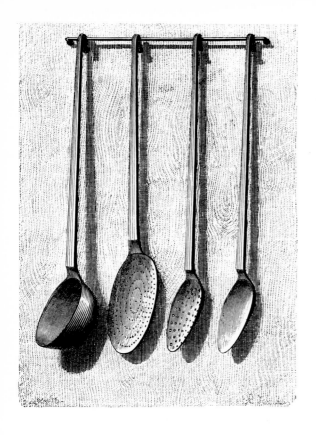

sible, try to use fresh tomatoes if they are the sweet, vine-ripened variety. (Two and one-half pounds of fresh tomatoes is the rough equivalent of two and one-half cups with their juice, or one twenty-eight-ounce can of tomatoes with their juice, although these measurements vary, depending on the type of tomato, climate, and the like.)

A sauté of oil and garlic or oil and onion is the starting point of a large number of pasta sauces that accompany dried-pasta dishes (*pastasciutta*).

Ragù are saporific, hearty sauces that usually start out with a *soffritto* of garlic or onion, and sometimes some type of salt pork or lard. Carrot and celery are often part of the opening mixture. Meat bones and other economy meats have traditionally been added, so *ragù* are cooked for an exceptionally long time to derive flavor from and tenderize these tough cuts. Within the category of *ragù* is the rustic variety that can include mushrooms, *prosciutto,* chicken livers, giblets, or sausages in addition to meat. In sauces such as these that cook for a long time, it is important to use a heavy pot and to simmer them over a very gentle flame.

In the north, milk- or cream-based sauces are prominent, such as *ragù bolognese.* Their sleek texture and richness are perfect anointments for the light, delicate fresh pasta the northerners prefer.

But remember, these are only basic sauces. Many pasta "sauces" are an integral part of the dish. They can consist of anything from bread crumbs, nuts, herbs, vegetables, eggs, or cheeses, to every kind of meat or fish, prepared in various ways and in various combinations.

The mother sauces are used in many different pasta (and other) dishes. *Besciamella* (béchamel) is part of many Italian dishes, from pasta to vegetables, and is the basis of many baked pasta dishes. *Pesto* goes in soups as well as with pasta. The simple, meatless tomato sauces are perhaps the most versatile of all, used with meat, fowl, fish, vegetable, and virtually any kind of pasta except for soup pasta. Bolognese sauce is almost always found between layers of *lasagne,* and is traditional with *fettuccine* and other noodles.

One last bit of advice about saucing spaghetti, best put by my mother when she said: "Italians are not like Americans—they're not hung up on swimming pools." In other words, *don't oversauce* your pasta.

Sugo di Pomodoro Fresco I

Sauce from Vine-ripened
Tomatoes I

Tomatoes must be the sweet, honest, sun-ripened garden variety for this sauce. When you are lucky enough to get them, the simplest sauce with the fewest herbs does them the greatest justice. To achieve an unadulterated tomato taste, purists sometimes leave out the basil and put in a whole clove of garlic, which they remove after the sauce cooks.

This is a lively, rustic sauce (due particularly to its un-sieved character), which goes well with both dried pasta and freshly made *gnocchi* or *ravioli*.

2½ pounds sweet, vine-ripened
 tomatoes
3 tablespoons virgin olive oil
2 garlic cloves, finely chopped (or
 left whole, see introduction)
½ teaspoon salt, or to taste
freshly milled black pepper to taste
2–3 fresh basil leaves, torn into
 small pieces (optional)
freshly grated *parmigiano* cheese
 at table

Immerse tomatoes in boiling water for 30 seconds. Immediately plunge the tomatoes into cold water. Peel them, cut in half, and remove the seeds. Chop them finely with a knife or hand chop-per. Heat the olive oil and the garlic until the garlic is soft but not colored. Add the tomatoes and stir. Sauté several minutes and then simmer at low heat, uncovered, for 15 minutes. The sauce will seem watery at first, but it will thicken as it cooks. Add the salt and pepper, and the basil, if you are using it. Stir. Simmer another 1–2 minutes. If using whole garlic, remove it before serving. Pour over just-cooked pasta. Pass the *parmigiano*.

Variation: Northerners tend to use onion rather than garlic in this sauce. Substitute 1 small white onion for the garlic. For a clearer tomato taste, do not chop the onion, but halve it and remove it when the sauce is finished cooking.

Sugo di Pomodoro Fresco II

Sauce (Sieved) from Vine-ripened Tomatoes II

This is a sauce that goes well on dried or fresh pasta, since it is both fruity and delicate. Tomato sauce must be sieved for *lasagne* and *pasticci*, stuffed pasta dishes (*tortelli*, *ravioli*, and others), or any pasta dish in which the sauce is used along with a cream, butter, or béchamel sauce.

2½ pounds sweet, vine-ripened
 tomatoes
3 tablespoons virgin olive oil
1 small white or yellow onion,
 finely chopped
1 small carrot, scraped and finely
 chopped
1 small celery stalk, finely chopped
1 teaspoon finely chopped fresh
 Italian parsley
1 teaspoon finely chopped fresh
 basil leaves
½ teaspoon salt, or to taste
freshly milled black pepper to taste
handful of fresh whole basil leaves,
 for garnish
freshly grated *parmigiano* cheese
 at table

Cut the tomatoes in half and remove and discard seeds, but do not peel them. There is flavor and vitamins in the skins, and since this sauce will later be sieved, it is best to leave them on. (Some Italian cooks also leave the seeds in the tomatoes, since they will be strained out when the sauce is put through the food mill. I think that the bitterness of the seeds can affect the taste of the sauce during cooking, however, so I remove them.) Chop the tomatoes.

Heat the oil, onion, carrot, and celery and sauté gently until the vegetables are soft, about 10 minutes. With the back of a wooden spoon, press down on the vegetables to release their flavors. Add the tomatoes and simmer, uncovered, for 20 minutes, until you have a thick purée. Add the chopped parsley and basil and stir. Let the sauce cool slightly. Pass the sauce through a food mill, using the fine attachment to produce a smooth purée. Season with salt and pepper. Reheat only until the sauce is hot, but not boiling (several minutes over medium heat). It is important not to overcook the sauce, or the fresh tomato taste will be spoiled. Serve over just-cooked pasta and scatter fresh basil leaves over each portion. Pass the *parmigiano*.

Pomarola

Neapolitan-style Tomato Sauce

FOR 1 POUND OF PASTA

Pomarola (in dialect, *pummarola*) is the classic Neapolitan sauce for spaghetti and macaroni. Because of the presence of unsieved vegetables, it is suited to the firmer textures of dried pasta.

2½ pounds sweet, vine-ripened tomatoes, or 1 28-ounce can peeled Italian plum tomatoes in purée, seeded and chopped, with their juice

3 tablespoons olive oil

2 medium-sized celery stalks, finely chopped

1 large carrot, scraped and finely chopped

1 small white or yellow onion, finely chopped

small handful fresh basil leaves, torn into small pieces

salt and freshly milled black pepper to taste

freshly grated *parmigiano* cheese at table

See Sauce from Vine-ripened Tomatoes I for directions on how to peel, seed, and chop fresh tomatoes. Heat the oil, celery, carrot, and onion and sauté gently until the vegetables are soft, about 10 minutes. Press down on the vegetables with the back of a wooden spoon to release their flavors. Add the tomatoes and simmer, partially covered, 20 minutes for fresh tomatoes, 35 minutes for canned tomatoes. Season with salt and pepper. Serve over just-cooked pasta. Pass the *parmigiano* cheese.

Sugo di Carne

Tomato Sauce with Pork

FOR 1 POUND OF PASTA

This is a particularly delicious and simple meat sauce. Pork is a "sweet" meat, a foil for the acidity of tomatoes. The slow, lengthy cooking time draws out the delicious flavor in the bones.

½ pound boneless economy pork

about 1 pound pork shoulder or neck bone

3 tablespoons olive oil

1 medium-sized yellow onion, finely chopped

1 teaspoon salt, or to taste

freshly milled black pepper to taste

1 28-ounce can peeled Italian plum tomatoes in purée, seeded and chopped, with their juice

freshly grated *parmigiano* cheese

Trim all the fat from the pork, then cut the meat into 1-inch cubes. Heat the oil and add the pork cubes and bone, onion, salt, and pepper. Sauté over medium heat, browning on all sides, about 15 minutes. Do not let the onion brown. If it begins to brown too quickly, lower the heat and cook the pork more slowly. Turn the meat over in the pan to brown it evenly on all sides. Add the tomatoes and stir, turning the heat down to medium low. Simmer, partially covered, for 1½ hours, stirring occasionally.

When the sauce is done, taste and adjust the seasoning. Allow the sauce to cool. Remove the meat from the bone and trim off any fat that remains. Purée the meat and the sauce in a food processor or blender. Reheat and serve over just-cooked macaroni, spaghetti, fresh noodles, or *gnocchi*. Pass the *parmigiano*.

Ragù
Meat Sauce

FOR 2 POUNDS OF PASTA

In French, a *ragout* is a stew made of any kind of meat, which is first cut up and browned, with or without various vegetables. The Italians borrowed the term, altering its spelling slightly to *ragù* and changing its nature to a long-simmered tomato-and-meat sauce. The classic Neapolitan *ragù* was originally made on a little outdoor stove set up along the roadside, on the street, or anywhere in the open air. The sauce was designed to accompany macaroni, which until modern times was street food. Making *ragù* was the beloved work of *portinai*, the doorkeepers or guards of shops and wealthy households. They had time to keep an eye on both the door and the sauce.

There are many variations of *ragù*—with chicken livers, salt pork, mushrooms, unsmoked ham, pork, beef, or veal, and combinations thereof. Here is a classic southern Italian version. Mixing pork with beef sweetens and softens the sauce.

1 pound chuck steak, in one piece
½ pound pork shoulder or large pork chop, in one piece
3 tablespoons olive oil
1 garlic clove, bruised
1 medium-sized white onion, very finely chopped
1 small carrot, scraped and very finely chopped
1 small celery stalk, very finely chopped
½ cup tomato paste
½ cup good dry red wine
1 35-ounce can peeled Italian plum tomatoes in purée, seeded and chopped with their juice
salt and freshly milled black pepper to taste
pinch of sugar, if needed
1 cup water
1 teaspoon chopped fresh basil, or ½ teaspoon dried basil
freshly grated *parmigiano* cheese at table

Trim all the fat from the chuck steak and pork, but leave meats in one piece. In a heavy pot or dutch oven, heat the oil and garlic and brown the beef and pork on all sides to a deep brown color. Remove meats to a plate and set aside. Discard the garlic. Add the onion, carrot, and celery and sauté over medium heat until soft. Stir in the tomato paste and sauté for 3 minutes. Return the meat (and any juices that have collected on the plate) to the pan and add the wine. Simmer, uncovered, for 3 minutes to evaporate the alcohol. Add the tomatoes and season with salt and pepper. If the tomatoes are acidic, add a pinch of sugar (no more). Add water and basil and bring to a boil. Immediately reduce heat to low and simmer, partially cov-ered, 1¾ hours, stirring now and then.

For a rustic sauce, serve the sauce unsieved. For a smooth sauce, remove the meat and sieve the sauce. A food mill will do a fine job. A food processor will make a slightly thicker sauce, since it doesn't actually strain any part of it. Serve the sauce over pasta; slice the meat and serve it either with the pasta or as a second course. Pass the *parmigiano*.

Sugo di Pomodoro all'Emiliana

Emilian Tomato Sauce

FOR 1 POUND OF PASTA

2½ pounds sweet, vine-ripened tomatoes, or 1 28-ounce can peeled Italian plum tomatoes, seeded and chopped, with their juice

5 tablespoons sweet (unsalted) butter

1 small white or red onion, finely chopped

1 medium-sized celery stalk, finely chopped

1 medium carrot, finely chopped

3 tablespoons tomato paste

2 tablespoons finely chopped fresh basil or Italian parsley

salt and freshly milled black pepper to taste

freshly grated *parmigiano* cheese at table

See Sauce from Vine-ripened Tomatoes I for directions on how to peel, seed, and chop fresh tomatoes. Gently heat the butter, onion, celery, and carrot until the vegetables are soft but not browned. Add the tomato paste and stir to blend in with the vegetables. Add the chopped tomatoes. Simmer, partially covered, over medium heat 25–30 minutes, stirring frequently, until a sauce consistency is formed. Add the parsley and allow the sauce to cool somewhat. Purée by pressing through a food mill. Season with salt and pepper. Serve over just-cooked pasta. Pass the *parmigiano*.

Salsa alla Bolognese

Bolognese Tomato and Meat Sauce

FOR 1 POUND OF PASTA

The Emilian version of *ragù* contains milk, which imparts sweetness and creaminess to the meat. This is an important sauce in Italian cooking. It is used in many different *lasagne,* and is also suitable for a wide array of macaroni dishes, for the meat is cradled within the curves of the pasta shapes. *Tagliatelle alla bolognese* (fresh spinach noodles with Bolognese *ragù*) is a classic dish for which Bologna's stupendous cooks are rightly famous. The traditional Bolognese *ragù* is most often made with ground beef, or combinations of beef, veal, pork, and sometimes *prosciutto* or chicken livers for flavoring. The last two optional ingredients in the recipe that follows should be added if the sauce is for noodles, not for *lasagne.*

5 tablespoons sweet (unsalted) butter

1 small white or yellow onion, finely chopped

1 small celery stalk, finely chopped

½ small carrot, scraped and finely chopped

¼ pound good-quality, lean beef, preferably chuck, ground twice

¼ pound good-quality, lean pork, preferably belly, ground twice

¼ pound good-quality, lean veal, ground twice

2 ounces *prosciutto crudo,* thickly sliced and finely chopped

½ teaspoon salt, or to taste

freshly milled black pepper to taste

½ cup good dry white wine

⅔ cup milk

⅛ teaspoon nutmeg, preferably freshly grated

1 28-ounce can peeled Italian plum tomatoes in purée, seeded and chopped, with their juice

1 white truffle (optional)

½ cup heavy cream (optional)

freshly grated *parmigiano* cheese at table

In a large, wide dutch oven or large, deep skillet, heat the butter, onion, celery, and carrot and sauté until the vegetables are soft but not browned, about 10 minutes. Turn the heat to very low and add the ground meats and *prosciutto.* It is very important that the meat not be seared; heat very gently, only enough to color it on the outside. Not searing the meat allows it to absorb the other flavors of the sauce and will make it more delicate and creamy. Break up and stir the meat as you heat it. It should be uniformly pink in color; do not brown it. Add the salt, pepper, and wine. Simmer very gently for several minutes until the alcohol evaporates and the liquid begins to be absorbed by the meat and vegetables. Stir in the milk and nutmeg. It is important to add the milk before adding the tomatoes for it to be absorbed directly by the meat. Cook gently for 10 minutes.

Add the tomatoes to the pan. When the sauce begins to simmer, turn the heat down as low as you can. If your burner cannot be regulated so low that only a few bubbles at a time break on the surface of the sauce, insert a flame tamer. Simmer in this way, partially covered, so that the sauce bubbles ever so gently, for about 4 hours, stirring it lightly now and then. If using a flame tamer, be sure that the heat isn't so low that the sauce doesn't simmer at all. Taste for seasoning and add an additional shade of nutmeg if necessary. If the sauce is being used on fresh noodles (not *lasagne*), and you have a mind to be extravagant, thinly slice the truffle (do not slice it before this point) and add it with the cream to the finished sauce. Stir and pour over cooked fresh pasta. Pass the *parmigiano*.

Ragù alla Toscana

Tuscan Tomato and Meat
Sauce

FOR 1 POUND OF PASTA

Because of the popularity of chicken in Tuscan cooking, chicken livers are widely used in the region's dishes. This typical Tuscan *ragù*, which combines beef with chicken livers, is an excellent sauce not only for fresh or dried pasta, but also for rice or *polenta*. I can't stress enough how important it is to use only the freshest, finest chicken livers and not the yellowish, spongy ones that are too often found in our supermarkets.

2 tablespoons olive oil
2 tablespoons finely chopped salt pork
1 small red onion, finely chopped
1 large garlic clove, very finely chopped
1 large carrot, scraped and very finely chopped
1 medium-sized celery stalk, including leaves, finely chopped
2 tablespoons finely chopped fresh Italian parsley
½ teaspoon fresh rosemary leaves, or ¼ teaspoon dried rosemary
¾ pound ground lean beef
2 tablespoons tomato paste
½ cup good dry red wine
2½ pounds sweet, vine-ripened

plum tomatoes, quartered, or 1 28-ounce can peeled Italian plum tomatoes in purée, with their juice
scant 1 teaspoon salt, or to taste
freshly milled black pepper to taste
3 fresh, plump chicken livers
1 teaspoon sweet (unsalted) butter or olive oil
freshly grated *parmigiano* cheese at table

Select a heavy saucepan. Heat the oil and the salt pork together over medium heat. When the pork fat has melted, add the onion, garlic, carrot, celery, and parsley. Crush the rosemary leaves in your hand to release the oils they contain and add them to the pan with the vegetables. Sauté gently for 7 or 8 minutes, or until the vegetables are soft, stirring with a wooden spoon to allow even cooking. Do not let them brown. Add the beef, breaking it up with the spoon and mixing it in with the vegetables. Sauté gently for 8–10 minutes, or until the meat is colored on the outside but still somewhat pink inside. Stir in the tomato paste and then the wine. Gently simmer for about 8 minutes to evaporate the alcohol. Pass the tomatoes through a food mill directly into the saucepan. Stir and season with salt and pepper. Simmer, partially covered, over very gentle heat for 40 minutes.

Trim the chicken livers of any fat, membranes, green spots, or discolorations and cut the into small pieces. Heat the butter or oil and sauté the livers in it until they are browned on the outside but still very pink on the inside. Then add them to the sauce and allow it to simmer an additional 5 minutes. Serve over freshly cooked pasta. Pass *parmigiano* at the table.

Pesto alla Genovese
Genoese Basil Sauce

This delicious uncooked sauce, which is now fashionable in America, originated in Genoa, in the Liguria region. It is among the oldest known Italian dishes, said to have come about from the combined influence of the Arabs, Persians, and Byzantines. The Genoese claim to make the best *pesto,* based on the highly aromatic properties of the basil that grows in their climate.

Classic *pesto* is made with unrefined olive oil, though modern tastes often prefer it made with lighter olive oil and sometimes butter. Like all Italian sauces, *pesto* should be added to pasta in conservative amounts. The Italians insist that it should be served with *trenette,* a narrow, thick homemade (usually eggless) noodle, for the unctuous character of the sauce is too overwhelming for more delicate egg noodles. *Pesto* is also for *linguine,* spaghetti, or even the larger *bucatini.* Saucing *tortellini* or other stuffed pasta with *pesto* creates too many conflicts with the flavors and textures of their fillings.

Traditionalists claim that the only way to experience true *pesto* is to make it fresh with a mortar and pestle. The hand method results in superior texture and it is quite simple to do with a good marble, ceramic, or hardwood mortar and pestle. For most Americans, *pesto* is easier to contemplate made with a blender or food processor, so here are recipes for both methods. A hand-pounded *pesto* is, however, something which all those who love Italian food should try.

Pesto must be made with fresh basil leaves. In America there are many varieties, from cinnamon basil to licorice basil, and from lettuce-leaf basil to sweet basil. What is usually sold in summer markets is sweet basil, which has large, crinkly leaves and a more minty fragrance and flavor than the basil grown in Italy.

There are many variations on *pesto.* It can be made with or without pine nuts or walnuts, toasted or untoasted; with or without butter; with the addition of a small quantity of parsley to quiet its natural sweetness. Some Italians put both *parmigiano* and *pecorino* cheeses in, while others, the Romans in particular, are horrified at the mere suggestion of introducing *pecorino* to *pesto.* A *pecorino* cheese is sharper and saltier than *parmigiano;* it would be a mistake to use it alone. I prefer using no *pecorino* at all, because I think that most *pecorino* cheeses imported to this country are too strong for *pesto* (see chapter 1 for information on these cheeses). According to well-known Italian cookbook author Alberto Consiglio, who writes of the matter in *I Maccheroni, con Cento Ricette,* traditional sources consider *pesto* made with *parmigiano* alone to be a concession to decadent, modern tastes. A blend is suggested in the recipe that follows. My readers can try their own variations and settle on their own favorite ways.

Pesto

Basil Sauce (Blender or Food Processor Method)

Use the same ingredients as for the mortar and pestle method. Put the basil leaves, garlic, pine nuts, salt, pepper, and oil into a blender or food processor. Blend to a smooth purée, stopping the machine once or twice to scrape the sides of the container with a rubber spatula so that all the ingredients are equally ground. Add the grated cheeses and the butter and whirl for about 15 seconds. Scrape the sides again and turn on the processor for another few seconds. Do not overdo the grinding in the food processor or your *pesto* will have very little texture. See mortar and pestle method for serving directions.

Note: For a *pesto* that is almost as quick to make, and with better texture, beat the grated cheeses and butter in by hand when you have finished processing the other ingredients.

Keeping and Freezing *Pesto:* *Pesto* will keep in the refrigerator for several months in a sealed glass jar. I have found that the best way to prevent a dark layer from forming on the top is to push a layer of plastic wrap onto the very surface of the *pesto*. This is far more effective than the traditional method of pouring olive oil on the surface. You can freeze *pesto* in the same way. But whether you are storing it in the refrigerator or freezer, it is important to leave out the cheeses, salt, and butter. Beat them in just before using the *pesto*.

Pesto

Basil Sauce
(Mortar and Pestle Method)

- 2 cups solidly packed fresh basil leaves
- 3 garlic cloves, cut into pieces
- ⅓ cup pine nuts, very lightly toasted
- generous ½ teaspoon salt
- 1–2 twists freshly milled black pepper
- ½ cup freshly grated *parmigiano* cheese
- scant ¼ cup freshly grated *romano* or *pecorino sardo* cheese
- ½ cup virgin olive oil
- 2 tablespoons sweet (unsalted) butter, softened to room temperature

Use a sturdy mortar and pestle, preferably of marble or ceramic, that is large enough to hold all the ingredients. The better hardwood mortars are also good. First crush the basil leaves, garlic, pine nuts, salt, and pepper, using a circular and steady motion to grind them. You will get a thick paste. Add the grated cheeses, using the same circular motion until they are incorporated into the basil paste. Now add the olive oil gradually, first in a trickle, mixing the paste with a wooden spoon. Beat the mixture continually as you drizzle in the rest of the oil. When it is incorporated, beat in the butter.

See the suggestions above for what types of pasta are best mixed with *pesto*. Save some of the hot water from the drained pasta and stir 1 tablespoon of it into the *pesto*. Then toss the pasta with some butter before combining it with the sauce.

Lo Stracotto

"Long-simmered" Beef
Sauce

FOR 1 POUND OF PASTA

There has been some argument in Italy about the healthfulness of sauces that are cooked for long periods of time (called *gli umidi*), that, in fact, depart from the general Italian practice of fast, simple cooking. The purpose of the lengthy cooking here is to leach slowly all the juices of the meat into a concentrated, dense flavor. Sometimes, *stracotto* is actually a stew, such as the Florentine version that contains mutton, some pork variety meats, the beloved Tuscan white bean, tomatoes, onion, garlic, cloves, herbs (usually thyme or marjoram), and red wine.

There are variations on *stracotto* in other parts of Italy, where pasta replaces beans and is cooked in the stew itself. This tomatoless, rich, pungent recipe is actually a cousin of that stew. It contains many of the same ingredients but is served over pasta. If spooned over macaroni, the bits of meat that have not disintegrated into the sauce nestle into the concaves of tubular or other hollow pasta (the Florentines love it with *rigatoni*). Over fresh noodles, this buttery sauce clings to the tender pasta ribbons—a lovely experience of flavor and texture.

1 ounce dried *porcini* mushrooms

1 cup warm water

1 pound very lean, good-quality boneless veal or beef

¼ pound (½ cup) sweet (unsalted) butter (see Note)

1 small yellow onion, finely chopped

1 medium-sized celery stalk, including leaves, finely chopped

1 small carrot, scraped and finely chopped

3 tablespoons finely chopped Italian parsley

¼ teaspoon powdered cloves

1 tablespoon unbleached white flour

¾ cup beef broth, or as needed

⅔ cup good dry red wine if using beef, or dry *Marsala* if using veal

salt and freshly milled black pepper to taste

3-inch strip fresh lemon peel

freshly grated *parmigiano* cheese at table

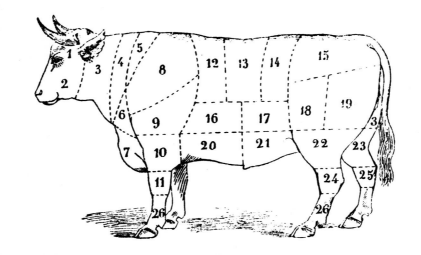

Soak the *porcini* in the water for 30 minutes. Meanwhile, trim any fat from the meat and cut it into ½-inch cubes. Remove the mushrooms from the liquid and rinse them under tap water only if they are still sandy. Pat the mushrooms dry and chop them. Reserve their soaking liquid, straining it through a paper towel or clean cloth.

Heat the butter with the onion, celery, carrot, and chopped *porcini*. Sauté gently for 5 minutes. Add the parsley and stir. Add the meat and sauté it gently until it is lightly browned on all sides. Add the cloves and the flour and stir to distribute evenly. Add the strained liquid from the *porcini,* the beef broth, and the red wine or dry *Marsala* (do not use sweet *Marsala* for this sauce) and season with salt and pepper. Pinch the lemon peel to release the oil in it and add it to the sauce. Stir, cover, and simmer at the lowest possible heat for 2½ to 3 hours. The temperature is low enough when only a few bubbles break on the surface of the sauce. If your burner gives uneven heat or cannot be regulated to a very low level, use a "flame tamer" between the pan and the flame.

At the end of the cooking time, the meat should have disintegrated into the sauce, thickening it. If the sauce is not thick enough at this point, remove the cover and allow it to reduce, always at very low heat. If the sauce seems too thick, add several tablespoons of beef broth, keeping the heat at the same gentle temperature. Serve over freshly cooked noodles or macaroni. Pass the *parmigiano* cheese.

Note: This recipe calls for an exceptionally large amount of butter, which makes the sauce very smooth and sweet. The quantity of butter can be cut in half, reduced to little as 4 tablespoons, if preferred.

Salsa Besciamella
Béchamel Sauce

MAKES 2 CUPS

The Italians brought the art of gastronomy to France. According to most historical records, when fourteen-year-old Caterina dé Medici married Henry II of France in 1533, she brought her Italian kitchen staff with her to Paris. Her Florentine cooks introduced a level of gastronomy hitherto unknown in that county. *Salsa besciamella* (or *besciamel*), historically, *balsamella,* has been part of the northern Italian cuisine, particularly that of Emilia-Romagna, for centuries. While reliable sources verify the sauce's Italian origins, "béchamel" is supposed to have taken its name from a certain Marquis Louis de Béchamel, *maître d'hotel* to Louis XIV.

Béchamel is a simple sauce, tricky only if the milk, which is always heated first, is not added very slowly and gradually. When it isn't, lumps result. The sauce should cook for fifteen to twenty minutes in all, to remove the raw floury taste. If lumps appear, they can be sieved out. A generous proportion of butter is essential to a good béchamel, which can be thickened by long simmering or thinned by adding more hot milk. The proportions given here make a sauce of the right consistency for *lasagne* and most other pasta dishes.

2¼ cups milk, heated just under boiling
4 tablespoons sweet (unsalted) butter
3 tablespoons unbleached white flour
¼ teaspoon salt
generous pinch of nutmeg, preferably freshly grated

Put the milk on to heat. Meanwhile, melt the butter in a thick-bottomed saucepan over low heat. Add the flour to the butter and stir with a wooden spoon to smooth out the lumps. Keeping the heat very low, let the flour and butter paste bubble, continually stirring. Do not let it brown. When it has bubbled gently for about 2 minutes, turn off the heat and let the paste rest for 3–4 minutes.

Return the pan to the burner and add the heated milk, a tablespoon at a time, stirring constantly. When you have used up ¼ cup milk, begin to add the hot milk a couple tablespoons at a time, until ½ cup milk is used up. If you are not an old hand at this, remove the pan from the heat as you add the milk, stirring continually as you do. Now add the milk in a trickle, very slowly and gradually, stirring all the while. If lumps start to appear, you are probably adding too much milk too quickly, or you have the heat on too high. Should this happen, turn off the heat and stir the sauce, pressing the lumps against the side of the pan. Continue to add the hot milk very gradually. When all the milk has been added, simmer the sauce over low heat for another 15 minutes or so until it has reached the proper thickness, stirring constantly. The sauce should coat a spoon when it is ready. Add the salt and nutmeg during the last 10–15 minutes of cooking.

Note: A bay leaf is often added to this sauce, but not generally when it is to be used in pasta dishes. To store the sauce, pour a little melted butter on the top to prevent a skin from forming, then cover tightly. Or put plastic wrap over the bowl and press it directly onto the surface of the sauce. It will remain fresh for up to 5 days in the refrigerator.

It is best to reheat béchamel in a double boiler, adding a teaspoon or more of hot milk (depending on how much sauce you are heating) and stirring with a wooden spoon or whisk to prevent lumping. When it is thoroughly heated, remove from the heat immediately. If the sauce still contains lumps (it most likely will), pass it through a sieve and use immediately.

Salsa di Pomodoro Crudo
Uncooked Tomato Sauce

FOR 1 POUND OF PASTA

Pasta tossed with an un-cooked tomato sauce is a wonderful way to enjoy the delightful fresh taste of summer's vine-ripened tomatoes. Because you will experience the raw flavor of every ingredient here, it is worthwhile to use virgin olive oil, for its fruity quality will come through clearly. You will achieve the best results by using a fleshy tomato, such as plum or Roma, and fresh rather than dried herbs. Make variations by adding red pepper flakes, different herbs, etc.

1½ to 2 pounds sweet, vine-ripened plum tomatoes

½ small red onion, very finely chopped (about 3 tablespoons)

6 tablespoons extra virgin olive oil

1 tablespoon fresh whole marjoram or oregano leaves

salt and freshly milled black pepper to taste

freshly grated *parmigiano* cheese at table (optional)

Immerse tomatoes in boiling water for 30 seconds. Immediately plunge the tomatoes into cold water. Peel them, cut in half, and remove the seeds and tough area around the stem. Chop the tomatoes and place them in a colander to drain off their excess juice. You should have about 2 cups chopped tomatoes.

Combine tomatoes, onion, oil, marjoram or oregano, salt, and pepper in a ceramic bowl and serve immediately or let marinate at room temperature for up to 6 hours. Serve at room temperature over just-cooked pasta. Grated *parmigiano* is optional.

Variation with Olives: Add ¼ cup black *niçoise* or *Gaeta* olives, sliced off their pits. Use 1 garlic clove, very finely chopped, in place of the onion.

Variation with Basil: Use ½ cup fresh whole basil leaves, torn into small pieces, in place of the marjoram. Use 1 garlic clove, very finely chopped, in place of the onion.

Variation with Mint: Use 2 tablespoons fresh mint leaves, torn into small pieces, in place of the marjoram. Omit the onion.

Variation with Capers: Add 1 tablespoon drained capers. If the capers are very small, leave them whole. If they are the larger variety, chop them coarsely. Use 1 garlic clove, very finely chopped, in place of the onion, and add 1 tablespoon chopped fresh basil. Two tablespoons flavorful black olives, such as *niçoise* or *Gaeta,* may also be added. Season with plenty of freshly ground black pepper.

4 PASTA SOUPS

Paste in Brodo

In a region called Bengodi where they tied the vines with sausages and where one can buy a goose for a farthing, and a gosling included, there is a mountain made of grated Parmigiano cheese on which men worked all day making pasta and ravioli, cooking them in capon's broth, and then rolling them down and who grabs most eats most . . .

—Giovanni Boccaccio,
Decameron, 1350

Three Pulcinellas, by Georg Friedrich Schmidt after Giambattista Tiepolo, 1751.

Preparations for a banquet in a mid-16th-century kitchen. Woodcut from Banchetti compositioni di vivande et apparec-chio generale, *written for the Este family, of Ferrara, by Christoforo di Messisbugo, 1549.*

There is something profoundly therapeutic in being able to "use up." While I love things that are new, I am happy in a more complete way when a naked bone, swathed in foil in the refrigerator, still has a vital purpose: the stock pot. This is not to say that just any old thing should find its way into a broth. *Al contrario,* or we might end up with the kind of soup Abraham Lincoln described as, "made by boiling the shadow of a pigeon that had been starved to death." A bone, a carrot, or whatever must still have some life to do any good.

Pasta and soup are meant to marry. Minestrone is the Italian soup of vegetables and pasta that most Americans know, and probably there are as many variations of it as there are cooks. But there are other types of pasta soups.

It is mostly the soups of the south that contain macaroni. They sometimes get so thick that they become almost a stew. In the central regions, the bean, of which Tuscans are inordinately fond, is sometimes joined by pasta in a thick, vigorous mixture. The soups of northern kitchens are typically fresh, flavorful broths in which stupendous fresh *tortellini* or *cappelletti* are boiled (see chapter 5).

There are soup-type macaroni *ad infinitum,* properly called *pastine.* They are the very small dried-pasta shapes, such as *anellini* ("little rings"), *semi di melone* ("melon seeds"), *tubettini* ("little tubes") and *acini di pepe* ("little pepper pods").

Which type of pasta to use depends on the soup. If it is robust but not too crowded, the slightly larger *ditalini* ("little thimbles") or *conchiglie* ("shells") are often used. In a more refined or a clear soup, the tiniest shapes are typical. Spaghetti can be broken up and used in soups, too. Fine egg noodles and filled fresh pasta should always be cooked in clear broth.

Broth (*brodo*) is made by starting out with meat and vegetables in cold water. It is all brought to a boil together, which lets the meat juices leach into the broth instead of being sealed into the meat by plunging into boiling water at the outset. The meat, though it has given flavor to the liquid, is still good and can be served as the second course, accompanied with a sauce. If your primary intent were to cook boiled meat, you would allow the water to boil first, then add the meat, and in this way, seal in the juices (see Mixed Boiled Meats in Broth, this chapter).

Here are some basic broths in which to cook small dried-pasta shapes or fresh stuffed pasta forms, as well as a number of hearty soup recipes.

Il Brodo di Pollo
Chicken Broth

MAKES ABOUT 2½ QUARTS

Supermarket-variety chickens are too bland to make rich-tasting chicken broth by themselves. Try to find boiling fowls (see Note), which stand up to boiling far longer than younger chickens and are far more flavorful. Most butchers carry them, as do many supermarkets, although they are less common in the fresh poultry section than they once were. Failing to find one, use a good quantity of economy chicken parts—backs, wings, necks. But keep in mind that for a properly flavorful chicken broth, nothing can substitute for boiling fowl.

4-pound boiling fowl, or 4 pounds economy chicken parts, such as backs, necks, and wings

1½ pounds chicken gizzards, trimmed of fat and quartered

1 medium-sized yellow onion, unpeeled

1 medium-sized carrot, scraped and cut in half

1 large celery stalk, including leaves

1 bay leaf

3 sprigs Italian parsley and stems from a bunch of parsley

about 4 quarts water

1 fresh or canned tomato, halved and seeded

¼ teaspoon whole black or white peppercorns

1 tablespoon salt, or to taste

Wash the fowl or chicken parts and gizzards. Put all the ingredients, except the tomato, salt, and pepper, in an 8-quart stock pot. The water should cover the chicken by several inches. Cover with the lid slightly ajar to allow steam to escape. Bring the stock to a boil. Add the tomato and pepper. You may also add the salt at this point if you will be using the stock within a day; salting stock in advance imparts a sour taste to it after that length of time. Lower the heat to a gentle simmer. Cook for 3–4 hours, skimming off the foam whenever it forms on the top (to get a clear broth you must be diligent about this).

The stock should cook gently for the entire cooking time, never returning to the boil. When it is finished, allow it to cool. Skim off as much of the fat as you can. Strain the broth through cheesecloth or a very fine sieve, preferably into a glass or ceramic bowl or vessel. You may want to pick some of the meat off the bones and save the carrots to add to your soup.

The stock can be kept in a covered jar in the refrigerator for 4 days. To use as a clear broth in which to serve filled pasta, use it within that time, remembering to add salt to taste. If you are planning to use it as a base for other soups or in sauces, you can continually replenish it by adding good new bones, more celery, carrot, parsley, and water, and simmering them for the same amount of time you did the initial batch. To keep the broth clear, do not add starchy vegetables such as potato or turnip, and be sure to strain it well before using. To keep the broth fresh, boil it every 4 days for about 10 to 15 minutes and store it in a tightly covered container in the refrigerator. If you prefer, you can freeze it, but add salt only when you are about to use the broth.

Note: If you can get them, the intestines and feet of the chicken add good flavor to broth. There have been restrictions on their sale in the United States for some time. Your butcher will no doubt be able to tell you whether they are available. Be sure to wash these parts thoroughly before using them.

Another way of getting rich-tasting chicken broth is to use the first broth as a base in which to cook another boiling fowl or chicken, either whole or parts. Wash the bird and place it in the strained broth. Bring to a boil and immediately reduce to a simmer. Cook, partially covered, until the fowl or chicken is cooked. Cooking time will depend on the type and weight of the bird used. If you wish to eat the chicken as a second course, remove it before it overcooks and falls off the bone. If you are using it only to strengthen the flavor of the stock, simmer at the lowest heat, partially covered, for 3–4 hours or more.

Brodo di Pesce
Fish Broth

MAKES ABOUT 2 QUARTS

It is best to leave the salt out of the broth until you are ready to use it. Even if you plan to use it right away, fish gives off its own salt, so it is best to taste for salt at the end of cooking.

4 pounds fish bones, including 1 large or 2 smaller fish heads (gills removed) from lean white fish, such as cod, flounder, sole, haddock, halibut, red snapper, sea bass, striped bass, or whiting

1 medium-sized white onion or several shallots, unpeeled

1 small carrot, scraped and cut in half

1 medium-sized celery stalk

3 sprigs Italian parsley, and stems from a small bunch of parsley

1-inch strip fresh lemon peel

1 cup good dry white wine

⅛ teaspoon whole white peppercorns

3 quarts water

salt to taste, when you are ready to use the broth

Wash the fish parts well with cold water. Put all the ingredients except the salt in an 8-quart stock pot. Cover with lid slightly ajar to allow steam to escape and bring to a boil. Immediately lower heat to a gentle simmer. Cook no more than 30 minutes, or the broth will become too strong.

Let the broth cool somewhat. Line a sieve with several layers of cheesecloth and strain the broth through it, preferably into a glass or ceramic bowl or vessel. This stock will keep in the refrigerator for 3 days, or it can be frozen for later use. Add salt when you are about to use the broth.

Il Brodo Misto
Meat and Chicken Broth

MAKES ABOUT 2½ QUARTS

I think the best broth is made with a combination of chicken and beef—good, fresh bones and a flavorful cut such as beef chuck.

2 pounds beef shin and marrow bones

olive oil, as needed

2-pound-piece beef chuck, short ribs, or shank

3-pound boiling fowl, or 3 pounds economy chicken parts, such as backs, necks, wings, and gizzards

1 medium-sized red onion, unpeeled and stuck with 3 cloves

1 medium-sized carrot, scraped and cut in half

1 large celery stalk, including leaves

1 sprig thyme, or ¼ teaspoon dried thyme

1 bay leaf

3 sprigs Italian parsley and stems from a bunch of parsley

about 4½ quarts water

1 fresh or canned tomato, or 1 scant tablespoon tomato paste

⅛ teaspoon whole black or white peppercorns

salt to taste, when you are ready to use the broth

Brown the shin and marrow bones in a little olive oil about 30 minutes, cooking gently on all sides. Add the beef chuck (or short ribs or shank) after the first 10 minutes. (If the bones are too large for a sauté pan, roast them for 45–60 minutes in a preheated 375-degree oven.)

Place the meats in a large pot with all the other ingredients and proceed as directed in the recipe for Chicken Broth, but cook the broth an additional hour. The bones will produce some fat, which should be skimmed from the top along with any foam that forms. Lift the meat out of the pot before straining the broth. Remove the broth you need for soup and return the meat to the pot with the remaining broth; it will keep the meat warm and moist until you are ready to serve it. Serve it warm as a second course with the Green Sauce for Boiled Meats on page 84.

Variation with Turkey: Substitute turkey parts, such as wings and legs, for boiling fowl or chicken parts, or use the carcass of a cooked turkey. Do not use the liver of the turkey, which will make the broth bitter. Crack the bones of the carcass before boiling, to release the flavorful marrow.

Variation with Tongue: Using beef tongue with a boiling fowl or with chicken or turkey parts makes a rich-tasting broth. Substitute a beef tongue weighing 2–3 pounds for the beef bones or beef chuck.

Bollito
Mixed Boiled Meats in Broth

FOR AT LEAST 8 PEOPLE

"Poor bollito," writes Ada Boni in *Il Talismano,* "born, like Desdemona, under a bad star, it gets limited sympathy." Such is the reputation of boiled meat, called by whatever name. But this is no ordinary boiled meal. It is a well-conceived, careful method of locking in all the moisture and flavor of several different meats at once, as they bathe in the mixture of their combined luscious flavors. It is a delicious food, one of my favorites. The resulting broth is deserving of freshly made *cappelletti* or *tortellini*.

The boiled meats follow as a second course, usually accompanied with *salsa verde,* a tangy green sauce of parsley, capers, anchovies, olive oil, and vinegar, or *salsa rossa,* a piquant tomato-based sauce. Sometimes both sauces are offered to the diner. In Rome, a sweet-and-sour sauce is often served. Traditional *bollito* includes a calf's head (or cheek), a fresh ham, a boiling fowl, pigs' feet and a pig's tail, and a special Italian sausage called *zampone,* which is a stuffed pig's foot. The delicious *zamponi* of Modena and Bologna are unavailable here, but you might find *cotechino,* a garlic-flavored pork sausage, in Italian specialty shops. Genuine *cotechino* is very tender,

but the variety we get here, usually domestically made, is often harder and may need to be presoaked for three to four hours. It gives a delicious flavor to the dish and is optional in this recipe, which is a simplified version of traditional *bollito*.

---

1 *cotechino* sausage (about 1½ pounds, optional)

1 large red onion, unpeeled

1 large carrot, scraped and cut in half

2 large celery stalks, including leaves

5 sprigs Italian parsley and stems from a bunch of parsley

1 bay leaf

2½-pound lean beef brisket, trimmed of all fat

3-pound boiling fowl or chicken, including gizzard but not liver

3 sweet, vine-ripened tomatoes, or 4 canned Italian plum tomatoes in purée, halved and seeded

¼ teaspoon whole black or white peppercorns

1 tablespoon salt

2 pounds veal shoulder, including bone, in one piece

2-pound veal tongue

If the *cotechino* is not very tender, put it in a pan large enough to hold it (do not cut or puncture it). Cover it with boiling water and let stand for 3–4 hours before you are ready to begin the *bollito*.

You will need an extraordinarily large pot, such as a canning kettle, to hold all of

the ingredients. It is much better for everything to cook together, but if it doesn't all fit, use 2 8-quart stock pots and divide the vegetables and herbs between them. Then, at the appropriate times, you will put the beef, boiling fowl, and tongue in one pot and the veal and chicken, if using, in the other.

Fill the pot(s) with plenty of water, enough to cover the meats when they are added. Add the onion, carrot, celery, parsley, and bay leaf. Bring the water to a boil and add the brisket and the boiling fowl. (If you are using a younger chicken, you will need to add it later.) The brisket and fowl will cook for a total of 3½ hours. When the water comes to a boil again, add the tomato, peppercorns, and salt. Reduce the heat to the gentlest possible simmer. Make sure to skim off the foam that forms on the surface throughout the cooking time. Wrap the (presoaked) *cotechino* in cheesecloth and secure with kitchen twine. After 30 minutes, put it in with the beef (and fowl). At the same time, add the veal shoulder (if you are using 2 pots, add it to the second one, making sure the water is boiling first). When the brisket has cooked 1½ hours,

add the tongue to it. After it has cooked for 1¾ hours, turn the brisket over. Fifty minutes before the brisket is finished, add the chicken, if you are using one in place of the fowl. (When done, chicken should be tender and still slightly rosy near the bone; it should not be shredding and falling away from the carcass.) Skim the fat from the broth.

When everything has cooked its proper time, adjust the seasoning and then remove the meats. If you have used 2 pots, combine the broths and strain. Peel the skin off the tongue and cut away the gristle. Use some of the broth for *tortellini* or *cappelletti* as a first course and return all the meats to the rest of the broth to keep them warm and moist. When the second course is ready to be served, slice the brisket, the tongue, the *cotechino,* and the veal shoulder. Carve the fowl or chicken. Boiled meats become cold very easily, so keep any meat you don't serve immediately in the broth. Serve each person some of each meat with the sauce that follows. Refrigerate any leftover meat in the broth.

Salsa per Bollito
Green Sauce for Boiled Meats

MAKES ABOUT 2¾ CUPS

This is the sauce my family has always served with *bollito*. A good homemade mayonnaise is essential to the sauce's success.

2 cups Mayonnaise (following recipe)
3 tablespoons finely chopped fresh Italian parsley
¼ cup very finely chopped sour dill pickle
2 tablespoons drained capers, chopped
3 tablespoons fresh lemon juice
1 small canned anchovy fillet, well mashed, or 1 teaspoon anchovy paste
freshly milled black pepper to taste

Mix all the ingredients together in a bowl, blending with a wooden spoon.

Maionese
Mayonnaise

MAKES ABOUT 2 CUPS

It is important that the bowl you use is warm and that all the ingredients are at room temperature, that is, out of the refrigerator an hour or more. Some of my Italian friends insist that it is so simple to make mayonnaise the traditional Italian way, using either a fork or a wooden spoon, that they have no use for whisks or electric beaters. (Whisks are, in any case, rarely used in Italian cooking and according to Italian traditionalists, a concession to French methods, which overemphasize the use of equipment and kitchen gadgetry.) My preferred way of making mayonnaise is to use an electric beater, which makes mayonnaise much faster than by hand beating, and as far as I'm concerned has absolutely no effect on the taste. Fresh mayonnaise tastes best when eaten immediately, but will keep well in the refrigerator for up to a week.

Novices at making mayonnaise often experience disaster because they do not add the oil to the eggs slowly enough—literally, drop by drop. This is the most crucial point in making mayonnaise, and as long as you adhere to it, you will find the process simple and gratifying. See the notation at the end of the method for salvaging curdled mayonnaise.

1 teaspoon salt
1 tablespoon fresh lemon juice
2 yolks from extra-large eggs
1½ cups light olive oil

Select a glass or ceramic bowl, not one made of wood, plastic, or metal. Dissolve the salt in the lemon juice and set aside. Place the yolks in the bowl. Using a wooden spoon, whisk, or electric mixer, beat the yolks, always in the same direction, until they are creamy. It is important to beat the yolks properly before adding the oil. Beat in the oil drop by drop, until the mixture starts to thicken. It is crucial not to add larger amounts of oil, or the mixture will separate. Each new addition of oil should be thoroughly absorbed before more oil is added. As the mixture begins to solidify and resemble mayonnaise, more oil may be added in slightly greater quantities. When all the oil has been absorbed into the egg, beat in a few drops of the lemon-salt mixture. When it has been incorporated, beat in the remainder of the lemon mixture. Taste for seasoning; you may want to add a little more lemon juice or salt.

If the mixture curdles, or separates, in the midst of making the mayonnaise, set it aside. In a warm clean bowl, place another egg yolk, also at room temperature. Beat it until it is creamy and add a few drops of oil, incorporating each well before adding the next. Now start adding the failed mayonnaise, drop by drop, beating it well into the yolk. Continue until all of the failed mayonnaise has been incorporated into the new yolk. At this point, return to the oil that remains from the initial batch of mayonnaise. Add it *slowly,* beating well after addition. Once the mixture begins to solidify, you may add the oil in a slow trickle, but be sure to incorporate well as you beat to prevent curdling again.

Minestra al Pomodoro alla Giustina

My Mother's Tomato Soup

FOR 4 PEOPLE

When my sisters and I were growing up, my mother often made this lovely, simple soup for us as a quick and nourishing lunch. Sometimes she used pasta (always *orzo*) and sometimes rice. I have since prepared it with cream, which makes it more elegant, although I prefer it without. It is very easy and very good, even when canned tomatoes are used.

¼ cup *orzo* ("barley")
¾ pound sweet, vine-ripened tomatoes, or 1 cup well-drained, canned peeled Italian plum tomatoes in purée
1 medium-sized yellow onion, grated
4 tablespoons sweet (unsalted) butter
1 6-ounce can tomato paste
½ large beef bouillon cube, or 1 regular-sized cube, crushed
½ teaspoon finely chopped fresh thyme or marjoram, chopped, or ¼ teaspoon dried thyme or marjoram
1½ tablespoons chopped fresh basil
4 cups water
¼ cup light cream (half-and-half), heated (optional)
1 teaspoon salt, or to taste
fresh whole basil leaves for garnish
freshly grated *parmigiano* cheese at table

If you are using fresh tomatoes, immerse them in boiling water for 30 seconds, then immediately plunge in cold water. Slip off skins. Seed and chop fresh or canned tomatoes. Set them aside for adding later.

In a large saucepan, heat the onion in butter until it is soft. Add the tomato paste and sauté for 1 minute. Add the bouillon cube and stir. Add the chopped herbs and stir in 2½ cups of water. Bring to a boil, then lower heat immediately. Simmer, uncovered, for 10 minutes. Add another 1½ cups water and simmer for another 10 minutes. Add the *orzo*, cover the pot, and simmer for 5 minutes. Add the tomatoes and simmer another 5 minutes, or until pasta is *al dente*. If using cream, stir in now. Season with salt and stir. Ladle soup into serving bowls; tear basil leaves into small pieces and sprinkle some on each bowl of soup. Pass the *parmigiano*.

Minestra con Ditalini e Zucca Gialla

"Little Thimble" Pasta with Yellow Squash Soup

FOR 6 PEOPLE

¼ cup *ditalini* ("little thimbles") or *tubettini* ("little tubes")
3½ tablespoons finely chopped salt pork
1 large yellow onion, finely chopped
1 large garlic clove, bruised
2 tablespoons olive oil
¾ pound new red potatoes, unpeeled and diced into small pieces

¾ pound yellow (summer) squash, diced into small pieces
2½ teaspoons salt
freshly milled black pepper to taste
6 cups water
2 teaspoons finely chopped fresh tarragon, or 3 tablespoons finely chopped fresh Italian parsley
freshly grated *parmigiano* cheese at table

In a large saucepan, heat the salt pork, onion, and garlic in the oil until they are soft. Stir to prevent the salt pork from sticking. Add the potatoes, cover, and cook 10 minutes at low heat, until the potatoes sweat, stirring occasionally as they cook to prevent sticking. Add the squash, salt, and pepper and stir in the water, Cover, bring to a boil, and add the pasta. Simmer 12 to 15 minutes, or until the pasta is *al dente*. Add the tarragon or parsley 5 minutes after the pasta. Remove the garlic clove and check for seasoning. Serve with *parmigiano*.

Note: This soup is remarkably tasty, even though there is no meat-broth base. The fresh flavor of the squash is more pronounced when it is cooked in water. For an even tastier dish, make the soup a day ahead, up the point where you add the pasta. The following day, reheat and add the pasta and herb to finish the soup.

Minestra di Zucchini

Zucchini Soup

FOR 4 PEOPLE

1 cup *acini di pepe* ("pepper-corns") or *orzo* ("barley")

1 medium-sized zucchini (enough for 2 cups, grated)

2 tablespoons very finely chopped salt pork and 1 tablespoon olive oil, or 2 tablespoons sweet (unsalted) butter and 1 tablespoon olive oil

1 small white or yellow onion, very finely chopped or grated on the coarse side of a grater (about 2 heaping tablespoons)

1 medium-sized celery stalk, including leaves, very finely chopped (about 2 tablespoons stalk and 1 tablespoon leaves)

½ teaspoon chopped fresh marjoram or thyme, or ¼ teaspoon dried marjoram or thyme

6 cups homemade chicken broth, or 4 cups good-quality canned chicken broth and 2 cups water, or 2 large chicken bouillon cubes and 6 cups water

salt and freshly milled black pepper to taste

1 tablespoon chopped fresh Italian parsley (optional)

freshly grated *parmigiano* cheese at table

Cut the unpeeled zucchini in half lengthwise and remove large or excess seeds. Dry well, grate on the coarse side of a grater, and set aside.

Heat the salt pork in the oil until it melts, or melt the butter in the oil. Add the onion and sauté until it is soft but not browned. Add the celery and celery leaves and the zucchini and sauté for 5 minutes. Add the marjoram or thyme and 1 cup of the broth. Simmer 5 minutes and add remaining 5 cups broth. Season with salt and pepper. Simmer for 10 more minutes and add the pasta. Cook for 10 minutes or until the pasta is *al dente*. Sprinkle with parsley, if you like, and serve with *parmigiano*.

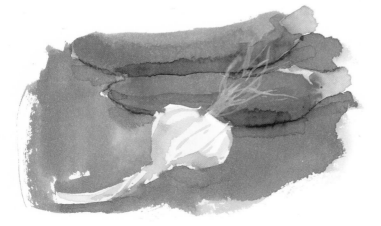

Minestra di Patate con Pasta

Potato Soup with Pasta

FOR 4 PEOPLE

My paternal grandmother nourished eleven children on this rustic soup, which was so thick it was more like stew. My mother, in her inimitable fashion, refined it into a lighter soup without compromising the flavors, which still left plenty of room for a second course.

½ cup *ditalini* ("little thimbles") or *tubettini* ("little tubes")

6 sweet, vine-ripened tomatoes, or 6 canned peeled Italian plum tomatoes in purée

2 tablespoons olive oil

1 rasher bacon, diced

1 small white or yellow onion, finely chopped

1 garlic clove, finely chopped

1 small carrot, scraped and finely chopped or grated

3 cups peeled and diced potatoes

1 teaspoon chopped fresh oregano, or ½ teaspoon dried oregano

8 cups (2 quarts) water

2 beef bouillon cubes, crushed

2 teaspoons salt, or to taste

¼ teaspoon freshly milled black pepper

1 tablespoon grated *pecorino* or *parmigiano* cheese

1 scallion, white and green parts, very finely sliced

If you are using fresh tomatoes, immerse them in boiling water for 30 seconds, then immediately plunge in cold water. Slip off skins. Seed and chop fresh or canned tomatoes. Set them aside for adding later.

In a large saucepan, heat the oil and add the bacon. Sauté until bacon is golden. Add onion, garlic, and carrot and sauté until wilted, about 5 minutes. Add the potatoes and sauté another 5 minutes over low heat. Stir in the tomatoes and oregano. Add 2 cups of the water and the bouillon cubes. Bring to a boil and reduce to a simmer. Cover and simmer 15 minutes over low heat. Add the remaining 6 cups of water and bring to a boil. Simmer another 15 minutes. Add salt and pepper. Add the pasta and cook another 8–10 minutes until *al dente*. Stir in the cheese and the scallion and serve.

Note: This soup tastes even better if made a day in advance and reheated.

Pasta e Fagioli
Pasta and Bean Soup

FOR 6–8 PEOPLE

Here is the traditional *pasta e fagioli* soup of *la cucina casalinga*. A cup of canned Italian plum tomatoes, or in summer, vine-ripened ones, is sometimes added. For me, this soup is a whole meal. I love to eat it with thick, fresh Italian bread.

½ pound *ditalini* ("little thimbles") or *tubettini* ("little tubes")

1 pound dried *cannellini* beans or navy beans

¼ cup olive oil

¼ pound salt pork, diced

1 large onion, chopped

3 garlic cloves

2 celery stalks, including leaves, chopped

1 tablespoon salt, or to taste

freshly milled black pepper to taste

4 sweet, vine-ripened tomatoes, or 1 cup canned peeled Italian plum tomatoes in purée, with their juice (optional)

2 tablespoons finely chopped fresh Italian parsley

freshly grated *parmigiano* cheese at table

Soak beans overnight in cold water to cover. Drain, place in a large pot, cover with 4 inches of cold water, and bring to a boil. Meanwhile, heat the olive oil and salt pork together in a small pan until the fat from the pork melts into the oil and the pork bits are golden. Add the onion, garlic, and celery and sauté gently until the vegetables are wilted.

When the beans have begun to boil, add this *soffritto* to the pot, along with salt and pepper. Cover and simmer over gentle flame until beans are tender, about 2 to 2½ hours. If the soup looks like it is drying out as it cooks, add more water. (This is a thick, hearty soup, but it should comfortably accommodate the beans and the pasta, and still have some broth to it.)

If using fresh tomatoes, immerse them in boiling water for 30 seconds. Remove and immediately plunge in cold water. Slip off skins, seed tomatoes, and chop. If using canned tomatoes, seed and chop them. In either case, add the tomatoes halfway through the simmering process. Add the pasta 10 minutes before the beans are finished. Stir in the chopped parsley and serve. Pass *parmigiano* at the table.

Minestra di Salsicce e Spinaci
Sausage and Spinach Soup

FOR 4 PEOPLE

¾ cup *farfalle* ("butterflies"), other small soup pasta, or broken noodles

1 pound fresh spinach, or 1 10-ounce package frozen chopped spinach, thawed

3 pork sausage links (about ½ pound)

1 medium-sized yellow onion, very finely chopped

¼ teaspoon fennel seeds, crushed in a mortar

1 tablespoon sweet (unsalted) butter

6 cups homemade or good-quality canned chicken broth

1½ teaspoons salt, or to taste

freshly milled black pepper to taste

freshly grated *parmigiano* cheese at table

If using fresh spinach, be sure to remove all the stems and discolored leaves. Wash it thoroughly to remove all sand. If using frozen spinach, use the chopped variety, which already has stems removed. Boil the spinach in plenty of water until it is limp, drain, and squeeze out excess water. Chop coarsely and set aside.

Remove the sausages from their casings. In a large saucepan, gently sauté the onion, sausages, and fennel seeds in butter for 5 minutes, stirring occasionally to break up the meat. Drain off excess fat and add the spinach to the pan. Sauté for 1–2 minutes and add 1 cup of broth, salt, and pepper. Simmer 2–3 minutes before adding the remaining 5 cups broth. Bring soup to the boil and add the pasta. Reduce to a simmer and cook for 5 minutes. Serve with *parmigiano*.

Variation: Use curly escarole in place of the spinach.

Orecchiette con Cavolfiore

"Little Ears" with Cauliflower

FOR 6 PEOPLE

Here is a variation of the traditional cauliflower and pasta soup of the Roman kitchen. It can be made with cauliflower or broccoli, because both vegetables have similar textures and strong, earthy flavors. I like to use *orecchiette* in this soup, because the way the little disks cradle the flowerets is very pretty. *Tubettini* ("little tubes"), *conchigliette* ("small shells"), *lumachine* ("little snails"), or other soup pasta would also do fine.

⅓ cup *orecchiette* ("little ears") or other soup pasta

1 head cauliflower or broccoli (about 1 pound)

2 tablespoons olive oil

2 ounces salt pork, very finely chopped

2 large garlic cloves, finely chopped

2 fresh sage leaves, finely chopped, or ¼ teaspoon dried sage

6 cups homemade chicken broth, or 3 cups good-quality canned chicken broth and 3 cups water

1 teaspoon salt

freshly milled black pepper

½ cup shelled fresh green peas or frozen green peas (not thawed)

freshly grated *parmigiano* cheese at table (optional)

Separate the cauliflower or broccoli into flowerets, then subdivide them into smallish flowerets. Cut several of the tender leaves into 1-inch pieces. Reserve the stalks for some other use.

In a large saucepan, heat the oil and salt pork together over low heat. When the fat is melted, add the garlic and cook over low heat until soft, stirring to prevent sticking. Add the cauliflower or broccoli and the sage. Sauté for 5 minutes over medium heat. Cover and cook gently for 5 minutes. Add the broth, and salt, and four or five turns of pepper from the mill. Bring to the boil. Add the peas and the pasta, cover the pot, and bring again to a boil. Remove the lid and cook an additional 5 minutes over medium heat, or until pasta is *al dente*. Taste for seasoning. Serve with *parmigiano,* if you like.

Variation: Sauté 2 sun-dried tomatoes, chopped, with the cauliflower or broccoli.

5 GNOCCHI AND STUFFED PASTA

Gnocchi e Paste Ripiene

The Greek gods once roamed the earth, feasting and making love. One night, Venus, Mars, and Bacchus stop at a little inn in the town of Castelfranco. They have a magnificent dinner and then retire to their room for the night. Mars and Bacchus arise at dawn and depart, leaving Venus alone. The innkeeper, overcome with curiosity, spies through the keyhole and seeing her naked, is overwhelmed by her beauty. He rushes to the kitchen, and to immortalize the vision of her, creates tortellini *in the shape of her navel.*

—an Emilian folktale

Mars and Venus United by Love, *by Paolo Veronese (1528–88).*

Prosciutto *goes into the filling of classic* tortellini.

Many kinds of *ravioli* and *tortellini* can be bought in America now. They are sold dried or frozen in the pasta shops that have sprung up all over, and even in supermarkets. What was before known as *ravioli* bore little resemblance to the delicious and delicate pasta pillows of the Italian kitchen. But while many of these newer stuffed *tortellini* and such are vast improvements, the dough is always too thick, and the fillings are often stingy and made of mediocre ingredients.

According to food historian Waverly Root, *rabiole,* a Genoese dialect word for "refuse" that evolved into *ravioli* at the beginning of the nineteenth century, were originally invented to use up leftovers. Sometimes the *cucina casalinga* makes use of leftover meat in this way, but in the best tradition of Italian stuffed pasta, the ingre-

Stuffed Fresh Pasta Shapes

Agnolotti
Stuffed dumplings made of round disks of pasta about 2 inches in diameter. Once the filling is in place, the disks are folded in half. The corners may or may not be pinched together. *Agnolotti* with pinched corners are also known as *tortellini. Agnolotti* are most commonly stuffed with meat.

Cappellacci
Larger versions of *cappelletti* made from 3-inch squares (or disks) of fresh pasta. *Cappellacci* are usually stuffed with a pumpkin filling and simply sauced with melted butter that has been flavored with a leaf or two of sage.

Cappelletti*
Small dumplings made from 2-inch squares. Once stuffed, two corners of the square are brought together to form a triangle, then the opposite corners are pinched together so that the dumpling resembles a three-cornered hat. They are filled with either meat or cheese and served in the broth they have cooked in accompanied with *par-*

migiano at the table, or with a cream, tomato, or butter sauce.

Pansotti
Literally, "pot-bellied." Triangular dumplings about 2 inches long, stuffed with cheese and spinach, swiss chard, or borage. Typical of the region of Liguria, where they are served with a creamy walnut sauce.

Ravioletti
Miniature versions of *ravioli* made from 2-inch squares of fresh pasta. These small stuffed dumplings are usually served in the broth they have cooked in, accompanied with *parmigiano* at the table.

Ravioli
Fresh pasta squares measuring 3 inches and containing meat, cheese, or vegetable fillings. Served with various sauces.

Tortelli (also Anolini)
Half-moon-shaped dumplings made from disks of fresh pasta 2 inches in diameter. They are usually stuffed with cheese or vegetable fillings and are served with various sauces.

Tortellini*
Round, navel-shaped dumplings made from disks of fresh pasta 2 inches in diameter. They are filled with either meat or cheese and served in the broth they have been cooked in accompanied with grated *parmigiano* at the table, or with a cream, tomato, or butter sauce.

Tortelloni
Larger versions of *tortellini* made from 3-inch disks or squares of fresh pasta. They are usually filled with cheese or spinach fillings and served with various sauces.

Cappelletti and *tortellini* are different words for the same little pasta envelope filled with meat or cheese. *Tortellini,* meaning "little pies," is the Emilian term; *cappelletti,* meaning "little hats," is what the people of Romagna, the eastern half of the region, call them. *Tortellini* are first cut into circles before they are shaped, which gives them a rounded navel-like shape. *Cappelletti* are cut into squares first, which give them a little peak when they are folded. Form them around your finger and pinch the corners together in the same way.

dients are fresh. The dough is as thin as can be made and still remain intact while acting as an envelope for the stuffing. The result is a little package that allows such careful and delicious stuffings as are made, to be instantly released and savored when bitten, in the best proportion of one texture to the other. The envelope must not be a doughy obstacle to the savory treasures within. As a result, the best filled pasta is not perfectly smooth, but vaguely lumpy, because the filling bulges through the ever-so-thin, but obedient dough that wraps it.

A classic Bolognese filling is a paste made with the best *prosciutto crudo, mortadella,* veal, pork, *parmigiano* and seasonings, including nutmeg. From town to town and cook to cook, the recipes vary on the classic theme, for the Emilians are tireless in the exercise of their culinary imaginations. I have included some of my favorite recipes from Emilian cooks I have known and others that have been inspired by them. While *tortellini* and such have been the special pride of the Emilians for centuries, this chapter is not exclusive to their recipes, for stuffed pasta is made throughout Italy.

Shopping for authentic ingredients may take some time and making fresh-filled pasta can take several hours. But if you would like to make something truly extraordinary, it will be well worth your trouble. You will find that there is little that can go wrong, for even these pasta dishes are fundamentally direct and simple. Once the pasta is stuffed, it is boiled very quickly in broth and eaten straightaway with a little grated *parmigiano,* or boiled in water and anointed with butter and cheese, cream and butter, or some other simple sauce. Heavy-handed sauces would spoil the delicacy.

Gnocchi (pronounced nee-oak'-kee) are an entirely different concoction from the stuffed *ravioli*-type pasta. They are probably the simplest of all pasta dishes to make at home. My mother made them when she had old potatoes on hand, which make the lightest *gnocchi* (they have less water content than fresh potatoes). *Gnocchi di patate* (potato *gnocchi*) are the most common type. Their specific origins are not certain, though they no doubt were created between the seventeenth and eighteenth centuries when potatoes were first cultivated in Italy, in the central region. There are classic variations made with semolina, spinach, and *ricotta,* and in this chapter, some of my own innovations.

In order to make the procedure for making *gnocchi* and stuffed pasta simple to follow, I have organized recipe methods somewhat differently in this chapter, separating the method for each recipe into numbered steps.

Illustration from Maccaronee, *by Merlin Cocai, 1521, in which sweet-filled* tortelli *and* ravioli *are mentioned.*

Gnocchi and Stuffed Pasta

tortellini(agnolotti)

cannelloni

tortelloni

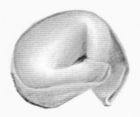

cappellacci

pansotti

ravioli

cappelletti

anolini (tortelli)

ravioletti

gnocchi

fazzoletti (crespelle)

Gnocchi di Patate al Gorgonzola

Potato Gnocchi with
Gorgonzola Sauce

FOR 6 PEOPLE

Most recipes for potato *gnocchi* call for the addition of eggs and sometimes baking powder. Eggs make the dough easier to work with by binding the ingredients, but also make it necessary to add more flour to absorb the moisture of the egg. Too much flour makes *gnocchi* very heavy. Eggs make them rubbery. This recipe prescribes neither baking powder nor eggs.

It is essential that the potatoes be *old* boiling potatoes, ones that have lost some of their water content. It is preferable to steam rather than boil them, again, to reduce moisture. Mash the potatoes with a ricer, food mill, or even a fork. The food processor makes cooked potatoes gluey, thus unusable for making *gnocchi*.

Gnocchi
2 pounds old boiling (not red or Idaho) potatoes
1¾ cups unbleached white flour
1 teaspoon salt
¼ teaspoon freshly milled white pepper
Sweet (unsalted) butter, for serving bowl
5 quarts water and 2 tablespoons salt, for cooking *gnocchi*

Gorgonzola Sauce
4 tablespoons sweet (unsalted) butter
6 ounces sweet (young) *Gorgonzola* cheese, crumbled
1 cup heavy cream
freshly milled white pepper to taste
¾ cup freshly grated *parmigiano* cheese

1. To make the *gnocchi,* steam the potatoes over boiling water until tender when pierced with a fork. Peel the potatoes as soon as they are just cool enough to handle. They must still be quite warm for making *gnocchi*. Turn the flour out on a large cutting board or work surface and sprinkle the salt and pepper over it. Make a "well" in the center of the flour. Mash the potatoes (see introduction) and drop them in the center of the well. Gradually draw the flour into the well, mixing it with the potatoes as you work the mass into dough. The amount of flour that will be absorbed is not predictable, but for the lightest possible *gnocchi,* the idea is to make a workable dough without using too much. You may use a little less or more than is called for here, so work it into the potatoes gradually. Once the dough is formed, knead it for 5 minutes. Divide it into quarters and refrigerate the portions you are not immediately working with until you are ready to use them. (Do not refrigerate the dough for too long or it will be unworkable.)

2. Working on a lightly floured board and using the palms of your hands, form a portion of the dough into a long, thin "rope" about ½ inch in diameter. To do this, roll the dough back and forth on the board until it is of even thickness. With a knife, cut the rope into ¾-inch lengths. Using the side of a grater, take each little piece you've cut, and holding it between your thumb and your forefinger, roll the piece of dough against the side with the large holes, pushing your thumb into it as you do so. A hollow, concave dumpling with pretty raised dots will be formed. You can also push the little pieces of dough against the floured surface of your board, again, using your thumb to push a hollow in the center of the little dumplings. The concave shape allows the *gnocchi* to cook thoroughly rather than remain doughy in the center while being cooked on the outside. Don't worry if the dough is a little sticky as you work with it. Lightly dust the grater with flour if the dough begins to stick. (If it is too sticky, you probably need to incorporate a little more flour in the dough.)

3. Have ready a slotted spoon and a perforated broiling tray or colander next to the stove. Choose a large, wide, shallow serving dish to hold the *gnocchi* once they've drained. Smear it with butter and keep it warm close to the stove. Bring water to a rapid boil, add salt, and drop in the *gnocchi*. Boil them until they float to the top. Retrieve them with the slotted spoon and place them on the tray or in the colander. You are, in essence, trying to "drip dry" them to avoid sogginess. After several minutes, transfer them to the serving dish. Do not layer the *gnocchi*; try to keep them from touching, to prevent them from clinging together.

You will find that it is quicker to form, cook, and drain one portion of dough at a time. Now, finish making the rest of the *gnocchi* with the dough that is left. When all the *gnocchi* are finished, put them in a 200-degree oven, loosely covered, while you make the sauce.

continued

continued

You will find that it is quicker to form, cook, and drain one portion of dough at a time. Now, finish making the rest of the *gnocchi* with the dough that is left. When all the *gnocchi* are finished, put them in a 200-degree oven, loosely covered, while you make the sauce.

4. To make the sauce, melt the butter in a saucepan and add the *Gorgonzola.* When the cheese has melted, add the cream. Heat to a slow simmer, stirring constantly with a wooden spoon. Cook for 4–5 minutes, at which point the sauce should thicken enough to coat the wooden spoon. Add the pepper and *parmigiano,* stir, and pour over the hot *gnocchi.* Serve at once.

Gnocchi di Patate Dolci con Salsa di Mandorle

Sweet Potato Gnocchi with Almond Sauce

FOR 6 PEOPLE

There is a pumpkin *gnocchi* made in Lombardy that is hard to duplicate here because our pumpkins are different from the Italian ones. Most pumpkin or squash varieties in North America absorb too much flour because of the high water content of the vegetable. As a result, the dough becomes heavy. Here is a recipe I have devised using American sweet potatoes, which absorb comparatively little flour. (It is best to use the true sweet potato, as it is smaller, yellower, and contains less water than the yam.)

Because of its inherent sweetness, this dish is a somewhat unorthodox inclusion in the Italian culinary tradition. But it is a festive and uncomplicated creation. The orange flavor in the pasta nearly sings to the almonds in the sauce. These *gnocchi* have a special affinity with pork, duck, turkey, and other game dishes, as long as there is no tomato sauce around. Read the general observations about potato *gnocchi* in Potato *Gnocchi* with *Gorgonzola* Sauce before beginning this one.

Gnocchi
1 pound sweet potatoes
1 cup unbleached white flour, plus additional few tablespoons if needed
¾ teaspoons salt
1 tablespoon freshly grated orange peel
¾ teaspoon nutmeg, preferably freshly grated
sweet (unsalted) butter, for serving bowl
5 quarts water and 2 tablespoons salt, for cooking *gnocchi*

Almond Sauce
3 tablespoons sweet (unsalted) butter
⅓ cup finely chopped (not ground) almonds (see Note)
1 cup heavy cream
freshly milled white pepper to taste
pinch of salt, or to taste

1. To make the *gnocchi,* preheat oven to 375 degrees. Prick the sweet potatoes in several places with a fork to help moisture evaporate when they are roasted. Place them directly on the oven rack, not in a dish, and roast until tender, about 1 hour. When they are cool enough to handle, peel them. Using a ricer, food mill, or fork, finely mash the potatoes while they are still quite warm. Do not put them in a food processor or blender.

The mashed sweet potatoes should measure 1 cup.

Turn the flour and salt out on a large cutting board or work surface and make a well in the center. Put the orange peel, nutmeg, and warm mashed sweet potatoes in the center. Draw in the flour gradually to form a dough. Following the directions for potato *gnocchi,* work the dough, form the *gnocchi,* boil them, drain them, and transfer to a serving dish. Place the serving dish in a 200-degree oven while you make the sauce.

2. To make the sauce, heat the butter in a heavy pan and add the chopped almonds.

Stirring with a wooden spoon, add the cream, pepper, and salt. Keep the heat very low, stirring now and then. When the sauce coats the wooden spoon, it is finished. It should take no more than 4–5 minutes. Serve over the *gnocchi.*

Note: If you are using whole unskinned almonds, blanch them in boiling water for 2–3 minutes. Peel off the skins and chop the nuts with a knife. Do not put them in the food processor, or they will be pulverized.

Forming, Cooking, and Storing *Tortellini* and *Cappelletti*

1. Make pasta dough according to the recipes in chapter 2. Roll it out as thinly as possible. Since it is critical that the dough not dry out as you work, keep the strips you have rolled out covered with a clean, damp towel until they are ready to be cut, stuffed, and sealed. Take care not to tear the dough as you roll it, or the filling will fall out when the little envelopes cook. You can "patch" dough you tear (refer to chapter 2). When you have rolled out the first quarter of the dough, cut it and stuff it according to the next step before rolling out the remaining pieces of dough, a quarter at a time.

2. With a knife or a pastry wheel, cut each length of rolled-out pasta into two-inch-wide strips. For *cappelletti,* cut each strip into two-inch squares. For *tortellini,* cut out disks two inches in diameter with a cookie cutter. Spoon a heaping one-fourth teaspoon of filling onto the center of each square (or disk). Dip your finger into water, milk, or beaten egg or egg yolk mixed with a little water and lightly run it along the inside edges, to help in keeping the little envelopes sealed shut. For *cappelletti,* fold the square in half, bringing two opposite corners together so that a triangle is formed. For *tortellini,* use the same amount of filling and fold the disk over to form a half-moon. Seal so that one side of the triangled edge (*cappelletti*) or curved edge (*tortellini*) is slightly below the other. Press to seal well. Now take the little "kerchief," or half-moon, and wrap it around your little finger to form the dumplings. Make them as uniform as you can, holding the peaked end up, with the "belly," or rounded side, away from you. Pinch the two corners together. Place the envelopes on a tray covered with a clean towel sprinkled with a little cornmeal or flour. Don't let them overlap or they will stick together. Turn them frequently so they dry evenly and don't stick to the tray. They should not be left to dry longer than three to four hours before being cooked or refrigerated.

3. To cook *cappelletti* or *tortellini,* bring the broth or salted water, depending on your recipe, to a boil and gently drop them into the water. Put a lid on the pot until the water returns to a boil. Do not let the water boil too rapidly or the envelopes may knock against each other and break. Cook for a total of three to five minutes once the water has returned to a boil, stirring gently as you watch over them. The best way to determine if they are done is to taste one. As soon as they are done, quickly lift them out, one by one, with a slotted spoon and transfer them to a warm buttered bowl. (See chapter 2 for additional directions on cooking filled pasta.)

4. There are two ways to refrigerate or freeze stuffed pasta. The first is to place the pasta in a plastic freezing container between sheets of aluminum foil or waxed paper and sprinkle lightly with cornmeal or flour. To prevent the pasta from sticking together, do not allow the pasta envelopes to overlap. Now, refrigerate or freeze them in the container. (Freezing them in bags will expose them to breakage from the weight of other objects in the freezer.) To cook filled pasta that has been refrigerated, drop into boiling salted water and cook for five to six minutes after the water has returned to the boil. To cook filled pasta that has been frozen, drop it directly from the freezer into boiling salted water and cook for seven to eight minutes after the water has returned to the boil.

The second way to refrigerate or freeze filled pasta is to half-cook the pasta envelopes first in salted water (see chapter 2). Drain and layer as described above. Refrigerate for up to five days, or freeze for up to two months. To finish cooking, slip the envelopes into lightly salted boiling water for two to three minutes. Frozen, they will take approximately five minutes once the water has returned to the boil. But the only real way to test for doneness is to taste one.

Tortellini Casalinghi in Brodo

Classic Tortellini in Broth

Given to me by Walter Cantoni of the Oreste restaurant in Modena, this is a classic Emilian recipe for *tortellini*. First make one recipe Chicken and Beef Broth, or even better, the broth in Mixed Meats in Broth, both in chapter 4. Then make the filling, and finally, the dough. You can also serve these *tortellini* simply with butter, warm cream, and freshly grated *parmigiano,* or just sweet butter and *parmigiano.* If serving in broth, allow ten to twelve *tortellini* for each person. For serving with sauce, figure on twice that.

Filling

¼ pound good-quality veal, cut into 1-inch dice

2 tablespoons sweet (unsalted) butter

¼ pound lean boneless pork, cut into 1-inch dice

2–3 slices *prosciutto crudo*

1½ ounces *mortadella*

½ cup freshly grated *parmigiano* cheese

1 egg

¼ teaspoon nutmeg, preferably freshly grated

½ teaspoon salt, or to taste

freshly milled white or black pepper to taste

Pasta Dough

1 recipe (about 2 pounds) Egg Pasta I or II (chapter 2)

freshly grated *parmigiano* cheese at table

1. To make the filling, very gently sauté veal in 1 tablespoon butter for 8 minutes until it loses its pinkness. Do not allow it to brown and get hard. The meat must remain soft, inside and out. Transfer the veal to a bowl and set aside. Heat the remaining tablespoon of butter and add the pork. Sauté the pork in the same manner for about 10 minutes, always over very gentle heat. Chop the *prosciutto* and *mortadella* very fine by hand, or very carefully in a food processor. They must not become pasty or pulverized. When the veal and pork have cooked, also chop them very fine. Combine the meats, cheese, egg, and seasonings. Bind the mixture well but do not beat and set aside.

2. Make the pasta dough and follow the steps for forming the *tortellini* that open this chapter.

3. Drop *tortellini* into boiling broth. Cover and allow to return to a boil. Cook for 3–5 minutes total cooking time. Ladle *tortellini* into bowls with broth. Serve with *parmigiano.* (For further information on cooking filled pasta, see step 3 in general directions for *tortellini* preceding this recipe.)

Cappelletti Zerbinati

Bruna Zerbinati's Cappelletti

Bruna Zerbinati claims to make the best *cappelletti* in all of Ferrara, and while I haven't tried them all, I do love these. She insists that you must use the local *salame* for this recipe. You won't find it here, but *soppressata* will do very well. It is important to buy the best-quality sausage for this recipe, for the filling should be aromatic and zesty, not greasy, heavy, and coarse. The *salame* and *pancetta* in the filling make these *cappelletti* more domineering than the *tortellini* in the preceding recipe, but they are still succulent.

First make any of the clear chicken or meat broths in chapter 4. If you prefer to accompany the *cappelletti* with sauce, also prepare it in advance. I suggest one of the smooth meatless tomato sauces in chapter 3. If serving in broth, allow ten to twelve *cappelletti* for each person. With sauce, twice that many is appropriate.

Filling

¼ pound pork, fat removed, cut into 1-inch dice

1 tablespoon sweet (unsalted) butter

¼ pound chicken breast meat, cut into 1-inch dice

continued

continued

2 ounces *pancetta,* finely chopped

2 ounces *salame* (see introduction), finely chopped

¾ cup freshly grated *parmigiano* cheese

¼ teaspoon nutmeg, preferably freshly grated

¼ teaspoon salt

1 small or medium egg

Pasta Dough

1 recipe (about 2 pounds) Egg Pasta I or II (chapter 2)

3 tablespoons sweet (unsalted) butter, melted, if serving with sauce

1. To make the filling, very gently sauté the pork in ½ tablespoon of the butter for 10 minutes until it loses its pinkness on the outside. Do not allow it to brown and get hard. The meat must remain soft, inside and out. In another pan, sauté the chicken gently in the remaining ½ tablespoon butter for 2–3 minutes. Combine the pork and chicken and add the salt. Allow the pork and chicken to cool. Chop the *pancetta* and *salame* very fine by hand, or very carefully in a food processor. They must not become pulverized or pasty. When the pork and chicken have cooled, chop them fine, too. Be careful not to chop so finely that the meats become

a paste. In a bowl, combine and mix all the meats, the *parmigiano,* nutmeg, salt, and egg. It is best to use your hands for this to arrive at the proper consistency.

2. Make the dough and follow the steps for forming the *cappelletti* that open this chapter.

3. To cook in broth, see preceding recipe for *tortellini,* or step 3 in general directions for *tortellini* and *cappelletti,* this chapter. To serve with sauce, boil the *cappelletti* in boiling, salted water for a total cooking time of 3–5 minutes. Meanwhile, put melted butter in a warm, large, wide bowl or baking dish. You do not want to pile the *cappelletti* on top of one another or they may stick together and break open. When they are cooked, remove them from the water with a slotted spoon. Place them carefully in the buttered bowl, being sure each of them is coated with enough butter to prevent them from sticking together and breaking. When all the *cappelletti* are cooked, add additional melted butter and *parmigiano,* or whatever sauce you have prepared.

Ravioletti Rossi al Pesto

Little Pink Ravioli Filled with Pesto

FOR 6 PEOPLE

These miniature *ravioli* are best boiled in chicken or fish broth. Stronger broths muddle the perfume of the *pesto.* The tomato-pink pasta is pretty with the pastel green filling.

Broth

1 recipe Chicken Broth or Fish Broth (chapter 4)

Filling

1 pound (2 cups) *ricotta* cheese

¼ recipe (about ¼ cup) Basil Sauce (*pesto;* chapter 3)

1 egg yolk

salt and freshly milled white pepper to taste

Pasta Dough

½ recipe (about 1 pound) Red (Tomato) Pasta (chapter 2)

freshly grated *parmigiano* cheese, or freshly torn Italian parsley leaves

1. Make broth and set aside.

2. To make the filling, put the *ricotta* in a sieve for 3–4 hours to drain off any excess liquid. It should be as dry as possible for the filling. In a bowl, combine the *ricotta, pesto,* egg yolk, and salt and pepper, forming an even mixture. Set it aside in the refrigerator, covered, until you are ready to use it.

3. Make the pasta dough and follow step 1 for making *cappelletti* (this chapter). Working with one strip of dough at a time, space little mounds of filling (generous ½ teaspoonfuls) 1½ inches apart in rows on a strip of pasta. Moisten the dough around each mound of filling with a little water. Place a second sheet of dough on top of the first and with your hands, press firmly all around the mounds of filling to seal the sheets together. With a knife or, preferably, a fluted-edged pastry wheel, cut the *ravioletti* row by row, first horizontally, then vertically, or vice-versa. Press down all around the edges of each *ravioletto* while the dough is still very soft to assure that each is well sealed. Work very quickly to prevent the dough from drying out.

4. Bring the broth to a boil, drop in the *ravioletti,* and cook about 3 minutes. Remember that they will continue to cook in the hot broth off the heat. Serve in soup dishes. With chicken broth, serve *parmigiano.* With fish broth, sprinkle with parsley.

Tortelli d'Erbette Rosetti

Tortelli Filled with Spinach
in Pink Cream Sauce

FOR 6 PEOPLE

These are a crescent-shaped pasta stuffed with greens, usually chard or spinach. It is a traditional dish that appears all over Italy, most often served with tomato sauce. This fashionable pink sauce is a nice variation on the classic theme and a pretty sight over the golden half-moons stuffed with bright green spinach.

Filling

1 pound (2 cups) *ricotta* cheese
2 pounds spinach
scant ½ teaspoon salt, for cooking
    spinach
2 egg yolks
¼ teaspoon nutmeg, preferably
    freshly grated
scant ½ teaspoon salt
generous sprinkling freshly milled
    pepper
½ cup freshly grated *parmigiano*
    cheese

Pasta Dough

½ recipe (about 1 pound) Egg
    Pasta I or II (chapter 2)

Sauce

1 recipe Béchamel Sauce (chapter
    3), plus additional ¼ cup milk
2 tablespoons tomato paste
2 tablespoons brandy

3 tablespoons sweet (unsalted)
    butter, melted
freshly grated *parmigiano* cheese
    at table

1. To make the filling, put the *ricotta* in a sieve for 3–4 hours to drain off any excess liquid. It should be as dry as possible for the filling.

2. Wash the spinach extremely well to remove sand. Cut off the stems and any yellow or limp leaves. Cook it in boiling water to cover, to which salt has been added, until tender. Drain well and squeeze out as much water as you can. Chop it very fine. It is best to do this by hand. If you are using a food processor, be careful not to turn the spinach into a mush.

3. In a mixing bowl, lightly beat the egg yolks. Add the nutmeg, salt, and pepper and mix well. Then add the spinach and drained *ricotta* and stir to form an even mixture. Set the filling aside in the refrigerator, covered, until you are ready to use it.

4. Make the dough. Follow step 1 (this chapter) for forming *tortellini,* but use a 2-inch round cookie cutter, preferably with a fluted edge. Lay the dough you have rolled out on a lightly floured board. Using the cookie cutter and beginning from the top corner of the sheet, cut rows of circles as close to each other as you can without interfering with the shapes of the other circles. Place 1 tablespoon of filling in the center of each circle and moisten edges with a little water to help seal. Fold in half, forming a half-moon. Press down to seal firmly. Transfer the *tortelli* to a tray lined with a waxed paper or foil and sprinkled with a little cornmeal or flour. Do not let the *tortelli* overlap or touch. Turn them over several times to let them dry evenly and to prevent them from sticking to the tray. Let them rest about 10 minutes. This is a rather

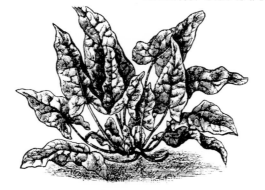

moist filling, so work quickly to keep the filling from soaking through the pasta.

5. Meanwhile, make the sauce. Prepare the béchamel. When it has thickened properly, mix a few tablespoons of the sauce with the tomato paste and then stir the mixture into the rest of the sauce. Stir until evenly blended and add brandy. Continue to heat the sauce, stirring constantly, until it has evaporated, about 3–4 minutes. Cover and remove from heat. Keep the sauce warm.

6. Drop the *tortelli* into boiling salted water, cover, and cook for a total cooking time of 3–4 minutes (see step 3 in general directions for cooking *tortellini* and *cappelletti,* this chapter). Meanwhile, put melted butter in a warm large, wide bowl. Taste the *tortelli* for doneness and remove with a slotted spoon to the dish. They should not be piled on top of each other too much, but should be spread out somewhat to prevent clinging and breaking. Smear with the melted butter and then the sauce. Serve immediately. Pass the *parmigiano*.

Tortelli di Pesce e Patate in Brodo

Tortelli Filled with Potato and Haddock in Broth

FOR 6–8 PEOPLE

An uncommon and delicious variation on classic *tortelli*.

Broth
1 recipe (2 quarts) Fish Broth (chapter 4)

Filling
1 medium-sized Idaho potato (about ¾ cup, mashed)

1½ pounds haddock or cod fillet, bones and skin removed

several sprigs Italian parsley

pinch of saffron powder (1 envelope), or ⅛ teaspoon saffron threads

1 egg, lightly beaten

1 teaspoon salt, or to taste

½ teaspoon dried green peppercorns, finely crushed

¼ teaspoon freshly milled white or black pepper

1 tablespoon finely chopped fresh Italian parsley

¼ cup freshly grated *parmigiano* cheese

Pasta Dough
½ recipe (about 1 pound) Egg Pasta I or II (chapter 2)

chopped fresh Italian parsley, for garnish

1. Prepare the broth and set aside.

2. To make the filling, boil the potato. When tender, peel and mash well with a potato masher, ricer, or fork. (Do not use a food processor or the potato will turn gluey.) Meanwhile, in a separate pan, bring enough water to boil to cover the fish fillets. Slip the fish fillets into the water, being careful not to stack them. Add parsley and cover the pan. Turn the heat as high as it will go. As soon as the water returns to the boil, reduce the heat to medium and remove the lid. The aim is to poach the fish only partially (about 3 minutes once water has returned to a boil). Lift the fillets from the pan with a slotted spatula and set them aside to cool off. Strain fish cooking liquid and add it to the fish broth; correct seasoning. When the fish is cool enough to handle, mash it with a fork. If using saffron threads, heat them first for about 1 minute in a hot oven or over medium heat in a pan for 1 minute. Crush them between your fingers. Combine saffron with the mashed potato, egg, seasonings, cheese, and fish and mix well without pulverizing. The filling should have a little texture to it.

3. Make the pasta dough. Roll out, cut, and stuff it as you would *Tortelli d'Erbette Rosetti* (step 4), substituting the fish and potato filling.

4. Bring broth to a boil and drop in *tortelli*. Cook as you would Classic *Tortellini* in Broth, this chapter. (See step 3 in general directions for cooking *tortellini* and *cappelletti*, this chapter, for further information.) Serve the *tortelli* and broth in soup plates. Sprinkle chopped parsley on each serving.

Variation: Boil the *tortelli* and serve with melted butter and torn fresh parsley leaves. Serves 4–6 this way.

Tortelloni con gli Asparagi

Tortelloni with Asparagus

FOR 4–6 PEOPLE

This is a recipe reminiscent of a dish I had in Franco Rossi's restaurant in Bologna. *Tortelloni* are larger than *tortelli*. Unlike many of the pasta-and-vegetable dishes fashionable now, the asparagus should not be undercooked and crisp. Tender-cooked asparagus are the best companion for this silky cream sauce.

Filling
1 pound (2 cups) *ricotta*
¾ cup freshly grated *parmigiano* cheese
2 egg yolks
¼ teaspoon nutmeg, preferably freshly grated, or to taste
¼ teaspoon salt, or to taste
⅛ teaspoon freshly milled white pepper, or to taste

Pasta Dough
½ recipe (about 1 pound) Egg Pasta I or II (chapter 2)

Sauce
1 pound fresh asparagus (see Note)
½ teaspoon salt, for cooking asparagus
4 tablespoons sweet (unsalted) butter
1½ cups heavy cream
¼ teaspoon nutmeg, preferably freshly grated
¼ teaspoon salt, or to taste
freshly milled white pepper to taste
¼ cup freshly grated *parmigiano* cheese

freshly grated *parmigiano* cheese at table

1. To make the filling, put the *ricotta* in a sieve for 3–4 hours to remove as much liquid as possible. The *ricotta* must be very dry. In a mixing bowl, combine the *ricotta, parmigiano,* egg yolks, and seasonings and blend to a smooth paste with a spoon. Cover and refrigerate.

2. Make the pasta dough. Roll it out according to the recipe for *tortelli,* this chapter. With a pastry wheel or knife, cut each strip of dough into 3-inch squares instead of circles. Put approximately 1 teaspoon of filling in the center of each square and moisten the edges of the square with a little water. Fold in half to form a triangle and press down firmly to seal well. Let the stuffed triangles rest according to the same procedure as for *tortelli.*

3. To make the sauce, first wash the asparagus well to remove any sand. Cut off any part of the shafts that looks woody or tough. Scrape off any discolored parts. The length you end up with will depend upon the tenderness of the asparagus. Arrange the asparagus flat in a wide skillet in boiling, salted water to cover. Cover the pan and cook for 10–12 minutes, or until tender. Lift the asparagus out of the bath and immediately plunge them into cold water, to set the color. Cut into 2-inch lengths, being sure to keep the tips intact. Cover and set aside in a warm place.

4. Melt the butter over low heat. Add cream, nutmeg, salt, pepper, and asparagus, except for 8 tips. Heat over low heat for 5 minutes, using a wooden spoon to stir

gently. Take care not to break the asparagus. Add *parmigiano,* check seasoning, cover, and keep warm.

5. Choose a large, wide, shallow serving dish (you may need 2 dishes unless you have an enormous one). Keep it warm. Cook *tortelloni* according to instructions for *tortelli.* Smear a thin layer of the sauce on the bottom of the serving dish. Drain the *tortelloni* with a slotted spoon and transfer them to the dish, laying them side by side without overlapping too much. Pour the rest of the sauce over them, making sure to coat every one. Decorate the top with the asparagus tips. Pass *parmigiano* at the table.
Note: Look for firm, smooth asparagus with tight tips. The thickness does not affect the tenderness.

Anolini Verdi con Sugo di Pomodoro e Panna

Spinach Anolini with Tomato Cream Sauce

FOR 6 PEOPLE

*A*nolini and *tortelli* are one and the same, the first being the Bolognese word and the second, the general Emilian and Tuscan term. *Anolini* are little stuffed crescents of fresh egg pasta.

Filling
1½ pounds (3 cups) *ricotta* cheese
pinch (1 envelope) of saffron powder, or ⅛ teaspoon saffron threads
½ cup freshly grated *parmigiano* cheese

Pasta Dough
½ recipe (about 1 pound) Spinach Pasta (chapter 2)

Sauce
Sauce from Vine-ripened Tomatoes II (chapter 3)
½ cup heavy cream

freshly grated *parmigiano* cheese at table

1. To make the filling, put the *ricotta* in a sieve for 3–4 hours to drain of any liquid. It should be as dry as possible for the filling. If using saffron threads, heat them for 1 minute in a hot oven or over medium heat in a pan, and crush them before adding to the other ingredients. In a mixing bowl, combine *ricotta, parmigiano,* and saffron and stir to form an even

mixture. Cover and set aside in the refrigerator.

2. Make the pasta dough. Roll out, cut, and stuff it as you would *tortelli* (step 4, page 98), substituting the cheese filling.

3. Prepare the Tomato Sauce. You can substitute 1 28-ounce can peeled Italian plum tomatoes in purée if sweet fresh tomatoes are not in season. After the sauce has been sieved, stir in the cream and reheat the sauce while you cook the *anolini,* according to the following directions.

4. Boil and drain the *anolini* following step 6 in the *tortelli* recipe. Smear *anolini* with sauce. Pass the *parmigiano*.

Cannelloni di Animelle

Cannelloni Filled with Sweetbreads

FOR 6–8 PEOPLE

*T*his delicate sweetbread mixture is a good filling for any of the pastas mentioned below, or for the crêpelike *fazzoletti* in Shrimp-filled Pasta "Handkerchiefs" with Béchamel Sauce.

Filling
1 recipe sweetbread sauce including the Béchamel Sauce (see *Tortellini* and Sweetbread Pie, chapter 8)

Pasta Dough
½ recipe (about 1 pound) Egg Pasta I or II, Spinach Pasta, Red (Tomato) Pasta, or Pink (Beet) Pasta (chapter 2)

Topping
reserved béchamel
½ cup shredded *fontina* or *fonduta* cheese
⅓ cup freshly grated *parmigiano* cheese

1. To make the filling, make the sweetbread sauce according to the recipe in chapter 8, following steps 1, 3, 4, and 5 except add only ¼ cup of the béchamel to the sweetbreads at the end of step 5. Reserve the rest of the béchamel (1¾ cups) for covering the *cannelloni.*

2. Make the pasta dough. Roll, cut, and precook the pasta according to step 3 in Emilian Onion Harmony (page 102).

3. Preheat the oven to 425 degrees. Butter a large rectangular baking dish (you may need 2, unless you have a very large one). Fill the *cannelloni* according to step 3 in Emilian Onion Harmony and arrange them in the baking dish. Do not let them overlap. Spread the reserved béchamel over the *cannelloni* and sprinkle the shredded *fontina* and grated *parmigiano* over the top. Bake in the preheated oven on the next-to-highest rack for 10–15 minutes or until golden. Let settle 10–15 minutes before serving.

Armonia di Cipolla all'Emiliana

Emilian Onion Harmony
(*Cannelloni* Filled with Onion, Sausage, and Asparagus)

FOR 6 PEOPLE

Another adaptation of a recipe from Franco Rossi's restaurant in Bologna, this dish is an exquisite combination of flavors and textures of the diverse ingredients.

Sauces

½ recipe Béchamel Sauce (chapter 3), plus additional ¼ cup milk

1 recipe Sauce (Sieved) from Vine-ripened Tomatoes II (chapter 3), using only half the onion and omitting basil

Filling

½ pound asparagus

¼ teaspoon salt, for cooking asparagus

4 tablespoons sweet (unsalted) butter

1 cup finely chopped white onion

1 pound good-quality lean sweet pork sausage meat (see Note)

1 teaspoon fennel seeds, crushed in a mortar (see Note)

1 teaspoon salt

¼ teaspoon freshly milled white pepper

½ pound fresh cultivated mushrooms, quartered and very thinly sliced

1 cup freshly grated *parmigiano* cheese

Pasta Dough

½ recipe (about 1 pound) Egg Pasta I or II (chapter 2)

sweet (unsalted) butter, for brushing on asparagus

1. First, make the sauces. Prepare the béchamel, adding the extra milk to make a thinner sauce. Then make the tomato sauce, reducing the onion and omitting the basil as directed. If sweet, vine-ripened tomatoes are not in season, substitute 1 28-ounce can peeled Italian plum tomatoes in purée. Cover the sauces and set aside.

2. To make the filling, wash and trim asparagus as described in *Tortelloni* with Asparagus. Blanch them for 3 minutes in boiling, salted water. Remove from the water and reserve the water. Immediately plunge the asparagus into cold water, to set the color. When they are cool enough to handle, set aside 4 of them and cut the remainder crosswise, including tips and stems, into ⅓-inch-thick slices. Slit the 4 reserved asparagus in half lengthwise and set aside.

   In a large skillet, heat the butter and the onion. When the onion is soft, add the loose sausage meat, crushed fennel, salt, and pepper. Sauté mixture at gentle heat for 4–5 minutes, using a wooden spoon to break up the meat. Do not let the meat get hard and brown. Cook until sausage is just barely pink. Add the mushrooms and sauté over gentle heat for 3–4 minutes. Add *parmigiano* and reserved sliced asparagus. Continue to sauté gently about 10 minutes, adding a little of the reserved asparagus cooking liquid only if the mixture gets dry.

3. Make the pasta dough and roll it out very thin. With a knife or fluted-edged pastry wheel, cut it into rectangles 3½ by 4½ inches. Drop the rectangle into a generous amount of boiling salted water 2 or 3 at a time, cover, and cook for a total of 1 minute. Retrieve them with a slotted spatula and immediately immerse them in a bowl of cold water to stop them from cooking further (do not put ice in the water, or it will make holes in the pasta). Lift the rectangles from the cold water and place in a single layer on a damp towel. Finish cooking all the pasta rectangles and cooling them off in the same manner. When all are cooked and on the towel, pat them with a dry towel. Put 2 generous tablespoons of the filling along the short end of each rectangle, covering a third of the area. Roll up each rectangle, starting at the filled end, to form a secure cylindrical bundle.

4. Preheat oven to 400 degrees. Choose a large, rectangular baking dish. (You may need 2 dishes, unless you have an enormous one.) Reheat the sauces you have prepared. Smear a very thin layer of tomato sauce on the bottom of the baking dish. Carefully place the *cannelloni* in the dish seam side up and side by side. Do not overlap them. Smear them with a layer of tomato sauce and over that, a layer of béchamel. (You may end up with extra sauce.) Butter the 4 reserved slit asparagus to prevent them from drying out and arrange them over the top decoratively. Slip the pan(s) on the next-to-highest rack in the oven. Bake 10–15 minutes, until the béchamel forms a golden crust. Do not overcook. Remove immediately. Let settle 10 minutes before serving.

Note: The sausage meat should be finely ground. If you can't find loose sausage meat, buy sausage and remove the casings. If only fennel-flavored sweet sausage is available, reduce the amount of fennel seeds called for to ½ teaspoon.

Fazzoletti coi Gamberi e Besciamella

Shrimp-filled Pasta
"Handkerchiefs" with
Béchamel Sauce

FOR 4–6 PEOPLE

Fazzoletti are also called *crespelle* or *manicotti* and are almost identical to crêpes. They can encase seafood, meat, cheese, and vegetable fillings (see the sweetbread filling in *Cannelloni* Filled with Sweetbreads, or the spinach and *mascarpone* filling in Spinach-and-*Mascarpone*-filled Pasta Handkerchiefs, both in this chapter). The "crêpes" can be made in advance, stacked, and refrigerated or frozen until ready to use.

Batter

⅞ cup unbleached white flour
pinch of salt
2 extra-large eggs
1 cup milk
1 tablespoon sweet (unsalted) butter, melted
1 tablespoon sweet (unsalted) butter, melted, mixed with 1 teaspoon vegetable oil, for cooking *fazzoletti*

Sauce

1½ recipes Béchamel Sauce (chapter 3)
⅓ cup freshly grated *parmigiano* cheese

Filling

2½ pounds shrimp in the shell
5 tablespoons sweet (unsalted) butter
4 medium-sized shallots, finely chopped
1 large celery stalk, finely chopped
7 ounces fresh cultivated mushrooms, quartered and thinly sliced

2–3 teaspoons good dry white wine, light stock, or water, if needed
generous ½ teaspoon salt
freshly milled white or black pepper to taste
2 tablespoons chopped fresh Italian parsley

1. Make the batter first, because it should stand at room temperature for at least 30 minutes. This will allow the flour to lose its elasticity and expand. (The batter can also be made in advance and kept in the refrigerator overnight. In this case, the butter should be left out of the batter until you are ready to use it.) Sift the dry ingredients together into a bowl. In a separate bowl, beat the eggs with a fork and add the milk gradually. Drizzle in the melted butter while you continue to beat. Make a "well" in the dry ingredients and gradually pour the egg-milk mixture into the well, pulling the dry ingredients into the well until they are thoroughly incorporated with the liquid ingredients. Do not overbeat the batter. If there are any lumps in it, sieve it. Cover the bowl and set aside.

2. Make the béchamel and set aside. (The *parmigiano* is used in step 5.)

3. To make the filling, shell the shrimp and remove the dark intestinal vein. Wash the shrimp, pat dry, and chop coarsely. Heat the butter and add the shallots and celery. Sauté gently until soft. Increase heat slightly and add the shrimp. Sauté for 1 minute, stirring to cook evenly. Add mushrooms. Sauté for another 1–2 minutes. If mixture seems too dry, add a little wine, stock, or water to moisten. Add salt and pepper and check for seasoning. Add parsley and stir well. Moisten the filling with 1–2 tablespoons of the béchamel. Remove from the heat and set aside.

4. Lightly brush a thick-bottomed 8-inch skillet or omelet or crêpe pan with the butter-and-oil mixture and place over medium heat. (Too much butter will make the *fazzoletti* greasy and heavy.) Pour ⅛ cup batter into the pan for each *fazzoletto*, keeping the heat at medium. Do not put more than this in the pan or the *fazzoletti* will be too thick and doughy. If you only have a ¼ cup measuring cup, fill it half full each time you need to pour batter into the skillet. Make 1 *fazzoletto* at a time, as you would a crêpe, tilting the pan to cover its entire surface with batter. If you find that you have an excessive amount of batter in the pan, pour it out immediately. Stir the batter in the bowl each time before using some to make another *fazzoletto*. Cook the *fazzoletti* until they are golden but not brown, about 1–2 minutes per side.

continued

continued

They should not be allowed to get crisp. Flip them with a spatula to cook them on the second side. You will need very little butter after the first coating of the pan. However, keep the butter-and-oil mixture on hand. Should the *fazzoletti* begin to stick, brush the pan very lightly with more of the mixture. Stack the finished *fazzoletti* on a plate until they are all cooked. If refrigerating them in advance of using, slip a piece of aluminum foil or plastic wrap between the layers.

5. Preheat the oven to 450 degrees. Butter 2 large baking dishes, each 9 by 14 inches. Place 2 tablespoons of filling in the center of each *fazzoletto* and spread it over the entire disk, except for 1 inch all around the edge. Starting from one end of the disk, roll the *fazzoletto* up, so that you wind up with a neat but fairly loose cylinder. Push any filling toward the center of the cylinder that is too near the ends and might fall out. Place the *fazzoletti* in the baking dishes seam side up and side by side. They may touch, but don't crowd them in. Reheat the béchamel without letting it boil. Sieve it if lumps have formed. Pour the béchamel over the *fazzoletti* and sprinkle with *parmigiano*. Bake for 10 or 15 minutes on the highest rack of the oven, or until the top is golden. Serve immediately.

Fazzoletti con Spinaci e Mascarpone

Spinach-and-Mascarpone-filled Pasta "Handkerchiefs"

FOR 4 PEOPLE

Sauce
1 recipe Béchamel Sauce (chapter 3)
⅓ cup freshly grated *parmigiano* cheese

Filling
½ pound (1 cup) *ricotta* cheese
1 pound spinach
scant ¼ teaspoon salt, for cooking spinach
1 cup *mascarpone* cheese
½ cup freshly grated *parmigiano* cheese
2 eggs, lightly beaten
¼ teaspoon nutmeg, preferably freshly grated, or to taste
salt and freshly milled black pepper to taste

Batter
see Shrimp-filled Pasta "Handkerchiefs" with Béchamel Sauce (preceding recipe)

1. Make the béchamel and set aside.

2. To make the filling, place the *ricotta* in a sieve to drain off excess moisture (about 30 minutes). Meanwhile, thoroughly wash the spinach to remove any sand. Remove any yellow or discolored leaves and all the stems. Boil the spinach in boiling, salted water to cover until tender but not overcooked. Drain well and squeeze out as much water as you can. Chop finely. It is best to do this by hand. If you are using a food processor, be careful not to turn the spinach to a mush. Combine the spinach, cheese, eggs, and seasonings in a large bowl and mix to distribute well. Take care not to add too much nutmeg or the mixture will become bitter. Set filling aside.

3. Make the batter and cook the *fazzoletti* according to the instructions in Shrimp-filled Pasta "Handkerchiefs" with Béchamel Sauce (step 4 on page 103).

4. Preheat the oven to 400 degrees and proceed to fill, bake, and sauce the *fazzoletti* exactly as described in step 5 of the shrimp-filled version. Serve.

6 FRESH NOODLES

Pasta Fresca

[Fresh] pasta should be cooked for as long as it takes to say three Pater Nosters.

—Bartolomeo Sacchi (Il Platina), *De Honesta Voluptate ac Valetudine* ("Of Honest Pleasure and Well-Being"), 1475

A monk eating noodles, by Torriglia, 19th century.

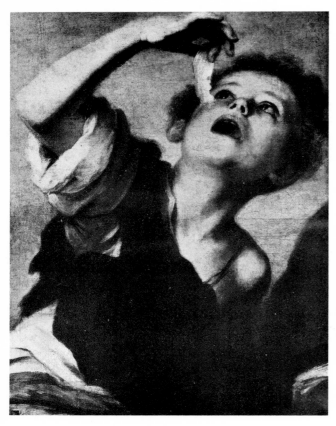

Detail from Boys Eating Pasta, *by Bartolomé Esteban Murillo (1618–82). Pinacoteca, Munich.*

A noodle made with ordinary flour and eggs is as different from dried macaroni made with semolina and water as a female human from a male human. One is wonderful for its delicacy and the other for its firmness. Both have like characteristics, but biology being what it is, and things being what they are, the inherent differences between fresh noodles and dried spaghetti just go to create that much more diversity in pasta cookery.

Fresh pasta is lighter than dried pasta and as such can mate with richer sauces. Its texture, because it is still porous and soft, easily absorbs sauces, resulting in a more subtle dish. Fresh noodles are meant for sauces containing cream, butter, and cheese, as long as they are not too heavy (a *ricotta* sauce, for example, is better with dried pasta).

There are two kinds of fresh pasta: homemade and store-bought. Commercial fresh pasta is not kneaded by hand, so it is rubbery instead of tender and absorbent and it is always too thick (fresh pasta should be extremely thin). The ingredients are often not as good as what you would use at home. For example, spinach powder sometimes replaces fresh spinach in green pasta and frozen or powdered eggs are often used instead of fresh ones.

Obviously, then, the best fresh pasta is what you make at home. For most noodles, it is important to roll the pasta dough out very thin or it will detract from the sauce and be too prominent and chewy. Certain noodles (*fettuccine* and *trenette,* for example) are slightly thicker than others, designed for heavier cream sauces and in the case of *trenette,* to carry unctuous *pesto.* See chapter 2 for different noodle thicknesses and widths, and directions for cooking them.

Very thin noodles such as *taglierini* are best in soups or with light tomato or stock-based sauces. They should not be accompanied with sauces containing large ingredients, as they will not easily settle among the fine strands. Wider noodles can handle the shapes of vegetables, shellfish, and meat, which will intermingle with the ribbons of pasta instead of rolling off to the sides and bottom of the dish. Refer to the basic sauces in chapter 3 for other sauces to serve on fresh noodles.

Fettuccine alla Moda d'Oreste

Fettuccine Oreste

FOR 4 PEOPLE

Modena restaurateur Walter Cantoni gave me this recipe. It has become one of my favorites. No one element is overpowering, but a perfect harmony of flavors—a "bouquet," to use Signor Cantoni's word—is achieved.

½ recipe (about 1 pound) Egg Pasta II, cut into *fettuccine* (chapter 2)

¼ pound fresh, plump chicken livers

6 tablespoons sweet (unsalted) butter

2 tablespoons shelled fresh petite peas or frozen petite peas (not thawed)

½ ounce dried *porcini* mushrooms, soaked, drained, and chopped (chapter 1)

2 garlic cloves, very finely chopped

2 tablespoons finely chopped Italian parsley

2 tablespoons olive oil

¼ cup cream

1 slice good *salame* such as *soppressata,* diced

6 tablespoons freshly grated *parmigiano*

salt and freshly milled black pepper to taste

1 white truffle (optional)

freshly grated *parmigiano* at table

Make pasta and set aside. Wash the chicken livers and trim off any fat, membranes, discolorations, and green spots. Dice (about ½-inch pieces) and sauté briefly (3–4 minutes) in 2 tablespoons of butter until they are just pink inside. Remove from the pan and set aside. Blanch peas in boiling water for 1 minute. Drain, rinse in cold water, and set aside. Gently sauté the *porcini,* garlic, and parsley in the olive oil for 3–4 minutes, or until garlic is soft. Set aside.

Meanwhile, put water onto boil for the pasta. When it reaches a rolling boil, add the pasta and salt and cook according to directions for cooking pasta in chapter 2. Have a heated serving bowl ready. At the same time, heat the remaining 4 tablespoons butter in a large skillet and stir in the cream. When the noodles are cooked, drain and add them to the skillet. Toss with 2 forks and add the sautéed livers, the mushroom mixture, the diced *salame,* peas, *parmigiano* and salt and pepper. Toss again. Transfer to the heated serving bowl. If using the truffle, shave and sprinkle on top. Serve with *parmigiano.*

Tagliatelle al Doppio Burro

Tagliatelle with "Double Butter"

FOR 4 PEOPLE

This classic cream sauce is also called *tagliatelle con la panna,* or *fettuccine* Alfredo when made with egg (not spinach) noodles. It is so simple, it should be put together at the very last, at the same time that the noodles are ready to be cooked.

½ recipe (about 1 pound) Egg Pasta I or II or Spinach Pasta, cut into *tagliatelle* (chapter 2)

8 tablespoons (¼ pound) sweet (unsalted) butter

¾ cup heavy cream

¼ teaspoon nutmeg, preferably freshly grated

freshly milled white pepper to taste

¾ cup freshly grated *parmigiano* cheese

freshly grated *parmigiano* cheese at table

Make pasta and set aside. Put water on to boil for the noodles. Meanwhile, bring water to the boil in the bottom pan of a double boiler. Heat the butter and half of the cream in the top pan for 2 minutes, or until combined. Be sure that the top pan does not actually touch the water in the lower pan. Add the nutmeg and several turns of pepper from the mill.

When the water comes to a rolling boil, add pasta and salt and cook according to directions for cooking fresh pasta in chapter 2. Have a heated serving bowl ready. When the pasta is ready, drain and turn it into a large skillet with the cream sauce. With 2 forks, toss until noodles are evenly coated with sauce. Place the skillet on the burner over very low heat. Add the remaining cream, the *parmigiano,* and pepper to taste, and toss very quickly over the heat in order to coat all the noodles (this should take place in less than 30 seconds). Turn into the heated bowl. Serve with *parmigiano.*

Fresh Noodle Widths and Shapes

Cannelloni

Rectangles measuring $3\frac{1}{2}$ by $4\frac{1}{2}$ inches, rolled out as thinly as possible (the last notch on the pasta machine). As with *lasagne,* these noodles are cooked in boiling water for 1 minute before being stuffed, sauced, and baked.

Farfalle (also Fiocchi)

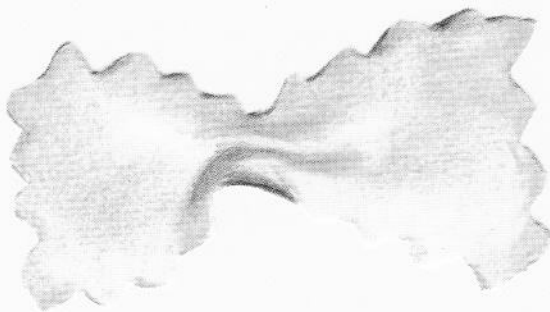

Literally "butterflies," or "bows." These are made by first forming 1-inch wide *pappardelle* (see instructions for cutting *pappardelle* below), then cutting the noodles into 2-inch lengths with a fluted pastry wheel. The short noodles are then pinched in the middle to resemble little bows, or butterflies. They are served with various light sauces. Smaller *farfalle* are well suited for simple broths served with *parmigiano.*

Fettuccine

Paper-thin (about $\frac{1}{32}$-inch thick) flat noodles, between $\frac{1}{8}$- and $\frac{1}{4}$-inch wide. If cutting by hand, roll up the disk of pasta dough loosely and using a knife, cut straight across the short side of the roll, cutting even $\frac{1}{8}$-inch segments along the entire roll. Then shake out the noodles to separate. To make *fettuccine* by machine, set the knob on the next to the last or the last notch (the setting will depend on the machine). Cut sheets of pasta dough into lengths about 14 inches long and feed into *fettuccine* cutting attachment. Because *fettuccine* are meant to carry rich, cream-based sauces, they are slightly thicker than *tagliatelle.*

Lasagne

Roll out pasta dough as thinly as possible. Cut 4-inch by 5-inch rectangles by hand, either with a knife, or fluted pastry wheel. These noodles are cooked in boiling water for 1 minute before they are layered between other ingredients in a baking dish.

Maltagliati

Refers to hand-cut noodles of usually short, irregular, triangular or diamond shapes, used in bean soups or with light sauces, including meat and tomato, or tomato sauces. Roll the pasta dough out as thinly as possible. Either roll up the disk (if pasta has been rolled by hand) or strip of dough loosely, so that it is about 3 inches wide. Using a knife, cut off both corners of each end of the roll of dough on a diagonal, so that each end comes to an arrowlike point. Then cut straight across the roll so that a triangle has been cut off. Cut off the corners again to form an arrowlike point, then cut straight across again and so on, until the whole roll has been cut up. Shake out all the cut noodles to separate them. The noodles will be about 3 inches long and somewhat unevenly shaped. Or, place the flat disk or strip of dough on a flat cutting surface, and using a fluted pastry wheel, make diamond or triangular shapes approximately 3 inches in length.

Pizzoccheri

Short, thin buckwheat noodles originating in Lombardy. Roll out as thick as for *fettuccine.* Cut noodles $\frac{1}{4}$ inch wide either by hand or by machine with a cutting attachment for *tagliatelle.* Then cut noodles into 3- or 4-inch lengths.

Pappardelle

Flat noodles $\frac{3}{4}$ to 1-inch wide, as thin as *tagliatelle,* with fluted edges. *Pappardelle* cutting attachments for pasta machines are available, but the noodles produced are uneven in width unless the sheet of dough that is inserted is precisely as wide as the roller (which is rarely the case). Cutting by hand with a fluted pastry wheel produces better results, as long as your hand can remain steady enough to cut the noodles all the same width. To cut *pappardelle* by hand, roll out the sheet of pasta dough, cut it in half so that the noodles are not excessively long (they should be about 14 inches long), and using a fluted pastry wheel, cut the noodles, taking care to make them equal in width. In Tuscany these noodles are traditionally accompanied with hare or duck sauce. Because of their broad width, they are well suited for sauces that contain meat, chicken livers, and so on. An alternative to cutting *pappardelle* by hand is to buy the cutting attachment for *lasagne ricce,* which does an excellent job of producing noodles slightly more narrow than the traditional *pappardelle* (about $\frac{1}{2}$ inch), with fluted edges.

Pici

A handmade ropelike egg noodle of the country table peculiar to certain parts of Tuscany around Siena. The dough is rolled out to a thickness of $\frac{1}{8}$ inch and then cut with a knife into 8-inch lengths $\frac{1}{8}$ inch wide. The strands are then quickly rolled between the palms of the hands and formed into yarn-shaped noodles. They must not be allowed to dry before being boiled. *Pici* are typically served with a thick tomato and meat sauce.

Tagliatelle

Very thin, delicate flat noodles about $\frac{1}{4}$ inch wide (the dough should be as thin as possible—thin enough to see through when it is held up to the light). They differ from *fettuccine* in that they are thinner and slightly wider. To cut by hand, see method for cutting *fettuccine,* above. To cut by machine, set the pasta machine on the last notch and roll the dough out as thin as can be. Cut the sheets of dough into lengths about 14 inches long and pass through the cutting attachment for *tagliatelle. Tagliatelle* are typically used with light cream sauces and other delicate sauces.

Taglierini (also Tagliolini or Capelli d' Angelo)

Very fine strands about $\frac{1}{16}$ inch wide and a bit thicker than paper thin; best made on the very narrow cutters of a pasta machine. When made fresh, these very slender noodles are generally used only in soups. They are too fine to use with most sauces.

Trenette

Narrow (about $\frac{1}{8}$ inch wide or less), fairly thick noodles most typically served with *pesto.* They are best made by machine. Roll the dough out as you would for *fettuccine.* Cut the sheets of dough into lengths about 14 inches long and pass them through the cutting attachment for *trenette.*

Tagliatelle con Prosciutto e Panna

Tagliatelle with Ham and Cream

FOR 4 PEOPLE

½ recipe (about 1 pound) Egg Pasta I or II, Spinach Pasta, Red (Tomato) Pasta, or Beet (Pink) Pasta, cut into *tagliatelle* or *fettuccine* (chapter 2)

8 tablespoons (¼ pound) sweet (unsalted) butter

¼ pound *prosciutto crudo*, thickly sliced and cut into strips 1½ inches long by ¼ inch wide

¾ cup heavy cream

⅔ cup freshly grated *parmigiano* cheese

freshly grated *parmigiano* cheese at table

Make pasta and set aside. Put water on to boil for the noodles. Put the butter and the prosciutto in a skillet large enough to accommodate the noodles later and place it over the pot with the boiling water to melt the butter. When the water comes to a rolling boil, add the pasta and salt and cook according to directions for cooking fresh pasta in chapter 2. Have a heated serving bowl ready. When the pasta is cooked, drain it and immediately transfer it to the skillet. Toss gently using 2 forks. Add the cream, and the *parmigiano*, continuing to toss until the ingredients are evenly distributed throughout. Transfer to heated bowl and serve. Pass the *parmigiano*.

Trenette Verdi col Sugo di Panna e Salsiccia

Spinach Trenette with Creamy Tomato-Sausage Sauce

FOR 4 PEOPLE

This recipe is reminiscent of an Emilian dish I love called *gramigna*, in which a round, hollow, fresh green noodle is served with a creamy sausage-and-tomato sauce. The noodles are difficult to make without the right tool. I substitute *trenette* or *fettuccine*, which are thicker than *tagliatelle*.

½ recipe (about 1 pound) Spinach Pasta, cut into *trenette* or *fettuccine* (chapter 2)

3 tablespoons finely chopped shallot or white onion

2 tablespoons finely chopped carrot

1 small celery stalk, finely chopped

2 tablespoons sweet (unsalted) butter

1 tablespoon olive oil

½ pound good-quality lean sweet Italian pork sausage meat, without fennel, finely ground

¼ teaspoon ground mace or nutmeg, preferably freshly grated

½ teaspoon salt, or to taste

freshly milled black pepper to taste

½ cup milk

1 cup canned peeled Italian plum tomatoes in purée, drained, seeded, and chopped

½ cup beef broth

¼ cup heavy cream

2 tablespoons sweet (unsalted) butter, melted

freshly grated *parmigiano* cheese at table

Make pasta and set aside. Heat the shallot or onion, carrot, and celery in the butter and oil until soft. Add the loose sausage meat, crumbling it with a wooden spoon to break it up. Add the mace or nutmeg, salt, and pepper and stir. Continue to sauté over gentle heat for 5–6 minutes. The sausage should color on the outside and remain pink inside. Do not brown it or it will become hard. (This is important to achieve a delicate sauce.) Add the milk and stir. (It is critical to add the milk to the meat before adding the tomatoes, for the meat will absorb the sweetness of the milk and acquire delicacy.) Cook until milk begins to simmer, always over gentle heat, about 10 minutes. Add the tomatoes and stir. Simmer over gentlest possible heat, partially covered, about 1½ hours, stirring in broth a little at a time throughout cooking time. Remove the lid during the last 10 minutes. Stir in cream at the end, heating it 2–3 minutes.

Meanwhile, bring water to a boil, add pasta and salt, and cook according to directions in chapter 2. Have a heated serving bowl ready. Drain pasta and place in the heated bowl. Toss with melted butter and the sauce. Pass *parmigiano* at the table.

Fettuccine con i Funghi Freschi

Fettuccine with Fresh
Wild Mushrooms

FOR 4 PEOPLE

Porcino (*Boletus edulis*), the famous Italian wild mushroom, is rarely seen in this country. Any serious mushroom stalker knows, however, that it does grow here. It was unusual to find any kind of fresh wild mushroom for sale here until recently. If you had a taste for them, you had to learn to pick them. Now they are becoming more and more common in specialty food shops, farmers' markets, and Asian stores, particularly on the West Coast where many wild mushrooms grow. Fresh *chanterelle, shiitake,* and oyster mushrooms are those most commonly available.

- ½ recipe (about 1 pound) Egg Pasta I or II, Whole-Wheat Pasta, or Chocolate Pasta, cut into *fettuccine, tagliatelle, pappardelle,* or *maltagliati* (chapter 2)
- 1½ pounds fresh wild mushrooms (preferably *chanterelles* or *chanterelles* combined with *shiitake* or oyster mushrooms)
- 8 tablespoons (¼ pound) sweet (unsalted) butter
- 3 garlic cloves, finely chopped
- 1½ cups heavy cream
- salt and freshly milled black pepper to taste
- 3 tablespoons finely chopped fresh Italian parsley
- 2 tablespoons sweet (unsalted) butter, melted
- freshly grated *parmigiano* cheese at table

Make pasta and set aside. Clean the soil off the mushrooms by using a soft brush or clean towel. If there is too much dirt to remove this way, wash them very quickly in cold water, using a wire basket or colander to dunk them quickly in and out of the running water. (Try not to soak them; this will alter their texture by making them soggy and less delicate.) Pat the mushrooms dry without bruising them and thinly slice them. In a large skillet, heat the butter and garlic. When the garlic is soft, add the mushrooms and sauté over medium heat for 8–10 minutes. Stir in cream. Season with salt and pepper. Add parsley.

Meanwhile, bring water to the boil, add pasta and salt and cook according to directions in chapter 2. Have a heated serving bowl ready. Drain the pasta and toss it in the heated bowl with melted butter and mushroom sauce. Serve with *parmigiano*.

Fettuccine con i Funghi Secchi

Fettuccine with Dried
Wild Mushrooms

FOR 4 PEOPLE

This is a truly lovely recipe for a delicate sauce of dried wild mushrooms that can be made any time of year in just a few minutes. I use three different kinds of mushrooms for a more interesting flavor. The types of dried mushrooms I've called for are the ones most commonly found in American markets. Other varieties can be used, depending on their availability. *Porcini* have a very strong flavor; use them in equal quantities with other mushrooms so they do not overwhelm their more subtle-flavored relatives. *Shiitake* mushrooms retain a firm, almost chewy texture throughout cooking, which makes them a good addition to the mixture.

- ½ recipe (about 1 pound) Chocolate Pasta, cut into *fettuccine, tagliatelle, pappardelle,* or *maltagliati* (chapter 2)
- 2 ounces mixed dried *porcini, chanterelles* (or morels) and *shiitake* mushrooms, in equal quantities
- 6 tablespoons sweet (unsalted) butter
- 3 tablespoons finely chopped shallots
- ½ cup good dry white wine
- 1½ cups chicken broth
- 1 cup heavy cream
- salt and freshly milled black pepper to taste
- 3 tablespoons chopped fresh Italian parsley

Make pasta and set aside. Cover the mushrooms in warm water to soak for 1 hour. Strain the mushroom soaking liquid through a paper towel and reserve. Chop the *chanterelles* and *porcini* very fine by hand (do not use a food processor). Slice the *shiitake* mushrooms into slivers. Melt the butter, add the shallots, and cook over medium heat for about 2 minutes until they soften. Add the mushrooms and continue to sauté for 5–6 minutes at low heat. Add the wine and simmer over medium heat to evaporate the alcohol (3–5 minutes). Add the broth and ½ cup strained mushroom liquid. Cook, uncovered, over medium heat for 12–15 minutes to reduce. Add the cream; when bubbles form around the edges (it should not boil), turn off the heat. Season with salt and pepper.

Meanwhile, bring water to the boil, add pasta and salt, and cook according to directions in chapter 2. Have a heated bowl ready. Drain the pasta and toss in the heated bowl with the sauce. Strew with chopped parsley, and serve with *parmigiano,* if desired.

Tagliatelle con Piselli, Salame, e Prosciutto

Tagliatelle with Peas, Salame, and Ham

FOR 4 PEOPLE

½ recipe (about 1 pound) Egg Pasta I or II, cut into *tagliatelle* (chapter 2)

4 tablespoons sweet (unsalted) butter

1 medium-sized yellow onion, very finely chopped

2 shallots, very finely chopped

1 medium-sized celery stalk, finely chopped

¾ cup shelled fresh petite peas, or ½ 10-ounce box frozen petite peas (not thawed)

1 teaspoon dried green peppercorns, crushed in a mortar

½ cup dry vermouth

1 cup chicken broth

2 tablespoons olive oil

2 ounces *prosciutto crudo*, sliced extra thick and cut into strips 1½ inches long by ¼ inch wide

3 slices *soppressata* or other good Italian *salame*, cut into strips 1½ inches long by ¼ inch wide

3 tablespoons Italian parsley, finely chopped

salt to taste

Make pasta and set aside. Heat the butter and add the onion, shallots, and celery. When soft, add the peas and green peppercorns. Stir and sauté gently for 1 minute, tossing to distribute. Add vermouth and broth. Increase heat to medium and simmer 3 minutes to evaporate the alcohol. In another pan, heat the oil and gently sauté the *prosciutto* and *salame* for 30 seconds. Combine with peas mixture and add parsley and salt to taste.

Meanwhile, bring water to a boil, add pasta and salt, and cook according to directions in chapter 2. Drain and place in heated serving bowl. Top with sauce, toss, and serve.

Pizzoccheri con Zucchini e Peperoni alla Giustina

Giustina's Buckwheat or Corn Pasta with Zucchini and Red Peppers

FOR 4 PEOPLE

Here is a sauce of my mother's invention to go with nutritious fresh buckwheat or corn pasta. The bright red and green of the pepper and zucchini splashed throughout the warm toasty brown of buckwheat or sunny corn pasta is a beautiful palette of colors. The combination of the pasta, grainy in texture and nutty in flavor, with the soft textures and sweetness of the vegetables is special.

½ recipe (about 1 pound) Buckwheat Pasta or 1 recipe (about 1 pound) Corn Pasta, cut into *tagliatelle* (chapter 2)

1 pound young, small zucchini (see Note)

1 medium-sized sweet red pepper, stem, seeds, and ribs removed (see Note)

2 medium-sized sweet, vine-ripened tomatoes

2 large or 4 medium-sized shallots, finely chopped

2 large garlic cloves, finely chopped

6 tablespoons olive oil

2 tablespoons chopped fresh mint, or 1 tablespoon dried mint

2 teaspoons chopped fresh thyme, or 1 teaspoon dried thyme

1 teaspoon dried green peppercorns, crushed in a mortar

1 teaspoon salt, or to taste

freshly milled black pepper to taste

Make pasta and set aside. Trim tough ends off zucchini and cut into lengths about 1 by 1¼ inches. Cut the pepper into pieces about the same size. Immerse zucchini in boiling water 1 minute. Remove and immediately plunge into cold water to stop the cooking. (This step keeps it crunchy and green.) Immerse the tomatoes in boiling water for 30 seconds and then immediately plunge in cold water. Remove skin, seed, and slice like the pepper. Heat the shallots and garlic in 4 tablespoons olive oil until soft. Add the sweet pepper and sauté 2–3 minutes over medium heat. Stir in the mint, thyme, green peppercorns, and salt. Add tomatoes and zucchini. Sauté 2–3 minutes over high heat, stirring. Remove from the heat and add remaining 2 tablespoons olive oil. Taste for seasoning.

Meanwhile, bring water to the boil, add pasta and salt, and cook according to directions in chapter 2. Drain and toss with the sauce in a heated bowl. Serve.

Note: You can use a large zucchini as long as the seeds are not too large and numerous, unless you scoop them out and discard them. A sweet yellow pepper can be used instead of the red pepper if you are preparing buckwheat noodles; it would not be colorful enough with the corn pasta, however.

Taglierini con Pesce al Limone

Taglierini with Fish and Lemon Sauce

FOR 4 PEOPLE

½ recipe (about 1 pound) Egg Pasta I or II, cut into *taglierini* or *tagliatelle* (chapter 2)

2 tablespoons sweet (unsalted) butter

2 medium-sized shallots, finely chopped

1 garlic clove, bruised

½ cup good dry white wine

⅓ cup water

3 very thin slices fresh lemon, with peel removed from 2 slices only

1 tablespoon finely chopped fresh Italian parsley

¼ teaspoon dried green peppercorns, crushed in a mortar

¼ teaspoon salt, or to taste

4 slices (each approximately ¼ pound) tile fish steaks (or other firm, white-fleshed fish, such as snapper, haddock, or grouper), with skin left on

Watercress sprigs, curly endive leaves, or other greens

Make pasta and set aside. In a skillet large enough to hold the fish later, heat the butter with the shallots and garlic clove until shallots are soft. Remove and discard the garlic. Add the wine and cook over medium-low heat for 2–3 minutes to evaporate alcohol. Add water, lemon slices, parsley, green peppercorns, and salt and stir. Add the fish to the sauce and reduce heat to very low. Spoon the sauce in the pan over the fish. Cover skillet tightly and cook for 5 minutes, removing the lid once to moisten the fish with the sauce. Turn the fish over and cook it another 5 minutes, repeating the same procedure. Lift the fish from the pan with a slotted spatula and put it on a platter lined with greens. Keep warm.

Meanwhile, bring water to the boil, add pasta and salt, and cook according to directions in chapter 2. Drain, add to sauce in skillet, and toss. Transfer to a heated bowl and serve at once; serve fish as a second course.

Pappardelle al Vitello

Pappardelle with Veal Sauce

FOR 4 PEOPLE

½ recipe (about 1 pound) Egg Pasta I or II, Yellow (Saffron) Pasta, or Chocolate Pasta, cut into *pappardelle*, *maltagliati*, *trenette*, or *fettuccine* (chapter 2)

4 tablespoons sweet (unsalted) butter

2 tablespoons olive oil

1½ tablespoons finely chopped shallots

½ pound fresh cultivated mushrooms, very thinly sliced

1 pound veal scallopini (cutlets), cut into strips 1 inch long by ¼ inch wide

½ cup good dry sherry

1½ cups chicken or veal broth

1 teaspoon chopped fresh thyme, or scant ½ teaspoon dried thyme

3-inch strip lemon peel (taking care to leave off white pith)

salt and freshly milled black pepper to taste

1 cup heavy cream

2 tablespoons chopped fresh Italian parsley

Make pasta and set aside. Heat the butter and oil, add the shallots, and gently sauté until soft, about 1 minute. Add the mushrooms and sauté quickly over high flame until limp (about 2 minutes). With a slotted spoon, remove from the pan to a small bowl. Add the veal to the pan and sauté gently over high flame until meat loses its color on the outside (about 2 minutes). Add the sherry to the pan and simmer over medium–high heat until the alcohol has evaporated (about 3–5 minutes). Add the broth and bring to a boil. Add the thyme. Reduce immediately to low and simmer, covered, for 15 minutes. Remove the cover, add the lemon peel, and return the mushrooms to the pan. Season to taste with salt and pepper. Simmer an additional 15 minutes until veal is tender and the liquid has reduced. Remove the lemon peel and add the cream. Heat, stirring, until bubbles begin to form around the edges, but do not let the cream boil. Immediately remove from heat.

Meanwhile, bring water to the boil, add pasta and salt, and cook according to directions in chapter 2. Drain and toss with sauce in heated bowl. Strew with parsley and serve.

Pappardelle col Radicchio Rosso

Pappardelle with Radicchio

FOR 4 PEOPLE

An extension of the Italian tradition of sautéing vegetables in olive oil and garlic and sometimes salt pork or *pancetta*, this memorable pasta dish features *radicchio trevigiano,* a slightly bitter, beautiful marbled scarlet winter lettuce that has become a darling of American cooks. As a result, *radicchio* is more common in our markets than it used to be and is almost always sold by Italian greengrocers. Much of it that is grown in this country is far less flavorful than that produced in the Treviso area. If it is disappointing or unavailable, you can make this dish with the slightly pungent broad-leafed escarole (not curly chicory) that is commonly found in vegetable markets.

½ recipe (about 1 pound) Egg Pasta I or II, cut into *pappardelle, fettuccine,* or *tagliatelle* (chapter 2)

½ pound medium-sized head *radicchio* or escarole

4 tablespoons sweet (unsalted) butter

2 garlic cloves, bruised

2 slices *pancetta,* chopped

¼ cup water

½ teaspoon chopped fresh marjoram, or ¼ teaspoon dried marjoram

salt and freshly milled black pepper to taste

2 tablespoons finely chopped Italian parsley

Make pasta and set aside. Core the *radicchio* or escarole. Slice the leaves crosswise into fine shreds; you should have about 2 cups. Set aside. Heat the butter and garlic and sauté the garlic until golden. Discard the garlic. Add the *pancetta* and sauté over moderate-high heat for 2–3 minutes. Add the *radicchio* or escarole and sauté briskly over moderate heat about 3 minutes. Add water, marjoram, salt, and pepper. Cook another 2 minutes. Turn off heat. Add parsley.

Meanwhile, bring water to a boil, add pasta and salt, and cook according to directions in chapter 2. Drain and toss with sauce in a heated bowl. Serve at once.

Note: This sauce is also suitable for spaghetti and other types of dried pasta, in which case substitute olive oil for the butter.

Tagliatelle ai Porri Secondo la Ricetta di Mia Mamma

My Mother's Beet Tagliatelle with Leeks

FOR 4 PEOPLE

½ recipe (about 1 pound) Pink (Beet) Pasta, Red (Tomato) Pasta, or Egg Pasta I or II, cut into *tagliatelle* (chapter 2)

2 large leeks

½ cup shelled fresh petite peas or frozen petite peas (not thawed)

2 medium-sized shallots, finely chopped (2 tablespoons)

1 medium-small white or yellow onion, very thinly sliced lengthwise

4 tablespoons sweet (unsalted) butter

½ cup sherry

1½ cups heavy cream

½ teaspoon salt, or to taste

freshly milled black pepper to taste

Make pasta and set aside. Wash leeks thoroughly to remove sand between the sheaths. Cut off and discard the green leaves. Divide each white portion lengthwise into eighths. Slice the eighths with a diagonal cut into 1½-inch lengths. Blanch for 2 minutes in rapidly boiling water with a good pinch of salt. Drain immediately and plunge into cold water to stop the cooking. Do the same with the peas if they are fresh, blanching for 1 minute only.

In a skillet large enough to accommodate the pasta later, heat the shallots, onion, and butter over medium heat until vegetables are soft. Add the leeks and peas, stir, and add sherry. Sauté over medium-low heat for 3–5 minutes to evaporate the alcohol. Add cream and cook 2–3 minutes. Season with salt and pepper.

Meanwhile, bring water to the boil, add pasta and salt, and cook according to directions in chapter 2. Drain and transfer the noodles to the skillet. Toss briefly over low heat, then turn into a heated bowl. Serve.

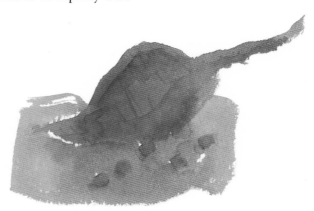

Tagliatelle Rosse con Salsa di Aragosta, Zafferano, e Panna

Tomato Tagliatelle with Lobster Saffron Cream Sauce

FOR 4 PEOPLE

It is always hard to answer the question, what is your favorite recipe? But if I could bring myself to make that choice, this would be a strong contender.

½ recipe (about 1 pound) Red (Tomato) Pasta, cut into *fettuccine* or curly *pappardelle* (chapter 2)

1 quart water

1½-pound live lobster

1 cup heavy cream

6 tablespoons sweet (unsalted) butter

½ cup plus 3 tablespoons finely chopped white onion

½ cup plus 2 tablespoons finely chopped carrot

2 large celery stalks, finely chopped

1 garlic clove, bruised

½ cup good dry white wine

3 large, sweet, vine-ripened tomatoes, or 6 canned Italian plum tomatoes in purée, drained and seeded

scant ½ teaspoon salt, or to taste

freshly milled white pepper to taste

⅛ teaspoon (2 envelopes) saffron powder, or ¼ teaspoon saffron threads

1 large shallot, finely chopped

3 tablespoons torn fresh fennel leaves or fresh Italian parsley

Make pasta and set aside. Bring water to a boil and drop in the lobster, head first. Cover the pan and when the water returns to a boil, cook for 5 minutes. Remove the lobster from the water and reserve the water.

Working over a bowl to catch any juices or roe, twist the tail and claw sections off. Pull off the legs and cut them into 2-inch pieces. Crack claws and tail and remove the meat. Cut the meat into medium-small pieces. Drop the meat into the cream and refrigerate. Add the lobster liquor in the bowl to the reserved cooking water and set aside. Discard the claw shells. Break up the other shells with a mallet and save. Save the coral. Discard the innards.

Heat 3 tablespoons butter and half of the onion in a large skillet. When the onion is soft, add half of the chopped carrot and celery and the garlic clove. Sauté gently for 5 minutes, stirring. Add the reserved shells and increase the heat to medium-high; cook, stirring, for 8–10 minutes, or until the shells have deepened in color. Should the vegetables begin to dry out, reduce the heat. Add the wine and lower the heat. Cook to evaporate the alcohol, about 5 minutes. Immerse the fresh tomatoes in boiling water for 30 seconds. Immediately plunge the tomatoes in cold water. Peel them, cut in half, and remove the seeds. Chop the fresh or canned tomatoes

and add to the skillet with the vegetables and wine. Add the salt and pepper. Cook, stirring, another 3 minutes. Remove the garlic. Add 3 cups of the lobster cooking liquid and bring this stock mixture to a boil. Lower the heat immediately and simmer gently, uncovered, for 1 hour. Skim any foam that rises to the surface.

Remove the stock from the heat. Strain the contents into a bowl through a fine wire sieve or a sieve lined with a double layer of cheesecloth. Press on the contents of the sieve to force out as much of the juices from the vegetables as possible. Pour the strained stock into a large skillet over medium-low heat and reduce it to about 1 cup without letting it boil. When it is reduced, add saffron. (If using saffron threads, crush them between your fingers before adding to the stock. If using saffron powder, add it directly to the stock.) Meanwhile, heat the remaining 3 tablespoons butter with the shallot and the remaining onion. When they begin to sweat, add the remaining chopped carrot and celery. Sauté gently for 5 minutes, stirring occasionally. Add the reduced stock and stir. Add the cream and lobster meat and coral and

just heat through—do not cook—4–5 minutes over medium-low heat. It is important not to overcook the lobster or it will lose its delicacy. Taste and adjust seasonings.

Meanwhile, bring water to a boil, add pasta and salt, and cook according to directions in chapter 2. Have a heated bowl ready. Drain pasta and add to the skillet with the sauce. Toss, using 2 forks to distribute sauce. Serve immediately in the heated bowl. Strew fresh fennel leaves or parsley on each portion.

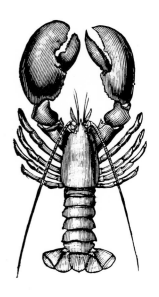

Tagliatelle alla Moda
Tagliatelle with Shrimp, Scallop, and Pernod Sauce

FOR 4 PEOPLE

½ recipe (about 1 pound) Egg Pasta I or II, cut into *tagliatelle* (chapter 2)

1 pound shrimp in the shell

1 pound bay scallops

6 tablespoons sweet (unsalted) butter

2 medium-sized shallots, finely chopped

¼ cup Pernod

2 cups heavy cream

⅛ teaspoon (2 envelopes) saffron powder, or ¼ teaspoon saffron threads

½ teaspoon salt, or to taste

2 tablespoons chopped fresh chives, or torn fresh fennel sprigs or Italian parsley leaves

2 tablespoons sweet (unsalted) butter, melted

Make pasta and set aside. Shell the shrimp and remove the dark intestinal vein down the back. Cut each shrimp in half lengthwise. Wash and pat dry thoroughly. Wash scallops and pat dry thoroughly. Set shellfish aside. In a skillet large enough to accommodate the noodles later, heat butter and shallots. When the shallots are soft, add the shellfish and quickly sauté over medium heat 1–2 minutes just to color them, stirring to heat them evenly. Add the Pernod and evaporate the alcohol over medium-low heat, simmering for 2–3 minutes. Meanwhile, heat the cream and dissolve the saffron powder in it. If using saffron threads, heat them first for 1 minute on a little dish in a hot oven, or for 1 minute in a pan on top of the stove. Crush the threads between your fingers into the cream. Add the saffron cream to the pan with the shellfish and cook over low heat 2 minutes. Remove shellfish with a slotted spoon to a warm dish, cover, and set aside. Reduce the sauce for about 5 minutes over medium-low heat. It should become thick enough to coat a wooden spoon. When it has thickened, return the shellfish to it and stir well.

Meanwhile, bring water to the boil, add pasta and salt, and cook according to directions in chapter 2. Drain and toss with the melted butter and chopped herb in a heated bowl. Transfer the noodles to the skillet with the sauce and toss well over very low heat. Return pasta to the bowl and serve.

Farfalle con i Fiori di Zucca La Chiusa
"Butterflies" with Squash Flowers La Chiusa

FOR 4 PEOPLE

A marvelous dish made for me by Dania Lucherini, owner-chef of La Chiusa Restaurant in Tuscany. The fragrance of fresh squash blossoms and fresh basil mated with the delicacy of homemade "butterfly" noodles still lingers. I have been able to make it here during the summer and early fall when squash flowers are still blooming. You will no doubt need a garden to make this recipe, since zucchini flowers are not as commonly eaten here as they are in Italy, and therefore not generally available in the market. Pick the male flowers when they're about two inches in length. (The female flowers are those with the baby squash attached, and should not be picked if you want your zucchini plant to bear fruit.)

This is such a delicate dish, it requires very light, homemade noodles. To make the *farfalle*, make *pappardelle* noodles first. Cut the ribbons into two-inch lengths. Pinch each little noodle in the middle to form a bow shape. Let the "butterflies" dry several minutes before dropping into boiling water.

½ recipe (about 1 pound) Egg Pasta I or II, cut into *farfalle* (see introduction and chapter 2)

4 tablespoons sweet (unsalted) butter

2 tablespoons virgin olive oil

1 small white onion, very finely chopped

10–15 zucchini male squash flowers

10 fresh basil leaves

2 tablespoons sweet (unsalted) butter, melted

3 tablespoons freshly grated *parmigiano* cheese

Make pasta and set aside. Gently heat the butter, oil, and onion together until the onion is soft. Meanwhile, remove the stems from the flowers. Gently wash the blossoms and pat dry. Tear each flower into ribbonlike pieces about the same size as the pasta bows. Include the inner parts of the flowers as part of the "ribbons." Add the flowers to the pan with the onion and sauté over medium-low heat about 3 minutes, or until the center parts of the flowers are tender. Tear the basil leaves into strips (do not chop or the basil will turn brown) and add them to the flowers.

Bring water to a boil, add pasta and salt, and cook according to directions in chapter 2. Drain and toss with melted butter, the sauce, and *parmigiano* in a heated bowl.

Pasta di Mais con Salsa di Coniglio

Corn Pasta with Rabbit Sauce

FOR 4 PEOPLE

I like the texture and flavor of corn noodles very much with game sauces, such as this sauce for rabbit. A sauce of quail, Cornish hen, or other small game would also be good.

1 recipe (about 1 pound) Corn Pasta, cut into *tagliatelle* (chapter 2), or commercial corn pasta (see Note)

1 recipe rabbit sauce (see Macaroni with Rabbit Sauce, chapter 7)

2 tablespoons sweet (unsalted) butter, melted

Make pasta and set aside. Make the rabbit sauce (it will take about 1 hour). Cook the pasta in boiling, salted water as directed in chapter 2. Drain the noodles and toss with the melted butter and the sauce in a heated bowl.

Note: While I like the flavor of commercial dried corn pasta, I have found that it becomes mushy when boiled, for it contains no wheat flour. The gluten in wheat flour is what holds the noodle together under boil. My recipe for corn pasta suggests mixing regular un-bleached white flour with cornmeal for a noodle that will remain intact.

Tagliatelle con Anitra Preservata alla De Marco

Tagliatelle with Confit of Duck De Marco

FOR 4 PEOPLE

An irresistible recipe from the De Marco Restaurant in Nantucket, Massachusetts. Chef Ralf De Santis combines tradi-tional flavors with a fresh ap-proach to duck sauce for pasta. Preparing a confit of duck makes the fowl very tender.

½ recipe (about 1 pound) Egg Pasta II, cut into *tagliatelle* (chapter 2)

2 ounces dried *porcini* mushrooms

1½ cups warm water

1 pound fresh cultivated mushrooms

8 tablespoons (¼ pound) sweet (unsalted) butter

¼ cup finely chopped shallots

1½ cups Barolo wine

1 tablespoon chopped fresh thyme

salt and freshly milled black pepper to taste

2 tablespoons sweet (unsalted) butter, melted

For the *Confit*

1 5-pound Long Island duck

lard (quantity will depend on quan-tity of duck fat)

1 cup water

¼ cup coarse (or kosher) salt for the duck *confit*

6 sprigs thyme

1 entire bulb of garlic, unpeeled and sliced crosswise

Make pasta and set aside. Next, make the *confit* of duck. Wash the bird well and pull out any fat inside the cavity. Reserve fat. Cut duck up with poultry shears in the following manner: Split the breast in half lengthwise. Remove the neck from the back and sever the legs and wings. Split the back into 3 crosswise pieces. Remove any additional loose fat pieces and all the skin from the duck pieces. Render all the fat and skin with an equal amount of lard and the water over moderate heat about 1 hour. Strain through cheesecloth, pressing firmly to force all the fat you can out of the sediment. Now separate fat from juices or sediment by ladling it off into another container. Mix the coarse salt with the thyme and garlic. Sprinkle the bottom of a deep ce-ramic or glass ovenproof dish that is narrow enough to crowd the duck pieces to-gether with some of the salt mixture. Pack in the duck pieces, skin side up, sprin-kling them with more of the salt as you arrange them. Sprinkle the remaining salt on top. Pour the strained rendered fat over the duck pieces. Cook the duck in a 350-degree oven for about 1 hour or until very tender. Remove the duck from the oven and scrape the fat off the pieces. Remove all bones and cut meat into long, thin strips; set aside.

Soak the *porcini* in the warm water for 30 minutes. Drain and strain the soaking liquid through a paper towel or clean cloth. Slice *porcini* and set aside. Dust the fresh mushrooms with a brush or towel to remove any earth (do not wash) and trim off the tough stem bottoms. Slice the mushrooms. Heat 3 tablespoons butter and the shallots together until shal-lots sweat, about 3 minutes. Add the sliced fresh mush-rooms and sauté 3–4 min-utes over medium-low heat until they have colored some-what. Add the wine. Cook about 10 minutes over me-dium heat to evaporate the alcohol. Add the *porcini* and their strained soaking liquid. Reduce to one-third the vol-ume, over medium heat. The sauce should become syrupy. Add the reserved duck strips, thyme, salt, and pepper. Simmer 10 minutes. Add the remaining 5 tablespoons butter and allow them to melt slowly.

Meanwhile, bring water to a boil, add pasta and salt, and cook according to direc-tions in chapter 2. Drain and toss with melted butter in a heated bowl. Spoon sauce over the noodles, toss, and serve.

<u>7</u> DRIED PASTA

I Maccheroni

Ceres, mother of Persephone
I have the urge
In my body,
Which torments me,
To sing
To praise
That which fills my stomach.

Bring me solace . . .
Help me, oh beautiful lady
Since I sing
The great glory
Of the beautiful macaroni. . . .

—Filippo Sgruttendio,
from *Le Laude de Li Maccarune*
("Praise to Macaroni")
Naples, 1646

Man eating spaghetti, artist unknown,
late 19th century.

Top: *Neapolitan spaghetti vendors, c. 1890.*
Bottom: *Italian immigrants taking a lunch break on New York's Lower East Side, c. 1920.*

Dried pasta, in Italian, *pasta secca,* or more colloquially, *i maccheroni,* occupies a hallowed and heroic place in Italian life. It is not surprising, for this staple has long nourished the peoples of southern Italy. Making *maccheroni* from flour and water was a way to preserve wheat, the primary grain crop of the Mediterranean basin. The pasta, once dried, kept for long periods. When cooked and combined with other ingredients available to the poor, it provided a hearty and wholesome repast.

Naples, located in one of the poorest regions of southern Italy, was so famous for pasta eating that its inhabitants were reknown throughout the country as *mangiamaccheroni* ("macaroni eaters"). All over the city spaghetti was hung to dry, like laundry, from the windows and on the rooftops. Vendors cooking spaghetti and macaroni in huge pots over makeshift stoves hawked their wares on the streets. One observer, the eighteenth-century traveler and adventurer Gorani, described such a Neapolitan scene:

> A common man goes to a macaroni vendor and asks for a wooden bowl filled with that boiling pasta on top of which one throws grated cheese. He takes the spaghetti with his hands and twirls them. . . . After having had his meal in public, and breaking into laughter, he goes to the lemonade vendor. . . . The seasoning is nothing but . . . pig fat melted into that great mass with a little salt.

A century later, in 1884, Matilde Serao in her *Ventre di Napoli* ("Womb of Naples"), describes the street life. The image of an impoverished populace to whom *maccheroni* was a mainstay of life persists. Large numbers of the poor were without livelihoods or steady work. *Lazzaroni* (beggars or street urchins) lived and slept in the open. Deprived of a place in which to cook their meals, they could buy a *maccheroni* supper from the street vendor for as little as a penny—far less than one twentieth of an Italian lire, or in our exchange, a small fraction of a penny. It is no surprise that the thousands of immigrants who left Naples brought pasta with them to America, where it remained the popular food of the Italians here.

For hundreds of years the Italians have ascribed a myriad of properties to *maccheroni,* mythic as well as culinary. In the *commedia dell'arte* (a popular entertainment between the sixteenth and eighteenth centuries), *maccheroni* is a central theme. One of the most celebrated characters is the colorful, wily Neapolitan servant, Pulcinella, who in England became "Punch" of Punch and Judy fame. He is scrawny and hunchbacked, his long hook nose part of his black mask (some versions of the myth claim that he was fathered by a chicken), and he is inseparable from his beloved *maccheroni*. He is often portrayed eating greedily with his hands from a large bowl of steaming macaroni, or else running with stolen spaghetti (sauce and all) trailing from his pockets. At once grotesque and funny, Pulcinella personifies the desperation of the hungry people of an impoverished and feudal land. *Maccheroni* assuaged their hunger and nourished their spirits.

The appetite for pasta was not confined to the masses. In the eighteenth century, the great chef Corrado introduced *maccheroni* to the Bourbon court in Naples. He became celebrated for his many spaghetti and macaroni innovations. Tomato sauce had not yet been invented, but Corrado's recipes were among the first to combine tomatoes (whole) with pasta. His *Il Cuoco Galante* ("The Gallant Cook"), written in 1765, is the first real recipe book of Neapolitan cooking, although it was no representation of the plebian diet. Corrado's kitchen reflected the international tastes of the aristocracy, and was primarily influenced by France.

There was a strong connection to France through the Bourbon court. In the mid–eighteenth century, Italian food in general was very much in vogue in upper-class French circles. And while *maccheroni* was never fully naturalized by the French (as other Italian inventions have been, from *besciamella* to *gelato*), the significance of this epic food was not lost on them. Alexander Dumas wrote: "It's true that macaroni was born in Naples . . . but today it is a European food, which has traveled like civilization. . . . It costs two cents a pound, which renders it accessible to thieves only on Sunday and holidays. . . ." Alfred de Musset put it on a scale with music when he lauded Naples as the place "where macaroni and music were born." Another eighteenth-century French poet, Tristan Corbière, made macaroni a metaphor for the sun:

The navel of the day spins
his burning macaroni
to the sound of the tarantella:
St. Lucia, Sir Aniello,
Saint Pia, the Devil,
With Pulcinella.

Among other men to have written in praise of *maccheroni* was the young Casanova, whose passion for it caused him to be called the Macaroni Prince by his contemporaries. Byron alludes to its love-inducing qualities in Canto II of *Don Juan,* in which Ceres and Bacchus feast on marmalade, eggs, oysters, and *vermicelli.* Rossini invented pasta recipes that are as well-known as his music. In 1816,

IL CREDENZIERE
DI BUON GUSTO
OPERA MECCANICA
DELL' ORITANO
VINCENZO CORRADO

NAPOLI MDCCLXXVIII.
NELLA STAMPERIA RAIMONDIANA.

Title page from Corrado's, The Steward of Good Taste *(second editon, 1778). His recipes were the first to combine tomatoes with pasta.*

*Pulcinella, on a donkey, eating macaroni,
artist unknown, 19th century.*

Francesco Barbaia, a celebrated Neapolitan impresario, invited the composer to his *palazzo* to write an opera based on *Othello* (Rossini had, after all, given the Romans *The Barber of Seville*). After six months of life in Naples amidst friends, feasting, and wine, the opera was still unwritten. Anxious for the masterpiece, Barbaia announced to the great composer that he would imprison him in his room with only one plate of pasta a day until the work was finished. After two days, Rossini threw the completed overture out his window to the pacing Barbaia. Later, he wrote: "I composed the overture for *l'Otello* in a little bedroom in Barbaia's *palazzo*, where the most harsh and ferocious of directors imprisoned me by force, with only one plate of *maccheroni* a day until I had finished the last note."

The Museum of the History of Spaghetti in Pontedassio preserves other such evidence of the Italian devotion to *maccheroni*. Giuseppe Verdi's wife once wrote from Russia, "It would take really perfect *tagliatelle* and *maccheroni* to put him in a good mood, amidst all this ice and all these fur coats." Mario Lanza said it was spaghetti that made him sing. Mario Puzo, author of *The Godfather* claimed, "Seven days without a plate of spaghetti drops me into a deep, dark well of physical anxiety."

The simple, gentle food that has been both the lifeline of the poor and the chosen fare of the rich and famous has transcended its regional origins and become a national dish in Italy. Italian emigrants have spread its popularity, but decades and generations later, the traditional and authentic recipes for cooking *maccheroni* have all but been forgotten outside of Italy. I set forth in this chapter recipes old and new, classic and modern, from the authentic Italian pasta kitchen.

There is great confusion about the proper words for dried pasta. Originally, or at least since the Renaissance, pasta of the dried variety, encompassing spaghetti and short dried pasta (*pasta corta*), was generally known as *vermicelli* ("little worms"). In modern times, *maccheroni* and *pasta secca* are terms used to denote all types of dried pasta. *Pastasciutta* ("dry pasta") refers to pasta, dried or fresh, prepared with any type of sauce, but not cooked in soup. In the English-speaking world, *maccheroni* became "macaroni," a label restricted to tubular, stubby-shaped varieties, while spaghetti signifies rods and strings. In English, all types of factory-made pasta are now termed, simply, "dried pasta."

In general, the taste and texture of dried pasta are suited to robust and rustic sauces. Traditionally, *maccheroni* have been combined with sauces made from ingredients and flavorings that are also characteristic of peasant cuisine—olive oil or salt pork, tomatoes, combinations of vegetables, beans, olives, anchovies, fish, economy cuts of meat, and innards. But it is essential to understand that each type of dried pasta, due to its characteristic size, shape, and thickness, absorbs and combines with sauces in different ways. Tomato sauces and simple "sauces" of butter and cheese combine easily with any type of pasta, dried or fresh. It is a mistake to suppose that all pasta sauces marry as easily with one type of pasta as another. It should also be realized that the density of dried pasta affects its taste to a startling degree. For example, the taste of angel's hair is very different from that of *rigatoni,* sauce not considered. The following categories offer guidelines for matching sauces to the various categories of dried pasta.

Rod or String Pasta

Long dried pastas, from the finest angel's hair to thick *bucatini* or *perciatelli,* are best combined with oil-based sauces. The oil easily covers each strand from end to end, keeping it well lubricated without oversaucing. They do not, however, combine well with most meat sauces, as the meat chunks fall to the bottom of the bowl instead of becoming uniformly distributed throughout the spaghetti. But more delicate sauces such as those made with diced chicken livers, or seafood sauces, which are generally of thin consistency, are fine with these pastas. Vegetable sauces in which the ingredients (artichokes, zucchini, or whatever) are sliced very thin are suitable for all but angel's hair.

Macaroni

Macaroni come in many shapes and sizes not just out of whimsy, but also because their various forms are meant to be accompanied by various types of sauces. Each shape is designed to cradle a sauce in a distinctive way. The thickness, texture, and form of various macaronis make them actually taste different from one another as well. The short, stubby varieties are easily lubricated by cream sauces. The large tubular types are perfect for capturing meat and beans and such, which nestle in all the little tunnels and grooves. Meat sauces and those containing nuts, beans, or vegetables such as broccoli or cauliflower are suited for such pastas as *ziti, penne,* and shells, which trap these ingredients inside their hollows. The very small pastas are used in soups (more about that in chapter 4).

Top: *Gioacchino Rossini.*
Bottom: *Giuseppe Verdi. Both Rossini and Verdi were ardent pasta aficionados.*

Matching Dried Pasta to Sauces

Acini di Pepe ("peppercorns") Use in broths, soups.

Anellini ("little rings") Use in broths.

Bucatini (long, thin hollow tubes) Use with *pesto* and with sauces containing *pancetta*, vegetables, cheeses.

Canestrini ("little baskets") Use with sauces containing small bits of meat or nuts, cream-based sauces such as *mascarpone* sauce with walnuts.

Capellini ("fine hair") Use in broths, with delicate sieved tomato sauces and other light, smooth sauces, in baked *pasticci*.

Cavatappi ("corkscrews") Use with *ragù*, meat sauces, creamy cheese and other cream-based sauces.

Conchiglie ("shells," same as *maruzelle*) Use with tomato sauces, simple butter sauces, meat sauces.

Conchigliette ("little shells") Use in light soups.

Creste di Gallo ("cockscombs") Use with tomato sauces, meat sauces, creamy cheese sauces, combine with small beans.

Ditalini (very small "little thimbles") Use in soups with lentils or peas.

Ditali Lisci (medium-small smooth "thimbles") Use in soups with beans.

Ditaloni (large "thimbles") Use in *minestroni*, *pasticci*.

Farfalle ("butterflies") Use with simple oil-based sauces, butter sauces, tomato sauces, and cheese sauces.

Farfalline ("little butterflies") Use in broths.

Farfalloni ("large butterflies") Use with simple oil-based sauces, butter sauces, tomato sauces, cheese sauces.

Fettuccelle ("little ribbons") Use with cream sauces.

Funghini ("little mushrooms") Use in broths, light soups.

Fusilli corti ("short twists") Use with *ragù*, meat sauces, *ricotta* sauces.

Fusilli lunghi ("long twists") Use with *ragù*, meat sauces.

Gemelli ("twins") Use with meat sauces, vegetable sauces, creamy cheese sauces.

Gnocchetti (small "dumpling," also known as *gnocchetti alla sarda**) Use with meat sauces, tomato sauces, *ricotta* and other cheese sauces.

Gnocchi (large "dumpling"*) Use with tomato sauces, simple butter sauces, meat sauces.

Linguine ("little tongues") Use with *pesto*, delicate oil-based sauces, white clam sauce.

Lumache (medium "snails") Use with *ragù*, tomato sauces, oil sauces, simple butter sauces, meat sauces.

Lumachine (small "snails") Use in *minestroni*.

Lumaconi (large "snails") Stuff and bake.

Maccheroncelli tagliati (thin, curled hollow macaroni) Use with meat sauces, sausage sauces, creamy cheese sauces.

Mafalde (long, wide, fluted noodle) Use with vegetable sauces, thick meat sauces, cream sauces, *ricotta* and other cheese sauces.

Marille (the new designer pasta shaped like a car door handle) Use with meat sauces, cream sauces, *pesto*.

Orecchiette ("little ears") Use in thick soups, with sauces made with *rapini* (broccoli rabe), vegetable sauces, meat sauces, *ragù*.

Orzo ("barley") Use in broths, light soups.

Penne ("quills") Use with tomato sauces, chunky tomato sauces, meat sauces, cream sauces.

Penne grandi ("big quills") Use with *ragù*, meat sauces, vegetable sauces.

Pennette ("little quills") Use with tomato sauces, meat sauces, cream sauces.

Perciatelli ("small pierced" macaroni) Use with *ragù*, meat sauces, baked *pasticci* with eggplant.

Radiatori ("radiators") Use with *ragù*, meat sauces, *ricotta* sauces.

Rigatoni ("large grooved" macaroni) Use with meat or sausage sauces, fresh tomato sauces, vegetable sauces, baked *timballi*.

Spaghetti ("a length of cord") Use with fillet of tomato sauce, oil-based sauces, *pesto*, fish sauces.

Spaghettini ("little lengths of cord") Use for *aglio e olio* (garlic and oil) sauce, delicate oil-based sauces, fish or clam sauces.

Stelline ("little stars") Use in broths.

Tagliatelle (from *tagliare*, "to cut") Use with cream sauces.

Trenette (long, narrow noodles) Use with *pesto*, simple oil-based sauces, fish sauces.

Tubettini ("little tubes") Use in light soups.

Vermicelli ("little worms") Use with tomato sauces, butter sauces, cheese sauces.

Ziti (long "bridegrooms") These should be broken into pieces before cooking. Use with *ragù*, meat sauces, vegetable sauces.

Ziti tagliati (cut "bridegrooms") Use with meat sauces, sausage sauces, vegetable sauces, baked *timballi*.

**Note: Do not confuse with homemade gnocchi.*

Spaghetti con Aglio, Olio, e Peperoncino

Spaghetti with Garlic, Oil, and Pepper

FOR 3–4 PEOPLE

This is one of the mother dishes of Italian pasta cookery, upon which so many others are based. For example, tomatoes, anchovies, or vegetables (zucchini, broccoli, cauliflower) can be added to this simple creation. The most important thing to remember is to use the best-quality virgin olive oil or the dish will be tasteless, except for the strong flavor of garlic.

¾ pound spaghetti of any type
⅓ cup virgin olive oil
5 large garlic cloves, very finely chopped
¼ teaspoon dried red pepper flakes, or to taste
2 tablespoons finely chopped fresh Italian parsley
salt to taste

Gently heat the oil, garlic, and red pepper flakes together until the garlic is soft but not crisp or the least bit colored. Meanwhile, cook the pasta in rapidly boiling salted water. When it is *al dente,* drain it and while dripping wet, transfer it to a heated bowl. Toss with the garlic and oil sauce and the parsley, add salt, and serve.

Spaghetti alla Carrettiera

Spaghetti, Pushcart Style

FOR 4–6 PEOPLE

Named for the drivers of the mule-driven carts that transported produce from the regions of Lazio and Tuscany into Rome, this dish has many versions. Some bear no resemblance to tomato sauce at all, but consist entirely of bread crumbs mixed with various herbs and onion or garlic. Use only fresh basil in this recipe.

1 pound spaghetti
1 28-ounce can peeled Italian plum tomatoes in purée, seeded and chopped, with their juice
1 cup firmly packed fresh basil leaves, finely chopped by hand
3 large or 4–5 medium-sized garlic cloves, finely chopped
5 tablespoons olive oil
salt and freshly milled black pepper to taste
freshly grated *parmigiano* cheese

Combine the tomatoes, basil, garlic, and 3 tablespoons olive oil and simmer over medium heat 20 minutes or until the tomatoes reach a saucelike consistency. Season with salt and pepper.
  Meanwhile, cook the spaghetti in rapidly boiling, salted water until *al dente.* Drain and toss with the remaining 2 tablespoons olive oil in a heated bowl. Pour on the sauce, toss, and serve. Pass the *parmigiano.*

Pasta con Salsa di Pomodoro Fresca alla Menta

Pasta with Fresh Tomato Sauce and Mint

FOR 4–6 PEOPLE

In this recipe, fresh tomatoes are simmered slowly without salt, oil, garlic, or onion, to keep their naturally sweet, clear flavor intact. The skin is left on to impart additional taste as well as nutrients to the sauce, and the sauce is seasoned after cooking. When puréeing the sauce, be sure to press every last bit out of the pulp to add thickness and extract vitamins.

4 pounds sweet, vine-ripened tomatoes, halved and seeded (about 4 cups)
½ teaspoon salt, or to taste
freshly milled black pepper to taste
3–4 tablespoons olive oil
1 pound spaghetti or medium-sized macaroni
2 tablespoons fresh mint leaves, torn into small pieces
½ cup freshly grated semisoft *pecorino* or *parmigiano* cheese

Put the prepared tomatoes in a pot and stew them over gentle heat, partially covered, for 45 minutes. Stir occasionally. If the tomatoes are excessively watery drain off some of the water when the sauce begins to cook. Strain the tomatoes through a food mill, pressing to get as much of the pulp as you can through the fine holes. Season with salt and pepper and 2–3 tablespoons olive oil.
  Meanwhile, cook the pasta in rapidly boiling, salted water until *al dente.* Drain and toss with the remaining olive oil in a heated bowl. Combine with the sauce and toss. Sprinkle with the mint. Serve with the grated cheese.

Variation: The classic flavoring for this type of sauce is basil, whose affinity with tomatoes is well-known. In Sardinia, where wild mint grows unrestrained, it is commonly used instead of basil, as I have chosen to do in this recipe. Use either herb, just be sure it is fresh.

Spaghetti Destefanis

Spaghetti with Raw
Tomatoes and Avocado

FOR 3–4 PEOPLE

A pleasant and rather surprising recipe given to me by the Destefanis family. Perhaps because of their travels around the world as a diplomatic family, they seem to be able to combine the best Italian eating traditions with an open mind to ingredients and ideas considered exotic in Italian cooking.

¾ pound regular or thin spaghetti
1 pound sweet, vine-ripened tomatoes (see Note)
1 ripe (but not spotty) avocado, peeled, pitted, and thinly sliced
1 large garlic clove, chopped extremely fine with a knife
⅓ cup virgin olive oil
½ teaspoon salt, or to taste
freshly milled black pepper to taste

Put water on to boil for the pasta. Immerse tomatoes in boiling water for 30 seconds. Remove and plunge in cold water. Slip off the skins. Cut the tomatoes in half lengthwise and remove the seeds. Thinly slice the tomatoes and put them in a large serving bowl with the avocado, garlic, olive oil, salt, and pepper. Cook the pasta until it is *al dente*. Drain and while dripping wet, transfer to the bowl and toss with the sauce. If the pasta is too dry, add a little more olive oil and toss again. Serve.

Note: Cherry tomatoes are a little tedious to clean, but when sweet tomatoes are out of season, you can substitute them.

Paolo's Variation: Add 1 tablespoon drained capers to the sauce.

Spaghettini con Carciofi e Olive

Spaghettini with Artichokes
and Olives

FOR 4–6 PEOPLE

If there is a dish that puts me in gastronomical heaven, it is this one. It cannot be made with anything but fresh artichokes—never frozen, canned, or heaven help us, the oily bottled ones. It is also important to use only good-quality *niçoise* olives, or black *Gaeta* as a second choice. You can use black *Kalamata* olives, but they must not be vinegary. Do not use the bland canned black olives that are preserved in water. (See chapter 1 for information on olives.)

1 pound *spaghettini* or other very thin spaghetti
5 large, very fresh artichokes
½ fresh lemon, or 1 tablespoon vinegar
½ teaspoon salt, for parboiling artichokes
3 tablespoons olive oil
3 garlic cloves, very finely chopped
1 teaspoon chopped fresh marjoram, or ½ teaspoon dried marjoram
3 tablespoons chopped fresh Italian parsley
2 tablespoons fine fresh white bread crumbs, lightly toasted
2 cups chicken broth
2 ounces black olives (see introduction), pitted and sliced (¼ cup)
½ teaspoon freshly milled black pepper
salt to taste
2 tablespoons sweet (unsalted) butter, melted

First, clean the artichokes. Rinse them under cold water and put in a large ceramic (not metal) bowl of cold water to which you have added the lemon juice or vinegar. Trim only a thin slice from the bottom of the stem to remove the dark skin. Pare off all the green skin on the stem. The flesh of the stem is good. With your hand, pull off the tough, outer leaves of the artichoke until you reach leaves that have tender, light-colored areas at their base. Snap off only the upper part of the inner leaves, which are dark green at the top and light greenish-yellow at the base. The inner rows of leaves are the tender part you want, so be careful not to cut away too much. The result will be that the trimmed choke will be higher in the center. Cut artichoke in half lengthwise, and with a small knife, cut out the hairy choke and any other tough inner purple leaves. Put the cleaned artichoke in the acidulated water until they are all trimmed, to prevent them from turning brown. Slice the trimmed artichokes very thin.

Parboil the artichoke hearts for 8 minutes in rapidly boiling water to cover

continued

continued

to which ½ teaspoon salt has been added. (If the artichokes are very fresh and tender, this step is not necessary. It is rare to find them so fresh outside the West Coast. If you do, add them directly with the crumbs.) Drain and set aside. Meanwhile, heat the oil and garlic and when the garlic is soft but not colored, add the marjoram, parsley, and crumbs. Continue to sauté for 1 minute, stirring as you do. Add ½ cup chicken broth, the olives, and the parboiled artichokes and sauté an additional 5 minutes. Add the remaining 1½ cups chicken broth and the pepper. Stir and simmer at medium-low heat, partially covered, until the artichokes are tender, about 10 minutes. Stir occasionally. Check for salt and seasonings.

Meanwhile, cook the pasta in rapidly boiling, salted water until *al dente.* Drain and while dripping wet, toss with melted butter in a heated bowl. Pour sauce over the top, toss, and serve.

Spaghetti con i Calamari
Spaghetti with Squid

FOR 4–6 PEOPLE

Although squid has long been used here as bait, few people considered them food until recently. Now eating squid is very fashionable and I am glad to see it. The lean little creatures are nearly 20 percent protein and practically no fat. A word of caution: They are as forgettable and rubbery when overcooked as they are delicious and tender when cooked properly (I cannot vouch for the ones that reputedly grow to sixty feet).

---

1 pound spaghetti, *spaghettini,* or *linguine*
1 pound squid
1 large clove garlic, finely chopped
2 medium-sized shallots, finely chopped
2 tablespoons olive oil
1 6-ounce can (¾ cup) tomato paste
1 beef bouillon cube
½ teaspoon fresh rosemary leaves
¼ teaspoon salt
¼ teaspoon freshly milled black pepper
1 cup water
½ cup good dry red wine
1 tablespoon finely chopped fresh Italian parsley
2 tablespoons sweet (unsalted) butter, melted

First, clean each squid in the following manner. Separate the head and the tentacles from the body by grasping the head below the eyes and pulling this top section from the body cavity in a smooth motion. Remove and discard the ink sack from the head portion. Place the squid body in a bowl of water, or hold it under running water, and peel off the speckled skin. Remove the cellophanelike "spine" from the body and clean out any insides remaining in the cavity. Rinse the body thoroughly to remove all traces of ink. Cut the head from the tentacles at the "waist," between the eyes and the tentacles. Discard the head portion containing the eyes and remove the hard "beak" from the base of the tentacles. Cut the body into ¼-inch-wide rings and the tentacles into strips. Dry the squid pieces thoroughly. This is important, for the excess water will cause the sauce to be thin.

Sauté the garlic and shallots in olive oil until they are soft but not colored. Add the tomato paste. Cook, stirring, for about 2 minutes. Add the bouillon cube, mashing it against the side of the pan to crush it. Gently stir it with the tomato mixture. Crush the rosemary in your hand and add it to the pan with the salt and pepper. Stir and add water and all but 2 tablespoons of the wine. Simmer 20 minutes.

Add the 2 tablespoons of wine and cook 5–7 minutes. Add squid and cook 5 minutes at gentle heat. The sauce may become thin after adding the squid, even if you have done the best you can to dry them. If so, remove the squid with a slotted spoon and reduce the sauce, always over gentle heat, until it regains its thickness. Return the squid to the pan and add the parsley. Check for seasoning and remove from the heat.

Meanwhile, cook pasta in rapidly boiling, salted water until *al dente.* Drain and while dripping wet, toss with melted butter in a heated bowl. Pour sauce over the top, toss, and serve.

Spaghettini alle Vongole, Versione Rossa

Spaghettini with Red
Clam Sauce

FOR 4–6 PEOPLE

1 pound *spaghettini* or spaghetti
5 dozen fresh littleneck (smallest) clams (see Note)
¼ cup olive oil
1 garlic clove, unpeeled and left whole
1 6-ounce can (¾ cup) tomato paste, or 1 tablespoon paste *and* 1 pound fresh sweet, vine-ripened tomatoes or same quantity canned Italian plum tomatoes in purée
2 large garlic cloves, finely chopped
¼ teaspoon salt, or to taste
freshly milled black pepper to taste
1 tablespoon chopped fresh Italian parsley

Scrub the clams vigorously to remove all sand. (If they are very sandy, leave them covered in salted water overnight so they can expel any sand within.) Rinse well with fresh water. Put 1 tablespoon olive oil, the whole unpeeled garlic clove, and the clams in a large pot and cover tightly. (Leaving the peel on the garlic clove will prevent it from browning and thus imparting a bitter flavor to the sauce.) Steam the clams over high heat, tossing now and then to allow equal exposure to heat. As soon as they open (4–5 minutes), remove them from the heat and allow them to cool. Reserve all the liquid. When they are cool enough to handle, remove the clams from their shells with a small knife. (Reserve some of the shells for use later.) If they are still sandy, rinse them in tepid water. Strain the liquid through a sieve lined with a clean cloth or paper towel to remove any sand. Discard the garlic. Put the clams back in their stock and set aside.

If using fresh tomatoes, immerse in boiling water for 30 seconds. Remove and immediately plunge in cold water. Slip off skins, seed tomatoes, and chop. If using canned tomatoes, drain well, seed, and chop. Set tomatoes aside. Heat the remaining 3 tablespoons olive oil and the chopped garlic together. When the garlic is soft, add the tomato paste or whole chopped tomatoes plus a tablespoon of paste. Stir well. Season with salt and pepper and add ½ cup of the clam liquid (reserve the rest for some other use). Simmer, uncovered, for 10–15 minutes over gentle heat. When the sauce thickens, add the clams and increase the heat to medium. As soon as the sauce starts to boil, turn off the heat. Check for seasoning and add several of the clam shells for character. Strew with parsley.

Meanwhile, cook pasta in rapidly boiling, salted water until *al dente*. Drain and place in a heated bowl. Pour sauce over top, toss, and serve.

Note: This recipe can be adapted for pre-shucked clams, or clam strips. Substitute 1 pound shucked clams (whole or strips) and ½ cup clam juice. Start by heating the olive oil and chopped garlic together and proceed from there.

Variation with Mussels: A Neapolitan variation is to use mussels (4 pounds) instead of clams. They should be plump and small, and should be soaked and scrubbed thoroughly to rid them of sand.

Linguine alle Vongole, Versione Bianca

Linguine with White
Clam Sauce

FOR 4–6 PEOPLE

1 pound thin *linguine* or spaghetti
5 dozen littleneck (smallest) clams (see Note)
¼ cup olive oil
1 garlic clove, unpeeled and left whole
4 garlic cloves, finely chopped
¼ cup dry white wine
¼ teaspoon salt, or to taste
freshly milled black pepper to taste
2–3 tablespoons fine fresh white bread crumbs, lightly toasted
1 additional garlic clove, finely chopped (optional)
¼ cup chopped fresh Italian parsley

Proceed as for *Spaghettini* with Red Clam Sauce, except use wine instead of tomato. Add the bread crumbs to the clam sauce to thicken it after you have added the whole clams. Toss with the parsley. If you like the strong flavor of garlic, toss in the additional chopped garlic clove at the end along with the parsley. Pour over freshly cooked *linguine* or spaghetti.

Note: See note in previous recipe about using pre-shucked clams or clam strips.

Spaghettini con Fegatini di Pollo

Spaghettini with Chicken Livers

FOR 2–3 PEOPLE

Chicken livers must be very fresh, plump, and firm to be good, and these qualities are critical to the success of this dish. Any livers that are discolored, soft, or spongy in texture should be discarded.

½ pound *spaghettini* or *linguine*
6 ounces fresh, plump chicken livers
2 large, sweet, vine-ripened tomatoes, or 4 canned peeled Italian plum tomatoes in purée, seeded, and ⅓ cup of their juice.
1 garlic clove, bruised
1 tablespoon olive oil
4 tablespoons sweet (unsalted) butter
2 medium-sized shallots, finely chopped
½ teaspoon fresh rosemary leaves
1 tablespoon tomato paste
¼ cup good dry red wine
¼ teaspoon salt, or to taste
freshly milled black pepper to taste
2 tablespoons sweet (unsalted) butter, melted
freshly grated *parmigiano* cheese at table

Wash the livers and remove any fat, membranes, green spots, and discolorations. Blanch them in boiling water for 1 minute, remove, and rinse in cold water. Allow them to cool completely and then cut them into quarters. If using fresh tomatoes, immerse them in boiling water for 30 seconds. Remove and immediately plunge in cold water. Peel and remove seeds. Coarsely chop fresh or canned tomatoes and set aside. Gently heat the garlic in the oil and butter and sauté until the garlic is golden. Add the shallots and sauté until soft. Remove and discard the garlic. Add the livers to the pan with the shallots and sauté until they are golden on the outside but still pink on the inside, about 3 minutes. Remove livers and shallots to a warm bowl. Crush the rosemary leaves in your hand to release some of the oils and add to the pan along with the tomato paste. Cook for 1 minute to "flavor" the tomato paste. Add the reserved tomatoes, wine, salt, and pepper and stir well. Cook gently until alcohol evaporates, about 3 minutes. Return the livers to the pan and heat gently for 2 minutes.

Meanwhile, cook the pasta in rapidly boiling, salted water until *al dente*. Drain and while dripping wet, toss with melted butter in a heated bowl. Pour sauce on top, toss, and serve. Pass the *parmigiano*.

Pastasciutta all'Ubaldo

Pasta with Green Tomatoes, Ubaldo's Way

FOR 2–3 PEOPLE

Another Destefanis family recipe. This is a way to use those sad little green tomatoes that have a bit of a rosy blush but never have had the chance to ripen fully on the vine. Use them soon after picking, when they have the most vitamins. Do not use very hard, immature green tomatoes, for they are too sour. This sauce should not be accompanied with cheese.

¾ pound spaghetti or macaroni
1 large garlic clove, bruised
¼ cup chopped fresh Italian parsley
5 tablespoons olive oil
1½ cups green tomatoes with blushes of pink, very thinly sliced

salt and freshly milled black pepper to taste
2 tablespoons sweet (unsalted) butter, melted

Sauté the garlic and parsley in 3 tablespoons of the oil for about 5 minutes. Add the remaining 2 tablespoons oil and heat it before adding the green tomatoes. Sauté the tomatoes briskly until they are tender but not falling apart, about 2–3 minutes. Season with salt and pepper.

Reduce heat to low, cover, and simmer for 5 minutes.

Meanwhile, cook the pasta in rapidly boiling, salted water until *al dente*. Drain and while dripping wet, toss with melted butter and plenty of pepper in a heated bowl. Add sauce, toss, and serve.

Spaghetti con Pane Grattugiato

Spaghetti with
Bread Crumbs

FOR 4–6 PEOPLE

In this rustic sauce that uses leftover bread, two things are essential: the crumbs must be freshly made and from good-quality bread, and the oil must be flavorful virgin olive oil.

1 pound spaghetti
stale Italian or white peasant bread, to yield ¼ cup crumbs
½ cup plus 3 tablespoons virgin olive oil
1 medium-sized onion, chopped
2 large garlic cloves, finely chopped
3 tablespoons chopped fresh oregano, or 1 tablespoon dried oregano, or to taste
⅓ cup chopped fresh Italian parsley
salt and freshly milled black pepper to taste

Toast the bread perfectly crisp and crush it into crumbs. In a pan large enough to hold the pasta later, heat ½ cup oil, onion, garlic, and oregano. Sauté until onion is soft. Add parsley, salt, and pepper; remove from the heat and set aside. In a separate pan, heat the remaining 3 tablespoons oil and add the toasted crumbs. Stir to coat them evenly with the oil so that they become crunchy. If they are too wet, add more toasted crumbs. (How wet they are will depend on the dryness of the bread you use.)

Meanwhile, cook the pasta in rapidly boiling, salted water until *al dente*. Drain so that pasta remains quite "wet." (This is important, for the water, with the oil, forms the sauce.) Reheat onion mixture and add pasta to the pan. Toss with 2 forks to distribute the sauce. Turn into a heated bowl, sprinkle crumb mixture on top, and serve.

Spaghetti alla Carbonara

Spaghetti with Eggs
and Bacon

FOR 4–6 PEOPLE

There are some who say that this dish originated during the last war when American GI's brought their rations of eggs and bacon to their Italian lovers, who cooked them with spaghetti. Actually, the idea of cooking pasta with eggs and bacon or sausage meat is not modern at all. *Carbonara* presumably refers to the generous sprinkling of coal-like (*carbone*) black pepper over the dish.

There are, however, other theories about the origins of *spaghetti carbonara*. A popular one is that it was an ancient dish of the common people and of the coal miners (*carbonari*), from which the term *carbonara* derives. Another explanation bandied about is that it was named for the *Carbonari,* a secret group of Italian patriots formed in the first decade of the 1800s that foreshadowed Italy's fight for liberty and unification.

The Italians make this dish with *pancetta*. Some Americans use the readily available smoked bacon, which produces a different result altogether. The taste of *pancetta* is far more subtle, since it is spiced and not smoked, and I prefer it. But both make good, if different, *spaghetti carbonara*. (See chapter 1 for information on substituting bacon for *pancetta*.)

1 pound spaghetti
3 large garlic cloves
2 tablespoons sweet (unsalted) butter
1 tablespoon olive oil
¼ cup good dry white wine (optional)
½ pound *pancetta* (or bacon), cut into ¼-inch dice
5 large eggs
2 tablespoons milk or heavy cream (optional)
¾ cup freshly grated *parmigiano* cheese
freshly milled black pepper
½ teaspoon salt, or to taste
3 tablespoons chopped fresh Italian parsley

Bruise the garlic with the side of your kitchen knife blade, pressing to release the oils but keeping the clove intact. In a skillet large enough to hold the pasta later, gently heat the butter, oil, and crushed garlic together. When the garlic begins to color, add the wine, if you are using it, and simmer for 2 minutes. Discard garlic. Remove the pan from the heat. In a separate pan, sauté the *pancetta* or bacon until it browns, but do not let it become crisp. Drain off all but 1–2 tablespoons fat, for there is a great deal of flavor in it. Set the skillet aside.

continued

continued

In a bowl, beat the eggs with milk or cream, if you are using it, the cheese, some pepper, and salt. Meanwhile, cook the pasta in rapidly boiling, salted water until *al dente*. Drain and while dripping wet and very hot, add it to skillet with the reduced wine sauce—the burner should be off—and toss. At the same time, reheat the *pancetta,* cooking it quickly 1–2 minutes until it is crisp. Quickly, while the pasta is still piping hot, add the egg mixture to it, tossing to distribute the sauce evenly. Allow the egg mixture to be cooked by the hot pasta, tossing well to distribute; do not let it scramble. Add the crisped *pancetta* and parsley to the pasta and toss again. Sprinkle liberally with pepper. Serve.

Note: There are different schools of thought about whether to use cream or not, whether to use wine or not, and whether to use *parmigiano* or a mixture of *parmigiano* and *pecorino*. To me, this is all a matter of personal preference.

Spaghettini alle Olive
Spaghettini with Olives

FOR 3 PEOPLE

Fans of *olivada*—the indescribable and beguiling olive *pesto* loved by Italians—will understand this dish. Put simply, it is among the most delicious, earthy, and satisfying of foods to combine with spaghetti. However, it should be made with only the best of olives and olive oil. The olives should be full, fleshy, imported black *niçoise* or *Gaeta* olives (*Kalamata* are too sour). Be very sure that they have not been suspended in water or preserved in a too sour-tasting vinegary brine. Never use canned olives.

This dish is best served as a small appetizer portion or alongside a main-course dish in place of potatoes or other starch. It has an affinity with almost all simply cooked foods. Offer it with virtually any poultry, meat, or fish dishes that are roasted, broiled, or sautéed—not fried or with cream or other rich sauces. Because of its intensity, it is best served in small portions. Raw (uncooked) virgin olive oil has a fragrance and aromatic flavor that is partially lost in cooking. In this recipe, and the one that follows, that flavor is fully experienced.

½ pound *spaghettini* or spaghetti
½ pound black *niçoise* or *Gaeta* olives
1 large clove garlic
½ teaspoon chopped fresh marjoram, or ¼ teaspoon dried marjoram
¼ cup virgin olive oil
2 tablespoons sweet (unsalted) butter, melted

Do not use a food processor or blender to chop any of these ingredients. They must be chopped with a knife or a *mezzaluna* chopper to achieve the proper texture. Cut the flesh of the olives off the pits. Chop coarsely. (There should be about 1 cup.) Grate the garlic on the fine side of a grater. In a bowl, combine the chopped olives, garlic, and marjoram. Mix with a wooden spoon. Add the olives, garlic, and marjoram. Mix with a wooden spoon. Add the olive oil a little at a time, blending the mixture with the spoon as you do (but do not mash the olives).

Cook the pasta in rapidly boiling, salted water until *al dente*. Drain, but not too thoroughly. The pasta should remain quite wet. Transfer it to a warm bowl and toss with melted butter. Toss the *olivada* with the pasta and serve hot, warm, or at room temperature.

Note: *Olivada* will last for a few weeks in the refrigerator if you cover it with olive oil, but always bring it to room temperature before using it. You can eat it the traditional way, on bread. Or you can use it for stuffed mushrooms, tomatoes, or the like.

Spaghetti al Pesto di Pomodori Secchi

Spaghetti with Sun-dried
Tomato "Pesto"

FOR 3 PEOPLE

In my mother's hometown, Decimoputzu, ripe plum tomatoes are hung along the walls or spread on the rooftops to dry in the sun. The tomatoes are gathered when they have lost all their moisture, preserved in sea salt in large terracotta urns, and stored for use in winter cooking. They are put in sauces, stuffings, soups, and stews. Now that authentic Italian cooking is coming into its own in America, sun-dried tomatoes are available in many food specialty shops and most Italian delicatessens. The pungent flavors in this recipe go well with the robust sweetness of pork. As in the recipe for *Spaghettini* with Olives, the fragrance and flavor of uncooked olive oil is fully experienced here. My comments in that recipe regarding suggestions for accompanying foods apply here.

½ pound regular or thin spaghetti
6 ounces (1 cup) sun-dried tomatoes, plus 1 tablespoon of the olive oil in which they are preserved (see chapter 1 to reconstitute dried tomatoes not preserved in oil)
½ cup Italian green *ponentine* or French green *piccholine* olives
1 large garlic clove, finely grated
1 very small white or red onion, very finely chopped (¼ cup)
½ teaspoon minced fresh thyme, or ¼ teaspoon dried thyme
pinch of salt, or to taste
¼ teaspoon red pepper flakes, finely crushed, or to taste
½ cup virgin olive oil
1 tablespoon sweet (unsalted) butter, melted

3 tablespoons freshly grated *parmigiano* cheese
1 tablespoon freshly grated *pecorino* cheese
¼ cup chopped fresh Italian parsley

Do not use a food processor or blender to chop any of these ingredients or they will become mushy. Use a knife or a *mezzaluna* chopper to arrive at the proper texture. With a sharp knife or scissors, chop the tomatoes coarsely. Cut the flesh of the olives off the pits and finely chop it. In a bowl, combine the chopped tomatoes, olives, garlic, onion, thyme, salt, and red pepper flakes. Add the olive oil and the tablespoon of oil from the tomatoes. Mix thoroughly with a wooden spoon without mashing the ingredients.

Cook the pasta in rapidly boiling, salted water until *al dente*. Drain, reserving 2 tablespoons of the pasta water. Be sure not to overdrain the pasta, for the excess water will help to keep the pasta moist and with the oil, forms the vehicle for the "sauce" of dried tomatoes. While still dripping wet, transfer the pasta to a warm bowl and toss it with the melted butter, the cheeses, and parsley. Add the 2 tablespoons pasta water that has been set aside to the tomato *pesto,* mixing it to a smooth consistency. Toss with the spaghetti and serve.

Note: This *pesto* will keep in the refrigerator for several weeks if it is topped with olive oil. Leave out the cheese and parsley, adding it to the sauce when it is combined with the cooked pasta.

Capelli d'Angelo ai Gamberi

Angel's Hair with Shrimp Sauce

FOR 4–6 PEOPLE

This is my favorite way to cook shrimp with pasta. It is reminiscent of the recipe in this chapter for *Spaghettini* with White Clam Sauce, but more elegant because of the addition of butter. As in that recipe, the bread crumbs that are added to the sauce thicken it and give it a pleasant texture that contrasts with the fine pasta and tender seafood. Use fresh medium-sized shrimp, or, if you are on the West Coast, the startlingly sweet Alaskan spotted prawns.

1 pound *capellini* (angel's hair) or other spaghetti

1½ pounds medium-sized shrimp in the shell

1 garlic clove, unpeeled and left whole

2–3 sprigs Italian parsley

small twist of lemon peel

4 garlic cloves, finely chopped

4 tablespoons sweet (unsalted) butter

¼ cup olive oil

¼ teaspoon red pepper flakes

½ cup good dry white wine

½ teaspoon salt, or to taste

freshly milled black pepper to taste

⅓ cup fresh fine white bread crumbs, lightly toasted

3 tablespoons chopped fresh Italian parsley

2 tablespoons sweet (unsalted) butter, melted

Shell the shrimp, reserving the shells, and remove the dark intestinal vein down the back. Cut each shrimp in half lengthwise. Wash and pat thoroughly dry. Make a stock with the shells by putting them in a pan with cold water to cover, the unpeeled garlic clove, parsley sprigs, and lemon peel. Bring to a boil. Immediately reduce heat and simmer gently, covered, until you are ready to use the stock, about 30 minutes (do not overcook stock). When done, strain the stock, pressing down on the shells to extract as much flavor as possible.

Heat the chopped garlic with the butter, olive oil, and red pepper flakes until the garlic softens. Add the shrimp and cook quickly over medium heat about 1 minute. Stir and turn them to cook them evenly. Do not cook them more at this point or they will lose their delicacy. Add the wine, stir, and immediately lower the heat. Add 1 cup of the strained stock and the salt and pepper. Simmer very gently, uncovered, for 4 minutes. Add the bread crumbs and 2 tablespoons chopped parsley, stir, and turn off the heat. Check for seasoning.

Meanwhile, cook the pasta in rapidly boiling, salted water until *al dente*. Drain and while dripping wet, toss with melted butter in a heated bowl. Add the shrimp sauce, toss, and sprinkle with the remaining 1 tablespoon chopped parsley. Serve.

Spaghettini con Acciughe e Cipolle

Spaghettini with Anchovies and Onions

FOR 2–3 PEOPLE

½ pound *spaghettini* or spaghetti

¼ cup olive oil

1 medium yellow onion, finely chopped (1 cup)

1 2-ounce can anchovy fillets, drained

1 tablespoon sweet (unsalted) butter, melted

3 tablespoons freshly grated *pecorino* (*romano* or *sardo*) cheese

freshly milled black pepper to taste

Heat the olive oil and the onion until onion softens. Add anchovies and sauté gently until they dissolve, stirring with a wooden spoon. Meanwhile, cook the pasta in rapidly boiling, salted water until *al dente*. Drain and while dripping wet, toss with melted butter and *pecorino* in a warm bowl. Top with sauce, toss, and sprinkle liberally with pepper. Serve.

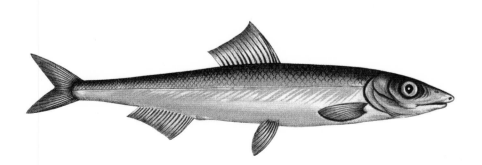

Capelli d'Angelo al Prezzemolo

Angel's Hair with
Parsley Sauce

FOR 4–6 PEOPLE

For this dish, it is very important to get the Italian flat-leaf parsley, which is far more flavorful than the ruffly-leaf type.

1 pound *capellini* (angel's hair) or other thin spaghetti
2½ cups Italian parsley leaves
½ pound (1 cup) sweet (unsalted) butter
2 garlic cloves, bruised
3 egg yolks
¼ teaspoon salt, or to taste
freshly milled black pepper
½ cup freshly grated *parmigiano* cheese

Remove the stems from the parsley before measuring the leaves. Wash the leaves, then dry them extremely well by blotting between paper towels. Using a chopping knife or a *mezzaluna* chopper, finely chop the leaves. Do not chop them in a food processor or they will become mushy, destroying the texture and altering the flavor of the dish. Set parsley aside.

Heat the butter and bruised garlic together, pressing on the cloves to release the garlic juice. Transfer to a heated serving bowl. Lightly beat the egg yolks, adding the salt to them as you do.

Cook the pasta in rapidly boiling, salted water until *al dente*. Drain; it is critical not to overdrain the pasta. While it is still dripping wet, transfer it to the heated bowl that contains the garlic butter. Add the *parmigiano* and egg yolks and toss to distribute evenly, making sure the eggs coat the pasta. Toss in the parsley and distribute it well, too. Sprinkle liberally with pepper and serve.

Spaghetti con l'Aragosta

Spaghetti with Lobster

FOR 3–4 PEOPLE

¾ pound spaghetti
2 cups water
1½-pound lobster
1 small yellow onion, unpeeled
1 celery stalk, including leaves
½ carrot, scraped
2–3 sprigs Italian parsley
2 pounds sweet, vine-ripened tomatoes, or equivalent (2 cups) canned, peeled Italian plum tomatoes in purée
1 tablespoon olive oil
1 large or 2 medium-sized garlic cloves, chopped
¼ teaspoon salt, or to taste
freshly milled black pepper to taste
2 tablespoons sweet (unsalted) butter
¼ cup dry vermouth
⅛ teaspoon (2 envelopes) saffron powder, or ¼ teaspoon saffron threads
1 tablespoon finely chopped fresh Italian parsley

Bring water to the boil, drop in the lobster, head first, and cover. When the water returns to a boil, reduce heat to medium and cook for 5 minutes. Remove lobster and let cool. Reserve stock and add to it the onion, celery, carrot, and parsley sprigs. Crack the lobster claws and the legs with a mallet. Working over a bowl to catch any juices or roe from the lobster, remove the meat from them and from the tail. Save the body shells and discard claw shells. Cut the meat into chunks, put the chunks in a bowl with the coral from the head, and cover the bowl. Refrigerate until ready to use. Cut the legs in small pieces and add them, the green tomalley, and the shells from the body to the stock, along with any juices in the bowl. Bring stock to a boil. Immediately reduce the heat to medium and simmer for 45 minutes or until reduced to ½ cup. From time to time, press on the shells with the back of a wooden spoon to extract the juices from them. Strain reduced stock and set aside.

While the stock is cooking, immerse the fresh tomatoes in boiling water for 30 seconds. Remove and immediately plunge in cold water. Slip off skins, seed, and finely chop. If using canned tomatoes, simply seed and chop. Heat the olive oil and garlic together. When the garlic is soft, add the tomatoes and their juice. Cook over low heat, uncovered, about 25 minutes until sauce thickens. Season

continued

continued

with salt and pepper.

Meanwhile, heat the butter and sauté the lobster meat gently for 1–2 minutes. Add the vermouth and simmer to evaporate the alcohol, about 2 minutes. Remove lobster pieces with a slotted utensil and set aside. Add the ½ cup reduced lobster stock to the vermouth butter, and then add the saffron powder. (If using saffron threads, first heat them for 1 minute in a hot oven, or gently in a pan on top of the stove. Crush them between your fingers before adding to the sauce.) Cook for another 5 minutes over medium heat. Combine the stock with the tomato sauce. If the sauce is too thin, reduce it further by simmering, uncovered, at medium heat for several minutes. Add the lobster, and sprinkle with parsley.

Meanwhile, cook the pasta in rapidly boiling, salted water until *al dente*. Drain and while dripping wet, toss with lobster sauce in a heated bowl. Serve.

Ditalini con Cicoria

"Little Thimbles" with Chicory

FOR 4–6 PEOPLE

Here is a simple dish that will particularly please vegetable lovers. Chicory is the same as curly endive, an inexpensive, common vegetable available year-round. Use the larger *ditalini* (no. 40 in some brands), not the small soup size.

½ pound *ditalini* ("little thimbles")
1 large head (about 1 pound) fresh leafy chicory (See Note)
6 tablespoons virgin olive oil
6 garlic cloves, very finely chopped
¾ cup water
½ teaspoon salt, or to taste
freshly milled black pepper to taste
2 teaspoons chopped fresh oregano, or 1 teaspoon dried oregano
1 16-ounce can imported white *cannellini* beans

Remove any wilted outer leaves of the chicory. Cut off the tough bottom and trim off any brown spots. Wash the chicory well and pat it dry, then cut into ½-inch-wide shreds or ribbons. Heat the oil and garlic in a large skillet over low heat. When the garlic is soft, add the greens. Coat them well in

the oil and garlic. Sauté for 5 minutes, stirring and tossing the greens constantly. Add water, salt, pepper, and oregano. Cover and cook for 5 more minutes over medium heat. Drain the beans and rinse them in cold water. Add them to the pan with the chicory. Stir and cook, covered, an additional 5 minutes over gentle heat.

Meanwhile, cook the macaroni in rapidly boiling, salted water until *al dente*. Drain and while dripping wet, toss with the chicory and beans in a warm bowl (there is no need to toss the pasta with butter for this recipe). Serve.

Note: There are several varieties of chicory, all of which can be used for this recipe. The most common are the broad-leaf type, also called escarole, and leafy chicory, also known as curly endive. The broad-leaf type is sweeter. The frilly type has a pleasantly bitter taste that I like, but that may not appeal to some people.

Pennette con Melanzane al Casaletto

"Little Quills" with
Eggplant, Casaletto Style

FOR 4–6 PEOPLE

A dish I nearly inhaled when it was first served to me in the Ristorante Casaletto outside Rome. The proprietor, Signora Pistolesi, insists that green peppercorns are critical to the flavor of this dish. Made with sweet garden tomatoes, fresh basil, and tender eggplants, it can be reproduced here. If fresh tomatoes are unavailable, canned Italian plum tomatoes may be used.

1 pound *pennette* ("little quills")

1-pound eggplant (see Note)

1 tablespoon salt, for eggplant

6 tablespoons sweet (unsalted) butter

1 cup good dry white wine

½ teaspoon dried green peppercorns, crushed in a mortar

2 pounds sweet, vine-ripened tomatoes or equivalent (2 cups) peeled canned Italian plum tomatoes in purée

3 large garlic cloves, very finely chopped

2 tablespoons virgin olive oil

salt to taste

pinch of sugar, if needed

2 tablespoons sweet (unsalted) butter, melted

⅓ cup freshly grated *parmigiano* cheese

10 fresh basil leaves, torn into pieces

freshly grated *parmigiano* cheese at table

Cut the top and navel off the washed, unpeeled eggplants. Cut crosswise into ½-inch slices. Sprinkle each slice on both sides with salt. Place in a colander upright for 30–40 minutes in order to allow bitter liquid to drain off. Pat dry and dice.

Heat the butter, add the eggplant, cover tightly, and cook for 20–25 minutes over medium-low heat. Lift the lid only to stir several times.

During the last 5 minutes, add the wine and cook, uncovered, until absorbed into the eggplant. Season with green peppercorns. The eggplant should be soft and creamy at this point.

While the eggplant is cooking, immerse the fresh tomatoes in boiling water for 30 seconds. Remove and immediately plunge in cold water. Slip off skins. Seed and chop fresh or canned tomatoes. Set aside.

Heat the garlic in the olive oil and when it is soft, add the tomatoes. Simmer over moderate heat for 12–15 minutes. Don't overcook or the fresh tomato flavor will be lost. (If using canned tomatoes, simmer a little longer, about 25 minutes.) Season with salt and add a pinch of sugar if the tomatoes are too acidic.

Meanwhile, cook the pasta in rapidly boiling, salted water until *al dente*. Drain and while still fairly wet, toss with melted butter and *parmigiano* in a warm bowl. Add the eggplant, tomatoes, and fresh basil and toss, combining well. Pass *parmigiano* at the table.

Note: Please read about eggplants in chapter 1.

Maccheroncini al Pecorino La Chiusa

Little Macaroni with Sheep's Cheese La Chiusa

FOR 3–4 PEOPLE

La Chiusa restaurant, in the Tuscan hills near Siena, is known for the impeccable freshness and quality of its ingredients. They are grown or produced on the premises, which is to say, on the *fattoria* ("farm"). From the grain for fresh pasta and the vegetables, to the wine and the olive oil, everything that is presented on the menu is grown or made there, with apparent skill and pride.

This simplest of classic Italian pasta dishes was prepared for me at the restaurant. What made it stupendous was the startling taste of the vine-ripened tomatoes and the local young *pecorino* cheese, which is semisoft and milder than the more aged *romano* and *sardo pecorino* that is imported to the United States. (Ask a cheese specialty shop for a young Tuscan *pecorino* or other young semisoft sheep's cheese, or try a young *asiago*.)

Consider making this dish only when sweet summer tomatoes and fresh basil are available. The tomatoes are cooked very quickly to retain their vitamins and their fresh flavor.

½ pound *pennette* ("little quills"), short spirals, or other small macaroni, or spaghetti

2 pounds sweet, vine-ripened tomatoes

3 tablespoons virgin olive oil

salt and freshly milled black pepper to taste

¼ cup freshly grated semisoft *pecorino* cheese (see introduction)

8–10 fresh basil leaves, torn into pieces

Immerse the tomatoes in boiling water for 30 seconds. Remove and immediately plunge into cold water. Slip off the skins, seed, and chop. Heat 2 tablespoons olive oil and add the tomatoes, salt, and pepper. Sauté briskly for 10 minutes until the tomatoes have lost their watery consistency.

Meanwhile, cook the macaroni or spaghetti in rapidly boiling, salted water. When it is *al dente,* drain it and while dripping wet, toss with the remaining 1 tablespoon olive oil in a heated bowl. Pour sauce over pasta and toss. Sprinkle with the cheese and basil. Serve.

Maccheroncini al Pepe e Pecorino

Little Macaroni with Pepper and Sheep's Cheese

SERVES 3–4 PEOPLE

½ pound *pennette* ("little quills"), short spirals, or short *ziti*

½ cup freshly grated semisoft *pecorino* cheese (see Note)

1½ teaspoons freshly milled black pepper

1 tablespoon olive oil

Have the grated cheese and milled pepper ready. Cook the pasta in rapidly boiling, salted water until *al dente.* Drain and while dripping wet, toss with olive oil in a warm bowl. Add cheese and pepper and toss again. Serve.

Note: See preceeding recipe for comments on the best type of cheese to use.

Penne al Gorgonzola

Penne with Gorgonzola

FOR 4–6 PEOPLE

1 pound *penne* ("quills") or short *ziti*

1 recipe *Gorgonzola* sauce (see Potato *Gnocchi* with *Gorgonzola* Sauce, chapter 5)

Prepare the sauce. Bring the water for the macaroni to a rolling boil and add the *penne* and salt. Cook until *al dente.* Drain and while dripping wet, toss with sauce in a warm bowl. Serve.

Maccheroni al Sugo di Coniglio
Macaroni with Rabbit Sauce

FOR 4–6 PEOPLE

If you know a butcher who hangs his game properly, you will have no trouble making this delicious dish. Rabbit should be hung from two to four days for the flesh to be tender. This sauce, which is typical of country cooking in parts of Italy where small game and various small birds are prized, can also be made with Cornish hen, squab, or quail.

1 pound *rigatoni* (curved tubes), *ziti* (long or short), or *penne* ("quills")

3-pound rabbit with liver, skinned, and cut into serving pieces

1 tablespoon salt, for washing rabbit

6 tablespoons olive oil

1 medium-sized yellow onion, finely chopped

2 large garlic cloves, finely chopped

2 teaspoons fresh rosemary leaves, or 1 teaspoon dried rosemary

2 tablespoons finely chopped fresh Italian parsley

1 medium-sized celery stalk, finely chopped

1 small carrot, scraped and finely chopped

½ teaspoon salt, or to taste

freshly milled black pepper to taste

½ cup good dry white wine

2 tablespoons tomato paste

1 cup chicken or beef broth

Wash the rabbit pieces and liver thoroughly with cold water to which salt has been added. Rinse well and pat dry thoroughly. Chop liver and set rabbit pieces and liver aside. In a small skillet, heat 3 tablespoons of the oil with the onion and garlic and sauté until soft, about 3–4 minutes. Add the rosemary (crushing it in your hand as you do), parsley, celery, and carrot. Sauté gently until soft but not browned. Remove from the heat and set aside.

In a very large skillet, heat the remaining 3 tablespoons oil and add the rabbit pieces. You may need to use 2 skillets so that the pieces are not too crowded. Brown them gently on all sides over medium-low heat, seasoning them with salt and pepper. When the rabbit is nicely browned all over (about 30 minutes), add the liver and sauté for 3–4 minutes, or until it is browned. Add the sautéed vegetables to the rabbit, stirring to mix all the ingredients. Again, you may need to divide the ingredients evenly between 2 pans if you don't have an extremely large skillet. Add the wine and cook for 3–4 minutes to evaporate the alcohol. Mix the tomato paste with a few tablespoons of the broth to dissolve it. Add it to the pan, mixing it in to cover all the pieces of meat. Cover and simmer over very gentle heat for 45 minutes, adding the broth gradually until you have used it all up. Keep the pan covered except to add more broth and stir. When the rabbit sauce has cooked for about 30 minutes, remove 2 or 3 of the rabbit pieces, cut the meat from the bone, chop it up, and return it to the sauce. Stir and replace the cover. Remove the cover during the last 10 minutes of cooking if the sauce looks somewhat thin. Taste for seasoning. Remove the rabbit pieces to a warm platter.

Meanwhile, cook the pasta in rapidly boiling, salted water until *al dente*. Drain and while dripping wet, toss with the sauce in a heated bowl. Serve pasta as a first course and the rabbit pieces as a second course.

Pasta Rosa alla Flavia

Pasta with Pink Vodka
Sauce, Flavia Style

FOR 4–6 PEOPLE

---

1 pound medium-sized macaroni
 (see Note)
3 tablespoons sweet (unsalted)
 butter
1 cup heavy cream
½ cup vodka
½ teaspoon red pepper flakes
¼ cup tomato paste
2 tablespoons sweet (unsalted)
 butter, melted
½ cup freshly grated *parmigiano*
 cheese

Heat the butter, cream,
vodka, red pepper flakes,
and tomato paste in the top
pan of a double boiler placed
over gently boiling water.
The water in the bottom pan
should not actually touch
the top pan. Stir mixture to
blend. Cook the sauce in
this manner, stirring, until
it is thick enough to coat a
wooden spoon, about 5 minutes.

Meanwhile, cook the pasta
in rapidly boiling, salted
water until *al dente*. Drain
and while dripping wet, toss
with melted butter, the *parmigiano,* and the sauce in a
warm bowl. Serve.

Note: This richly colored
sauce is also good on fresh
pasta. Prepare ½ recipe (1
pound) Egg Pasta I or II or
Spinach Pasta, cut into *tagliatelle.* See chapter 2 for
these recipes and for directions for cooking fresh pasta.

Penne Grotta Verde

Penne "Green Grotto"

FOR 2–3 PEOPLE

½ pound *penne* ("quills") or short
 ziti
1 large garlic clove, bruised
¼ cup virgin olive oil
2 large or 3 small green sweet
 peppers, stems, seeds, and ribs
 removed and then thinly sliced
2 tablespoons sweet (unsalted)
 butter, melted
salt and freshly milled black pepper
 to taste
handful of fresh basil leaves, torn in
 small pieces
1 tablespoon sweet (unsalted)
 butter, melted
3 tablespoons freshly grated *parmigiano* cheese, or to taste
freshly grated *parmigiano* cheese
 at table

Heat the garlic in the oil until it colors, pressing with a
wooden spoon to extract the
juice. Discard garlic. Add
the sweet peppers and sauté
for 15 minutes. Add the butter, salt, pepper, and basil.
Gently sauté another 5
minutes.

Meanwhile, cook the
pasta in rapidly boiling,
salted water until *al dente.*
Drain and while dripping
wet, toss with melted butter
and *parmigiano* in a warm
bowl. Toss with the pepper
sauce and serve with additional *parmigiano.*

Maruzzelle al Mascarpone e Noci

"Small Seashells" with
Mascarpone and Walnuts

FOR 2–3 PEOPLE

When I lived in Britain,
I quickly discovered
Elizabeth David's wonderful
classic, *Italian Food.* From its
pages I learned this quick
and elegant dish, which is as
much at home on a simple
table as at an elegant dinner.
I have been making it ever
since. It is best made with
mascarpone, the sweet Italian
cream cheese. However, fresh
cream cheese or even French
crème fraîche can be substituted. Commercial brands
of American cream cheese
contain additives that make
them thick and gummy. I do
not find them a satisfactory
substitute.

---

10 ounces *maruzzelle* ("shells")
4 tablespoons sweet (unsalted)
 butter
½ pound *mascarpone*
¼ cup freshly grated *parmigiano*
 cheese
¼ cup walnut meats, lightly
 toasted

Gently heat the butter; when
it is melted add the *mascarpone.* Stir with a wooden
spoon to make a creamy-
smooth mixture, but do not
let it heat longer than 4–5
minutes, or it will become
too thin.

Meanwhile, cook the mac-
aroni in rapidly boiling,
salted water until it is *al
dente.* Drain and while dripping wet, turn it into a warm
bowl. Toss it with the *mascarpone* sauce and the *parmigiano.* Add the walnuts and
toss again. Serve.

Pasta in Salsa di Zafferano alla Flavia

Pasta with Saffron Cream Sauce, Flavia Style

The brilliant yellow of saffron speckled with green parsley makes this a beautiful dish.

1 pound medium-sized macaroni
⅛ teaspoon (2 envelopes) saffron powder, or ¼ teaspoon saffron threads
1½ cups heavy cream
2 tablespoons sweet (unsalted) butter

4 egg yolks, lightly beaten
½ teaspoon salt
freshly milled white pepper to taste
2 tablespoons sweet (unsalted) butter, melted
⅓ cup freshly grated *parmigiano* cheese
1 tablespoon fresh Italian parsley leaves, torn into pieces

If using saffron threads, heat them for 1 minute in a hot oven or gently on top of the stove. Combine the saffron powder or threads, cream, butter, egg yolks, salt, and pepper in the top pan of a double boiler placed over gently boiling water. The water in the bottom pot should not actually touch the top pan. Mix the sauce with a whisk or wooden spoon, taking care not to let the egg curdle. The sauce is ready when it is thick enough to coat a wooden spoon, about 5–10 minutes.

Meanwhile, cook the pasta in rapidly boiling, salted water until *al dente*. Drain and while dripping wet, toss with melted butter, *parmigiano,* and sauce in a warm bowl. Serve. Sprinkle torn parsley on individual portions.

Note: If you prefer, serve this sauce with fresh pasta. Make ½ recipe (1 pound) Egg Pasta I or II and cut into *tagliatelle*. See chapter 2 for these recipes and for directions for cooking fresh pasta.

THE ATLANTIC MACARONI CO.

MILLERS AND MANUFACTURERS OF MACARONI FANCY PASTE & EGG NOODLES

MACARONI PLANT CAPACITY 100,000 LBS. DAILY OF ALIMENTARY PASTE

295-303 VERNON AVE.
LONG ISLAND CITY
NEW YORK

8 FESTIVE AND BAKED SPECIALTIES
Paste al Forno

The lackeys in green, gold, and powder entered, each holding a great silver dish containing a towering mound of macaroni. . . . The burnished gold of the crusts, the fragrance of the sugar and cinnamon they exuded, were but preludes to the delights released from the interior when the knife broke the crust; first came a mist laden with aromas, the chicken livers, hard-boiled eggs, sliced ham, chicken, and truffles in masses of piping hot, glistening macaroni, to which the juice gave an exquisite hue of suede. . . .

from *Il Gattopardo* ("*The Leopard*"), a 1958 novel by Giuseppe di Lampedusa about the Bourbon states of Naples and Sicily in the 1860s

Pasta-making at the Este court in Ferrara.

At the Time of Medici, *by C. Becker,*
1890.

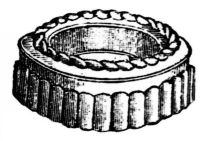

A "pastiche," says the dictionary, is a composition made up of a selection from different works (as in literature or music). *Pasticcio* is the Italian word for it and the Italians are fond of saying *che pasticcio!* meaning, "what an awful mess!"

In gastronomic terms, a *pasticcio* is not a mess at all. In fact, it is quite a pretty thing, a "composition" of pasta and other things cooked separately from it—chickens' breasts and livers, sliced truffles, ham, sweet sausages, wild mushrooms, and the like—between layers of silky cheese and béchamel or other sauces. Whereas Americans are likely to think of tuna noodle when they hear casserole, Italians are likely to think of a *timballo,* a *timpano,* or a *lasagne.* A *timballo* ("drum") has a crust, like a pie. A *timpano* (also, *sformato*) is a molded pasta. Besides being the generic word, a *pasticcio* is the term for a particular "composition," one with a crumb topping instead of a crust. A *lasagne* is a dish of layered wide noodles.

Pasticci are among the oldest kinds of pasta dishes. Before modern times, when cooking was not just a service to the growling belly (at least, not in Italy), but a pleasurable part of life's daily activities, a *pasticcio* was almost always an elaborate concoction. *Pasticci* were served by Pope Clement VII at a formal dinner he gave for his niece, Caterina de'Medici. One *timballo* was moistened with the drippings of a roast and mixed with meat and grated cheese; another was anointed with butter, honey, sugar, cinnamon, and saffron. History shows that the French were willing subjects on culinary matters. But probably because of her propensity for wholesale political assassination, Caterina's ways didn't catch on in France and the *pasticcio* retreated to Italy.

A *pasticcio* can be simple or complicated, but it is almost always a festive dish consisting of short, stubby pasta or small filled pasta with other ingredients cooked *al forno*—"in the oven." My mother still reminisces about the *timpano* that was made on special occasions when she was growing up in Sardinia. It consisted of homemade macaroni with tomato sauce and cheese baked in a mold with some delicate thing in the hole in the center, such as sautéed chicken or duck livers or sweetbreads.

In making *pasticci* it is important to use good-quality imported Italian pasta, which will hold up to being cooked twice—first boiled on the stove and then baked in the oven. These substantial dishes are intended as a main course. They should be followed by a vegetable course.

Timballo di Tortellini con Animelle

Tortellini and Sweetbread Pie

FOR 6 PEOPLE

Renaissance recipes for *timballi* prescribe a sweet pastry crust encasing a savory filling. The crust was not meant to be eaten, but only to impart a subtle sweetness to the contents of the "drum." The *timballo* is still made this way. Because I like to eat the crust with the pasta, I prefer an unsweetened classic short crust like the one below. The *tortellini*, the sauces, and even the crust can be made several days in advance and refrigerated.

Because of the complexity of this recipe and the one that follows, I have presented the method in steps, as in the recipes in chapter 5 for *gnocchi* and stuffed pasta forms.

Sauce
1 pair (about 1 pound) veal sweetbreads
1 tablespoon salt, for cooking sweetbreads
1 recipe Béchamel Sauce (chapter 3)
5 ounces fresh cultivated mushrooms
2 tablespoons sweet (unsalted) butter
3 medium-sized shallots, finely chopped
¼ pound ham, sliced about ⅛ inch thick and cut into 1½-inch long strips
¾ teaspoon salt, or to taste
pinch of freshly milled white pepper
¼ cup good dry sherry
1 cup freshly grated *parmigiano* cheese

Pasta
cheese *tortellini* made with ½ recipe (1 pound) Egg Pasta I or II (chapter 2) and 1 recipe of the filling used for *Tortelloni* with Asparagus (chapter 5)
2 tablespoons sweet (unsalted) butter, melted

Pastry Crust
10 tablespoons (6 ounces) sweet (unsalted) butter, chilled, or equal amounts butter and lard, chilled
2 cups unbleached white flour, chilled
½ teaspoon salt, plus a pinch
1 extra-large egg
⅓ cup ice water
1 egg yolk, beaten with pinch of salt, for glazing crust

sweet (unsalted) butter and flour, for preparing pan

1. To prepare the sweetbreads for the sauce, wash them and then soak in several changes of ice water for 1 hour. Place in a pan, add water to cover to which 1 tablespoon of salt has been added, and bring to a boil. Immediately reduce heat and simmer, uncovered, for 3 minutes. Drain and plunge the sweetbreads into ice water until they have cooled off. Drain well. Trim off cartilage, fat, and all thick membranes, tubes, and dark or discolored spots. Using your hands, break up the sweetbreads into their natural small sections without tear-ing the fine membranes that connect them. Chill in the refrigerator before slicing.

2. Meanwhile, prepare the pasta. First make the filling and then the dough for the *tortellini*. Shape them according to directions for *tortellini* in chapter 5.

3. To make the pastry crust, cut the butter or butter and lard into 4 or 5 pieces. Mix the flour and salt. Rub the shortening into the flour by hand, in a food processor, or in an electric mixer with a paddle on lowest speed, until pieces the size of your thumbnail are formed. The pieces should not be smaller than this. Beat the egg in a measuring cup and mix in the ice water. Slowly add the liquid to the flour and shortening and stir by hand until the dough holds together when you pinch it. If there is too much liquid for the dough, do not use it all. If you are using a food processor, engage it for only 5 seconds and do not allow the dough to actually form into a ball in the bowl. Quickly gather the dough up with your hands into 2 balls, one about twice the size of the other. For a properly flaky crust, it is very important not to overwork the dough. Press each ball into a thick disk and wrap loosely in plastic wrap (to allow a little air to enter packages). Chill for 2 hours.

4. Make the béchamel, cover as directed, and set aside.

5. To make the sauce, cut the chilled sweetbreads into slices 1 inch thick. Clean dirt from the mushrooms with a soft brush or clean towel. Do not wash them unless they are excessively gritty. (Water alters the texture of mushrooms.) If you must, rinse them in a colander quickly with very cold tap water. Pat thoroughly dry. Cut in half and thinly slice crosswise; set aside. In a large skillet, heat the butter, add the shallots, and sauté gently until soft. Add the ham and sweetbreads and season with salt and pepper. Sauté 2–3 minutes over medium heat until colored. Add the mushrooms and sauté another 2 minutes. Add the sherry. Reduce over medium heat for 2 minutes, stirring. Add 1 cup of the béchamel and simmer gently for 5 minutes.

6. Drop the *tortellini* into 5 quarts of boiling, salted water and cover. When water returns to a boil, cook for 1 minute. Lift them out of the water with a slotted spoon

continued

continued

into a warm bowl. Coat them with the melted butter, half the *parmigiano,* and the remaining béchamel, which has first been reheated. Take care not to break the *tortellini.* Cover and set aside.

7. Preheat the oven to 375 degrees. On a lightly floured surface, roll each disk out into a circle about ⅛ inch thick. The larger disk will be adequate to line an 8-inch spring-form pan; the smaller disk will roll out to about 9 inches in diameter to form the lid, with enough overhang to join it to the bottom casing. Work quickly to prevent overworking the dough. (If the dough is too cold, it will be difficult to roll. If this is the case, allow it to rest at room temperature for 5 minutes or so before roll-

ing out.) Butter an 8-inch spring-form pan and dust it with flour. Roll the 8-inch pastry disk around your rolling pin and transfer it to the spring-form pan. Unroll it gently, centering it over the pan. Gently push the pastry round into the bottom of the pan and press the dough against the sides to shape it, taking care not to break it. Do not trim excess dough, allow it to join the pastry lid later. Gently reheat the sweetbread mixture and spoon one third into the crust. Sprinkle with some of the *parmigiano.* Top with a third of the *tortellini.* Continue layering in that order, ending with a layer of *tortellini* sprinkled with *parmigiano.* Drape the second pastry round over your rolling pin and center it over the *tim-*

ballo. Unwrap from pin to rest evenly on top of pan. Crimp the edges of the top and bottom crust together with your fingers; do not allow the crust to overlap the pan edges, for you will be removing the pan ring before serving. Cut off any excess pastry and reserve the scraps. Cut a small hole out of the center of the top pie crust and combine the removed dough with the pastry scraps into a small ball. Flatten with the palm of your hand, roll out and cut into a decorative pastry flower. Place the "flower" over the hole, leaving vents for steam to escape. Brush the entire crust with beaten egg yolk. Bake for 30 minutes in the preheated oven or until crust is golden.

8. When the *timballo* is done, remove it from the oven and let it settle for about 10 minutes before unmolding. To unmold, unfasten the snap of the spring-form pan and remove the ring. Carefully transfer the *timballo* to a round platter. Present the *timballo* whole at the table, then cut into wedges and serve.
Note: The *timballo* can be made in a deep casserole, but you will not be able to unmold it.

Pasticcio di Maccheroni, Pollo, e Prosciutto

Pasticcio of Macaroni, Chicken, and Ham

FOR 6 PEOPLE

- 10 ounces macaroni, such as *penne* ("quills"), short *ziti*, or spirals
- ½ pound fresh, plump chicken livers
- 1 pound (boned weight) chicken breast, skinned
- ½ pound fresh cultivated mushrooms, quartered and thinly sliced
- 9 tablespoons (¼ pound plus 1 tablespoon) sweet (unsalted) butter
- salt and freshly milled black pepper to taste
- ¼ pound cooked ham, cut into ¼-inch dice
- 1 medium-sized yellow onion, finely chopped
- 1 small carrot, scraped and very finely chopped
- 1 medium-sized celery stalk, finely chopped
- sweet (unsalted) butter, for preparing the dish
- ½ cup fine fresh white bread crumbs, lightly toasted
- 2 eggs
- ¼ teaspoon nutmeg, preferably freshly grated
- 2 cups light cream (half-and-half)
- ¼ cup chicken broth
- ½ cup freshly grated *parmigiano*

Wash the livers and trim off any fat, membranes, and green spots. Pat dry and cut into quarters; set aside. Wash and pat dry the chicken breast. Trim off any fat and cut meat into thin 2-inch-long strips; set aside. Dust the mushrooms with a soft

continued

continued

brush or cloth to remove sand. Do not wash them unless they are excessively gritty. If you must, rinse them quickly in a colander under cold tap water and dry thoroughly. Quarter them and then thinly slice them. Sauté the mushrooms quickly in 2 tablespoons butter over medium heat until they start to color (3–4 minutes). Season with a few pinches of salt and pepper. In a separate pan, sauté the ham, onion, carrot, and celery in 3 tablespoons butter until vegetables soften. Remove them from the pan and set aside. Add 2 more tablespoons of butter to the pan and gently sauté the sliced chicken. It should color on the outside but still remain moist and somewhat pink on the inside. Remove the chicken from the pan, transfer it to a dish, and cover. Add 1 tablespoon butter to the pan, heat it, and add the livers. Sauté them quickly for 2–3 minutes until they are colored on the outside but still pink and moist inside. Season with a pinch of salt and pepper. Remove from the skillet and set aside. Combine the mushrooms and the sautéed vegetables, keep the livers and chicken separate.

Preheat the oven to 375 degrees. Cook the pasta in plenty of boiling, salted water until it is about 2 minutes short of *al dente*. It should be firm but still crunchy. Meanwhile, generously butter a large baking dish and sprinkle it with all but 2 tablespoons of the crumbs. Beat the eggs with the nutmeg, cream, chicken broth, and all but 1 tablespoon of the *parmigiano*. Season with about 1 teaspoon salt and a few pinches of pepper. Drain the pasta and rinse lightly with cold water. Toss the pasta with the egg mixture and pour half of it into the prepared baking dish. Spread half the vegetable and ham mixture over it. Dot with all the liver and chicken. Add the remaining pasta over that and finish it off with the remaining half of the vegetable mixture. Mix the remaining 2 tablespoons crumbs with the remaining 1 tablespoon each of butter and cheese and sprinkle it on top. Bake for 15 minutes on the next-to-highest oven rack. Finish the *pasticcio* off under a hot broiler for several minutes until a golden crust is formed. Let settle for 5–10 minutes and serve.

Timballo di Maccheroni
Timballo of Macaroni

FOR 6 PEOPLE

This dish is inspired by an eighteenth century recipe for a *timpano di maccheroni* that appears in Vincenzo Corrado's *Il Cuoco Galante.* In the original recipe, the *ziti* are first boiled in beef broth, drained, and mixed with a sauce of beef or pork and tomatoes. A deep dish is then lined with a slightly sweet pastry and filled with alternating layers of *ziti* in its sauce, grated *parmigiano,* and a thick *ragù* of sausages, sweetbreads, and strips of *prosciutto.* Then a crowning lid, and the pie was baked.

First make a *ragù* (½ recipe Meat Sauce, chapter 3), using all pork instead of beef; cut the pork into small pieces. Boil and chill a pair of sweetbreads as in *Tortellini* and Sweetbread Pie, slice them and sauté in a little butter. Separately sauté ½ pound fresh, plump chicken livers, trimmed and quar-

tered until they are colored on the outside but still quite pink inside. Make a pastry crust like the one for the sweetbread pie. Make ½ recipe Béchamel Sauce (chapter 3), omitting the nutmeg; cover and set aside. Cook ¾ pound *rigatoni* (curved tubes), short *ziti, penne* ("quills"), or other medium-sized macaroni in boiling, salted water until not quite *al dente.* The pasta should be firm but not crunchy. Drain and toss with the béchamel and ⅔ cup freshly grated *parmigiano* cheese. Combine the *ragù,* the pork from the *ragù,* the sweetbreads, the livers, and the macaroni. Turn the mixture into the pastry casing. Seal as in sweetbread pie. Bake in a preheated 375-degree oven for 30 minutes, or until golden. Remove from the oven and let stand for about 10 minutes before unmolding. Remove pan ring and present *timballo* whole at the table. Cut into wedges and serve.

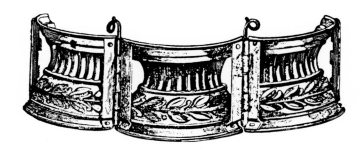

Timpano alle Melanzane

Timpano of Eggplant
and Macaroni

FOR 4 PEOPLE

A simply delicious, rather easy-to-make *pasticcio*.

6 ounces *perciatelli* (*bucatini*) or thick spaghetti

1½ pounds eggplant (see Note)

1 tablespoon salt, for sprinkling on eggplant

¾ cup vegetable oil, or as needed

4 good-quality lean sweet Italian pork sausages, partially frozen (about ¾ pound)

¼ cup olive oil

1 garlic clove, bruised

3 tablespoons tomato paste

5 fresh basil leaves, torn in small pieces, or ½ teaspoon dried basil

1 28-ounce can peeled Italian plum tomatoes in purée, seeded and all but 4 of the tomatoes coarsely chopped, with their juice

salt and freshly milled black pepper to taste

½ recipe Béchamel Sauce (chapter 3), omitting nutmeg

1 tablespoon sweet (unsalted) butter, melted

¼ cup freshly grated *parmigiano* cheese

You will need 1 very large globe eggplant or 2 medium-sized ones. Wash and remove the stem but do not peel. Cut into thin, lengthwise slices and sprinkle with salt. Place them in a colander standing up, for 30–40 minutes, to allow bitter liquid to drain off. Pat dry. Heat the vegetable oil, which should be 1 inch deep, in a frying pan and fry the eggplant slices on both sides until golden brown. Drain on paper towels.

Cut the sausages lengthwise into thin slices (partially freezing lets you slice them quite thin). Remove the casings. Heat the olive oil with the garlic. When the garlic is golden, discard it. Add the sausage slices and gently sauté for a few minutes on each side until golden. Remove sausages and set aside. Stir in tomato paste and basil. Add the chopped tomatoes and their juice. Simmer 10 minutes. Slice the 4 reserved whole tomatoes into thick ribbon lengths, add them to the sauce and simmer for another 3 minutes. Season with salt and pepper. Remove sauce from the heat and set aside. Meanwhile, make the béchamel and set aside.

Cook the pasta in rapidly boiling, salted water until about 2 minutes short of *al dente*. It should be quite firm but not crunchy. Drain the pasta, rinse it lightly with cold water, and toss with the melted butter. Set aside.

Preheat the oven to 400 degrees. In a deep baking dish, preferably glass (to be able to see the pretty alternating layers of purple, red, and white), layer the ingredients as follows: 3–4 tablespoons of tomato sauce on the bottom; next, a thin layer of the eggplant, a few tablespoons of tomato sauce, and some sausage; then, a smear of *béchamel* (2–3 tablespoons) and a sprinkling of *parmigiano*; finally, a thin layer of pasta. Repeat layering in this order until all the ingredients are used up. The top layer should be eggplant smeared with a few tablespoons of tomato sauce, sprinkled with *parmigiano*. Bake for 15 minutes. Let settle about 10 minutes.

Note: See chapter 1 for information on selecting eggplants.

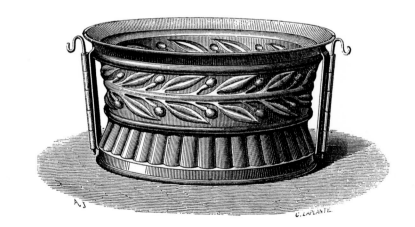

Lasagne Rosse ai Quattro Formaggi

Tomato Lasagne with Four Cheeses

FOR 6–8 PEOPLE

This smooth, cheesy lasagne can be made with tomato, beet, spinach, or egg pasta. The dry *lasagne* noodles sold in boxes are just not delicate enough for dishes such as the two that follow, both of which contain creamy sauces.

Pasta Dough
½ recipe (about 1 pound) Red (Tomato) Pasta, Spinach Pasta, Pink (Beet) Pasta, or Egg Pasta I or II (chapter 2)

Sauce
1½ recipes Béchamel Sauce (chapter 3)

½ pound *fontina, fonduta,* or *gruyère* cheese, shredded

½ pound *mozzarella* cheese, shredded

½ pound sweet *provolone* or *Gouda* cheese, shredded

1 cup freshly grated *parmigiano* cheese

2 tablespoons sweet (unsalted) butter

1 tablespoon sweet (unsalted) butter, for greasing dish

Use a 9- by 14-inch baking dish for the *lasagne*. Make the pasta dough. You will have enough for about 10 very thin noodle layers. Roll out the pasta extremely thin and cut it into 3- by 4-inch rectangles. They should fit into the pan exactly when laid side by side (a standard 9- by 14-inch baking dish has an 8- by 12-inch interior bottom surface.) Precook the noodles as for *cannelloni* in Emilian Onion Harmony (chapter 5). While the precooked noodles are resting, covered, on damp towels, make the béchamel.

Preheat the oven to 400 degrees. Combine the three shredded cheeses in a bowl. Have the grated *parmigiano* handy in another bowl. Smear the baking dish with 1 tablespoon butter. Smear a layer of the béchamel on the bottom of the dish. Put a layer of *lasagne* noodles over the béchamel, making them touch without overlapping. You should cover the surface area of the baking pan completely with the noodles. Smear a thin layer of béchamel over the noodles and scatter a handful of the soft cheeses over it. Sprinkle some *parmigiano* over that. Lay down another layer of noodles, always making sure there are no gaps and no overlapping. Repeat the process of spreading the béchamel, then the soft cheeses, and finally the *parmigiano*. End with a layer of *lasagne* noodles topped with béchamel. Drizzle the melted butter over the *lasagne*. Bake for 20 minutes or until golden. Let settle 10 minutes and serve.

Lasagne Verdi

Spinach Lasagne

FOR 6 PEOPLE

No discussion of *lasagne* would be complete without mention of *lasagne verdi*. One variation on this dish alternates layers of yellow and green egg pasta for a most lovely effect. And various kinds of *ragù* can be sandwiched between the layers. The sauce can include mushrooms, for example. If fresh *porcini* are in season, they may replace meat in the sauce altogether. Or the *ragù* can contain sausage, *prosciutto,* chicken livers, *pancetta,* even nuts or lemon peel (but not all at once). Some *lasagne* sauces contain several meats and chicken and very little tomato. But this *lasagne* is always made with two sauces—*ragù* and béchamel. For the dish to be delicate, it is important that the *lasagne* noodles be very thin homemade pasta.

Pasta Dough
½ recipe (about 1 pound) Spinach Pasta (chapter 2)

Sauces
1½ recipes Béchamel sauce (chapter 3)

1 recipe Bolognese Tomato and Meat Sauce (chapter 3)

1 cup freshly grated *parmigiano* cheese

1 tablespoon sweet (unsalted) butter

Make the 2 sauces first. While the tomato and meat sauce is simmering, make the pasta. You will have enough for about 10 very thin noodle layers. Roll out the pasta very thin. Cut and precook as directed in Tomato Lasagne with Four Cheeses.

Preheat the oven to 350 degrees. Smear a 9- by 14-inch baking dish with the butter. Spead a thin layer of the *ragù* on the bottom. Cover with a layer of noodles, making them touch without overlapping. Spread a layer of the *ragù* over it and on top of that, a layer of béchamel, smoothing it with the back of a wooden spoon. Sprinkle a little *parmigiano* over it and repeat the process, adding another layer of noodles, *ragù,* béchamel, *parmigiano,* and so on until all the ingredients are used up. End with a layer of béchamel sprinkled with *parmigiano*. Bake on the next-to-highest oven rack for 30 minutes. The top of the *lasagne* should be golden. If it is not, pass the *lasagne* under the broiler for several minutes. Let settle 10 minutes and serve.

9 REGIONAL SPECIALTIES
Ricette Regionali

"... Often [pasta] shapes denote a place of origin common to the pasta and the eater. ... [In Italy] a native place is not just a particular landscape; it is also the opinion of how the world should be formed; what the weather should be like, what the water should taste like, how people should speak, and how pasta should be cooked."

—Professor Peter Kubelka, essay on the nature and meaning of pasta in *Pastario*, 1985

Bay of Naples, *by H. Rmbg., 1801.*

If there was any circumstance that interrupted Italian culinary history as much as the invasion of the barbarians in A.D. 600, it was the impact of the Second World War. It did not send gastronomy underground, except during those tragic lean years of fighting. But in its aftermath Italy became "modernized," and the cultural differences that had so marked northerners from southerners, Tuscans from Neapolitans, had less and less meaning. Country populations whose kitchen traditions are always purest—elementally connected as they are to the harvest, to husbandry, and to local history and custom—shifted as modern life became more centered around industry and city life.

A traveler in Italy sticking to menus created especially for tourists is particularly unaware of the quiddities of local cuisine. One might journey through the length and breadth of the country and never realize the rich and diverse details of Italy's regional kitchens. Even despite the increasing homogeneity of life in Italy, there are recipes so intrinsic to every region, so much a part of local custom, that they are not likely to be found anywhere else. Some such pasta dishes are impossible to duplicate in foreign kitchens because their nature or the quality of their ingredients is peculiar to local air, climate, and harvest. But here are some specialties that I consider to be original to certain regional Italian tables and possible to make in American kitchens.

[A case in the Bologna court records] judged on June 23, 1909 concerned a postman who, in a Bologna restaurant, had assaulted a visitor from Venice imprudent enough to have run down tortellini. *The Venetian wound up in the hospital and the postman in jail, sentenced to six months—* without tortellini, *the court specified, from which it may be assumed that Bologna has no statute forbidding cruel and unusual punishments.*

—Waverly Root
The Food of Italy

Milanese Women, *by Jules Boilly, 1827. Lithograph by Engelman.*

Malloreddus con Lo Spezzato d'Agnello della Nonna

Malloreddus with Lamb, Sardinian Style

FOR 4 PEOPLE

My Sardinian grandmother used to make this typical rustic regional dish with lamb from the family's flock and the artichokes that grew on the island. *Malloreddus* are a Sardinian macaroni made simply with semolina, a pinch of saffron, and water. They are not usually available here, though I have found them in the form of dried pasta in some Italian grocery stores over the years. Substitute *cavatelli*. This is served as a main course.

1 pound *malloreddus* or *cavatelli* (short, curled forms)

2 pounds (untrimmed weight) lamb shoulder

2 large fresh artichokes

3 tablespoons olive oil

2 medium-sized yellow onions, very coarsely chopped

1 large garlic clove, finely chopped

2 teaspoons chopped fresh mint, or 1 teaspoon dried mint

1½ cups water

1 tablespoon chopped fresh Italian parsley

salt and freshly milled black pepper to taste

1½ cups shelled fresh or frozen green peas (see Note)

Have the butcher trim the fat from the lamb and cut it into bite-sized pieces with a saw (the meat is to be cooked on the bone). Clean the artichokes according to directions for Spaghetti with Artichokes (chapter 7), but do not slice them. Instead, cut them into sixths and leave them in the acidulated water until you are ready to cook them.

In a heavy dutch oven, put 2 tablespoons of the oil, the meat, onions, and garlic. Sauté over low heat just enough to color the meat. When it loses its pink color inside, add the mint and 1½ cups of the water. Cover tightly and simmer gently 1½ hours, stirring occasionally.

Sauté the artichokes in the remaining 1 tablespoon oil for 10 minutes, then add to the meat mixture along with the parsley. Simmer another

10 minutes and check for salt and pepper. At this point, the artichokes should be nearly tender. If they are still quite hard, simmer gently, covered, for a few more minutes. Add unthawed frozen peas and cook another 5 minutes. If using thawed frozen peas, add during last 3 minutes of cooking. If using fresh peas, add at the last minute.

Meanwhile, cook pasta in rapidly boiling, salted water until *al dente*. Drain and while dripping wet, toss with meat sauce in a warm bowl. Serve.

Note: Use fresh peas only if they have been picked very recently, preferably the same day—or better, within several hours. Such peas barely need cooking, so add them 1–2 minutes before the sauce is done. If you have fresh peas that are not straight from the garden, add them about 3 minutes before the sauce is done. Fresh peas that need more cooking than that are not worth eating. Bear in mind that fresh peas deteriorate very rapidly once they are picked, losing all their sweetness and turning starchy and tough. Frozen peas are better than old fresh peas.

"I Cavatieddi" con i Rapini

Cavatelli with Turnip Greens

FOR 6 PEOPLE

A delicious dish from Puglia, a region from which many *contadini* emigrated to America, including my own paternal grandparents. The same dish is also frequently made with *orecchiette* ("little ears"), which are available here in dried form in many Italian food shops. The quality of the olive oil is very important to this and other very simple *pastasciutta* dishes bound by olive oil. *Rapini*, a variety of turnip greens, also goes by the name *rape* (pronounced raap'-eh) or broccoli rabe.

1 pound *cavatelli* (short, curled forms)

1 pound *rapini* (turnip greens)

¼ cup virgin olive oil

4 medium-sized garlic cloves, finely chopped

¼ teaspoon red pepper flakes, or to taste

freshly grated *parmigiano* cheese at table

Wash the greens. Remove and discard any yellowed leaves. Cut off and discard tough stem portions and leave the more tender stems. Cut into 3-inch lengths. Add *rapini* and pasta to rapidly boiling, salted water. Stir several times as pasta cooks.

continued

continued

Meanwhile, in a skillet large enough to hold the cooked pasta later, gently heat the oil with the garlic and red pepper flakes. Do not let the garlic brown. Turn the burner off when the garlic is lightly golden. When the pasta is *al dente,* drain (be sure not to over-drain). Add the pasta and greens to the oil and garlic in the skillet. Toss to distribute the ingredients evenly. Taste for salt, transfer to a warm bowl, and serve. Pass the *parmigiano.*

Note: This dish is also typically made with fresh *orecchiette* formed from semolina dough (Semolina Pasta, chapter 2; halve the recipe). To form the *orecchiette,* shape the dough on a lightly floured board into long "ropes" about a ½ inch in diameter. Slice the ropes crosswise into ½-inch pieces. Place a piece in the slightly cupped palm of your hand. With the thumb of your other hand, flatten each little piece into a concave disk, turning the disk a little as you work so the sides flare. Spread the little disks out on a dry towel until you have finished forming all of them.

Cover them with a slightly damp towel to keep them from drying out. They must not dry or they will not be tender when cooked.

First cook the *rapini* in the boiling, salted water for about 10 minutes. Then drop in the *orecchiette* all at once and cook them together until they are tender, about 5 minutes. Taste one for doneness and cook longer, up to 9 or 10 minutes, if necessary. Because of the thickness of these homemade macaroni, they take longer to cook than other types of fresh pasta. Drain the pasta and the greens, but do not over-drain. Proceed as you would if using dried pasta.

Ziti con Sugo di Rape
Ziti with Rapini

FOR 4–6 PEOPLE

Though this dish might seem similar to *Cavatelli* with Turnip Greens, it is quite different due to the opulent flavoring imparted by the anchovies. Once dissolved in the olive oil, the anchovies are unrecognizable in both form and flavor, but produce a wonderful sauce. I have made a convert of every anchovy hater to whom I have fed this dish. The shape of the *rapini* goes well with a narrow, short tube-type spaghetti. Do not serve this dish with cheese.

1 pound short, slim *ziti*
1½ pounds *rapini* (turnip greens)
½ cup virgin olive oil
1½ 2-ounce cans anchovy fillets

Wash the greens. Discard any yellowed leaves. Cut off and discard all tough stem portions. Use tender stems and the richly colored leaves. Cut into pieces about 2 inches in length. Add *rapini* and pasta to rapidly boiling, salted water. Stir several times as pasta cooks.

Meanwhile, heat the olive oil. Add the anchovies and the oil from 1 can. The anchovies will dissolve completely in the oil, forming a sauce for the *ziti*. When pasta is *al dente,* drain it (be sure not to overdrain) and transfer to a warm bowl. Pour the anchovy sauce over the *ziti* and toss. Serve.

Note: Broccoli can be used interchangeably with *rapini* in this recipe. Wash and trim the broccoli, removing any yellow leaves and tough parts on the stem. Separate the flowerets from the stalk. Cut the stalk into finger-sized slices. Drop all the broccoli pieces into the boiling, salted water with the pasta. Proceed as for *ziti* cooked with *rapini*. Do not serve with cheese.

Vermicelli con le Melanzane

Vermicelli with Eggplant

FOR 6 PEOPLE

A very old Sicilian way of cooking pasta attributed to the Arabs who dominated the island for two hundred years. The eggplant, which is native to India, was introduced to Sicily and Europe by the Arabs. To select the sweetest specimens, read about eggplants in chapter 1. The creamy color of the pasta combined with the deep, glistening purple of the sauce make this dish as beautiful as it is delicious.

1 pound *vermicelli* or spaghetti
1 pound dark purple eggplants
1 tablespoon salt

1 cup olive oil, plus ¼ cup preferably virgin olive oil
¼ cup fresh Italian parsley leaves, torn into pieces
freshly milled black pepper

Cut unpeeled eggplants into strips the length of your finger and about ¼ inch thick. Sprinkle the pieces uniformly with the salt. Place them in a colander standing up, for 30–40 minutes to allow bitter liquid to drain off. Pat dry.

Heat 1 cup olive oil in a pan. When it is hot, deep fry the eggplant pieces until crisp and golden. Turn them over once to fry them on the other side. Remove them from the oil and drain on paper towels. Discard the oil or save it for some other use. Keep the eggplant warm. Put the ¼ cup virgin olive oil in the bottom of a warm bowl.

Meanwhile, cook the pasta in rapidly boiling, salted water. When it is *al dente,* drain it. Transfer it, still dripping wet, to the bowl with the olive oil and toss. Add the eggplant, parsley, and a liberal sprinkling of black pepper and toss again. Serve.

Maccheroni e Finocchiella

Macaroni with Fresh Fennel

FOR 4–6 PEOPLE

A recipe characteristic of the region of Calabria. Fennel has a strong anise flavor, an unusual but delicious taste with pasta. As with the *rapini* sauce recipes in this chapter, the quality of the olive oil is very important.

1 pound medium-sized macaroni, such as shells or short *ziti*
1½ pounds fresh fennel, including feathery leaves
1 teaspoon salt, for boiling fennel
⅓ cup plus 2 tablespoons virgin olive oil
1½ tablespoons salt
¾ cup freshly grated *parmigiano* cheese
freshly milled black pepper to taste
freshly grated *parmigiano* cheese at table

Wash the fennel thoroughly without detaching the ribs from the bulbs. Cut away any brown spots and tough parts on the base of the bulbs, as you would with celery. Cut off the leaves and chop enough of them to measure ½ cup; set aside. Parboil the fennel in 4–5 quarts rapidly boiling, salted water for 8–12 minutes, or until tender but still firm. The length of time will depend on how old the fennel is. Remove from the water

continued

continued

with a slotted spoon and set aside. Reserve the water in the pot. When the fennel is cool enough to handle, squeeze out some of the excess liquid. Reserve the liquid in a separate bowl. Cut the fennel crosswise into thin ribbons.

Gently heat ⅓ cup oil and add the fennel and ¼ cup of the reserved chopped leaves. After several minutes, add the little bit of reserved water squeezed from the bulb. Sauté gently for another 2–3 minutes. Do not overcook the fennel or it will dry out. Keep warm.

Meanwhile, bring the water in the pot back to a boil. Add salt and the pasta. Cook until *al dente*. Have a warm serving bowl ready with the remaining 2 table-spoons oil. (The uncooked olive oil gives a lovely, rich flavor to the pasta.) Drain the macaroni and while drip-ping wet, toss it together with the oil and *parmigiano*. Add the cooked fennel and the remaining ¼ cup chopped fennel leaves. Sprinkle liberally with black pepper and toss well. Serve with additional *parmigiano* at the table.

Pici
Pici

FOR 6–8 PEOPLE

A specialty of certain parts of Tuscany around Siena, *pici* (some-times called *pinci*) are thick, handmade fresh egg noodles of the country table. They are unlike other noodles found in central or northern Italy, being similar to the old noodle of Sicily and Naples that was handmade and rather coarse. It is con-jectured that during the Re-naissance, *pici* traveled to Tuscany from the south and have remained there ever since.

The dough is made with fewer eggs than regular egg pasta, and also with water, for it must be elastic yet soft enough to be formed into the little "ropes" by hand. Because of their thickness, *pici* must be cooked imme-diately and not allowed to dry, or they will become too hard. They are most often served on Sundays and holi-days *alla ragù*. First make a *ragù* or other meat sauce such as Tuscan Tomato and Meat Sauce or Tomato Sauce with Pork, both in chapter 3, or the sauce prepared for Macaroni with Rabbit Sauce in chapter 7.

4 cups unbleached white flour
pinch of salt
¾ to 1 cup water
1 egg
3 tablespoons olive oil
2 tablespoons sweet (unsalted) butter, melted

Prepare a *ragù* (see recipe introduction).

Follow steps 1–3 in Chap-ter 2 (Making Fresh Pasta: Method), adding ¾ cup water to the well with the egg and oil. Add up to ¼ cup more water if needed to make the dough soft and pliable. Roll the dough out about ⅛ inch thick on a lightly floured board. With a knife, cut it into strips ⅛ inch wide, making each of them about 8 inches long.

Roll each strip between the palms of your hands to shape it into a thin, knitting-needlelike form. Spread the *pici* out on clean towels until you have finished forming all of them. Cover them with a slightly damp towel to keep them soft. *Pici* must not dry.

Have the *ragù* ready and warm on the stove. Bring water to a boil, add *pici* and salt (about 2 tablespoons), and cook according to direc-tions in chapter 2. *Pici,* how-ever, take much longer to cook than other types of fresh pasta because of their thickness. Test for doneness and drain. Toss with melted butter in a warm bowl. Pour the *ragù* over the top, toss, and serve.

Fettuccine con Salsa di Noci

Fettuccine with Walnut Sauce

FOR 6 PEOPLE

Salsa di noci is Liguria's traditional accompaniment for *pansoti,* a large, three-cornered *ravioli* stuffed with spinach, swiss chard, or borage. These pasta pillows are similar to the *Tortelli* Filled with Spinach (chapter 5), except for their shape. The walnut sauce is also often used with fresh noodles, particularly *fettuccine* or *trenette,* both of which are thick enough to carry its creaminess. *Salsa di noci* has an unusual base of bread crumbs and a kind of soured milk, which is not available here. I have substituted cream mixed with *mascarpone,* an Italian cream cheese, because I think it produces a close facsimile.

½ recipe (about 1 pound) Egg Pasta I or II, cut into *fettuccine* or *trenette* (chapter 2)

1 slice stale white bread, crusts removed

⅓ cup milk

1 cup walnut meats, lightly toasted

2 tablespoons pine nuts, lightly toasted

½ cup heavy cream

⅓ cup *mascarpone* cheese

¼ teaspoon salt

freshly milled white pepper to taste

¼ cup olive oil (light, not virgin)

3 tablespoons sweet (unsalted) butter, melted

2 tablespoons freshly grated *parmigiano* cheese

freshly grated *parmigiano* cheese at table

Make pasta and set aside. Soak the bread in the milk and when the bread is soft, remove it and squeeze it dry; discard the milk. Add the bread to the toasted walnuts and pine nuts and pound all together in a mortar with a pestle, or grind in a food processor. Combine the cream, *mascarpone,* salt, and pepper and beat with a whisk or a wooden spoon. Add the cream mixture to the nuts and bread mixture and stir. Gradually add olive oil, stirring as you do to amalgamate it with the sauce.

Meanwhile, bring water to a boil, add pasta and salt, and cook to directions in chapter 2. Drain, and while it is still somewhat wet, toss with melted butter in a warm bowl. Add the *parmigiano* cheese and distribute evenly. (If you are using the sauce with fresh filled pasta [see cooking directions, chapter 5], coat the pasta envelopes with the melted butter in a warm bowl as soon as they are drained, leaving them somewhat moist so that the butter distributes easily. Smear with the sauce and sprinkle with *parmigiano.*) Serve immediately. Pass *parmigiano* at the table.

Maccheroni Strascinati

"Dragged" Macaroni with Eggs and Sausage

FOR 4–6 PEOPLE

This hefty, delicious recipe, adapted from Ada Boni's *Il Talismano,* is native to Umbria, a region where pork is favored and fennel is a popular flavoring. *Strascinati* refers to the way the piping hot macaroni is mixed with the raw eggs—quite literally, dragged through until the eggs are cooked by the heat of the pasta.

½ pound *rigatoni* (curved tubes)

1 teaspoon olive oil

2 tablespoons sweet (unsalted) butter

1 pound good-quality lean, sweet Italian sausage meat

scant ½ teaspoon fennel seeds, finely crushed in a mortar

about 1¼ cups beef broth

½ cup freshly grated *parmigiano* cheese

2 tablespoons sweet (unsalted) butter, melted

2 extra-large eggs, beaten

2 tablespoons milk

¼ teaspoon salt

1 tablespoon chopped fresh Italian parsley

freshly grated *parmigiano* cheese at table

It is important that the macaroni be a good, imported Italian brand to hold up under the cooking method in this recipe. Heat the oil and the butter over gentle heat. Add the loose sausage meat, using a wooden spoon to break it up in the pan into small pieces. Be careful not to actually brown it, or it will become hard. Instead, heat it gently only until it loses its raw red color on the outside while remaining a soft pink on the inside, about 6–7 minutes. Still over gentle heat, add the fennel seeds and ½ cup

continued

continued

of the broth. Cook gently for 10 minutes, stirring occasionally.

Meanwhile, boil the pasta in rapidly boiling, salted water until it is only partially cooked, about 4–5 minutes. It should still be hard but not crunchy. Drain and toss with melted butter and ¼ cup of the *parmigiano* and add to the sausage mixture in the pan. Gently toss with a wooden spoon to coat all the macaroni evenly with the sausage and liquid. Stir constantly to bathe the pasta in the broth, but be careful not to break it up. Add the additional ¾ cup broth, a few tablespoons at a time, stopping when the pasta is fully cooked (*al dente*). You may not need all the broth you have. Remove the pan from the burner.

Meanwhile, mix the beaten eggs with the milk, salt, parsley, and remaining ¼ cup cheese. Immediately add the eggs to the macaroni in the pan and remove from heat. Toss to distribute everything thoroughly, using a wooden spoon to quickly "drag" the pasta mixture through the raw eggs. The heat of the pasta will cook the eggs. Taste and adjust seasoning. Turn into a warm bowl and serve. Pass additional *parmigiano* at the table.

Pizzoccheri della Valtellina

Buckwheat Noodles with Cabbage and Potatoes

*P*izzoccheri are the characteristic buckwheat noodles of Valtellina, in Lombardy. Here they are combined with several different flavors in a hearty but surprisingly light vegetarian pasta dish. Spinach or swiss chard is sometimes used instead of cabbage.

½ recipe (about 1 pound) Buckwheat Noodles (chapter 2)

6 quarts water

1 tablespoon salt, for cooking vegetables and pasta

2 or 3 medium-sized potatoes, peeled and sliced about ¼ inch thick

½ pound savoy cabbage, cut into strips ½ inch wide by 2½ inches long

4 tablespoons sweet (unsalted) butter

1 garlic clove, bruised

6 fresh sage leaves, very finely chopped, or ½ teaspoon dried sage

1 leek, well washed of sand and sliced, or 1 large red onion, coarsely chopped

½ cup freshly grated *parmigiano* cheese

¼ teaspoon salt

¼ pound *Taleggio, fontina,* or *bel paese* cheese, sliced and cut into finger-sized pieces

Make the buckwheat noodles. Have ready a 9- by 14-inch baking dish or other ovenproof baking dish large enough to accommodate all the ingredients. Bring water to a rolling boil. Add salt and the potatoes, cover the pot, and return to the boil. Remove lid and with water still at boiling, cook for 4 minutes. Add the sliced cabbage. Cover the pot again and bring to a boil. Remove lid and boil for 5 minutes. Add the noodles and cover. Bring to the boil again. Im-

mediately drain everything together and reserve the stock. Put the pasta and vegetables in a large bowl. Preheat the oven to 450 degrees.

Meanwhile, heat the butter, garlic, sage, and leek or onion and sauté until soft but not browned. Discard the garlic. Add the sautéed mixture, *parmigiano,* and salt to the *pizzoccheri* and vegetables and toss well. Put a layer of the noodle mixture on the bottom of the baking dish. Put a layer of the soft cheese over it and then alternate layers of *pizzoccheri* and soft cheese, ending with a layer of cheese. Sprinkle 2–3 tablespoons of the reserved stock on the top, or enough to moisten the casserole. Place casserole on the next-to-highest rack in the oven for 5 minutes, just enough to melt the cheese. Do not overcook. Let settle for a few minutes. Serve.

Note: Dry *pizzoccheri* noodles can be bought loose or boxed from some Italian food stores. If using dried pasta, add it when you add the cabbage. Cover, bring to a boil, and cook 8–12 minutes or until pasta is not quite tender. Proceed as directed in recipe.

Cappellacci con la Zucca

Cappellacci Filled
with Squash

FOR 8 PEOPLE

Ferrara, in the region of Emilia-Romagna, is home to this extraordinary dish. Its principle ingredient is a type of Italian squash (*zucca gialla*) similar in appearance to our pumpkin. The flesh of the squash is firmer and sweeter than that of American pumpkins, however. I have found the butternut squash to be a good substitute. Sweet squash is an unusual taste in Italian cooking, but this dish always makes converts of skeptics.

A similar dish, called *tortelli di zucca,* is made in the town of Mantua in Lombardy. The filling includes squash, a little apple purée, eggs, nutmeg, and *parmigiano* or *grana* cheese.

1 recipe (about 2 pounds) Egg Pasta I (chapter 2)

4 pounds butternut squash (2½ cups prepared)

1⅓ cups freshly grated *parmigiano* cheese

½ teaspoon nutmeg, preferably freshly grated

½ teaspoon salt

¼ teaspoon freshly milled white pepper

½ pound (1 cup) sweet (unsalted) butter, melted

To prepare the squash for the filling, preheat oven to 350 degrees. Cut each butternut squash in half lengthwise. Remove and discard seeds and stringy fibers. Place the halves on a baking sheet, face down, and bake for 45 minutes, until tender. (In a microwave, this is done in 9–11 minutes.) Remove the squash from the oven and let cool until it can be handled. Then pare the skin and put the flesh in a fine sieve. Drain for 1 hour to remove excess moisture. Purée squash with a ricer, through a food mill, in a food processor, or mash very finely with a fork. Combine the squash with ⅓ cup of the *parmigiano,* nutmeg, salt, and pepper and blend to a smooth consistency.

Make the pasta dough and roll it out as for *tortellini* (chapter 5), but cut the circles about 3 inches in diameter. Put a little mound of filling in the center of each disk and form the *cappellacci* in the same way as for *tortellini,* into little "hats"; they will just be larger. Spread them out on waxed paper or foil-lined trays to dry, turning them every few minutes to prevent them from sticking. This is a moist filling, so keep in mind that you cannot leave the *cappellacci* out too long or the filling will seep through the dough.

Cook the *cappellacci* in boiling, salted water according to step 3 in the general directions for *tortellini* and *cappelletti* found in chapter 5.

(They may also be frozen in the same manner as *tortellini;* see step 4 of same section.) Drain and place in a warm bowl with melted butter; make sure all of the *cappellacci* are coated with the butter. Sprinkle with remaining 1 cup *parmigiano.* Serve.

Variation: *Cappellacci* are sometimes served with sage-flavored butter, a lovely combination.

Weights and Measures

Dry Measures

1 pound = 16 ounces = 453 grams

2.2 pounds = 1000 grams = 1 kilogram

1 ounce = 28 grams

3.5 ounces = 100 grams = 1 ectogram

Liquid Measures

1 cup = ½ pint = 8 fluid ounces

1 tablespoon = ½ fluid ounce

1 teaspoon = ⅙ fluid ounce

1 pint = 16 fluid ounces

1 quart = 2 pints = 32 fluid ounces

4 cups = 1 quart

4 quarts = 1 gallon

Miscellaneous

4 cups flour = 1 pound

2¼ cups sugar = 1 pound

4 cups grated or shredded cheese = 1 pound

2½ pounds fresh tomatoes =
2½ cups peeled and seeded tomatoes with their juice

2½ pounds fresh tomatoes =
1 28-ounce can Italian plum tomatoes

1 35-ounce can Italian plum tomatoes =
3 cups peeled and seeded tomatoes with their juice

1 stick butter = 8 tablespoons = ½ cup

3 pounds solid shortening = 7 cups

7 ounces uncooked spaghetti or macaroni = 4 cups cooked

2 teaspoons fresh herbs = 1 teaspoon dried

*Pulcinellas at the Roman Carnival, by
Bartolomeo Pinelli, 1835.*

Credits

W. GRAHAM ARADER III, NEW YORK

ii (*Nova Italiae Delinatio,* ["New Map of Italy"], by Joan Blaeu, *Atlas Major,* Amsterdam, 1664), 14T (by Pierre Antoine Poiteau, in *Histoire Naturelle des Orangers,* Paris, 1818–20), 27, 38 (in *Les Liliacees,* Didot, Paris, 1802–16), 39 (in *Histoire Naturelles des Plantes Grasses,* A.P. Decandolle, Paris, 1798–1805), 42B, 48, 53, 126

From *A Curious Herbal,* by Elizabeth Blackwell, London, 1737–39: 7, 34, 112

From *Hortus Eystettensis,* illustrated by Wolfgang Kilien and others, published by Basil Besler, Eichstatt, 1613: 36, 37, 40TB, 46, 78

From *Ictyologie ou Histoire des Poissons,* by Berlin and Paris, 1782–87, engravings by Marcus Elieser Bloch: 47, 99, 131

MUSEO STORICO DEGLI SPAGHETTI, COLLEZIONE AGNESI, PONTEDASSIO (IMPERIA), ITALY

2, 3, 5, 6, 11B (c. 1940 illustration for Liebig stock cubes), 15, 17T, 18LR, 19, 22, 23, 26TB, 28, 31, 49, 52 (from plate III of *Description et Details des Arts du Meunier, du Vermicelier et du Boulanger,* by M. Maulin, 1767), 60 (c. 1940 illustration for Liebig stock cubes), 61, 66, 105, 117, 120, 130 (by De Vito, 19th century), 133, 134, 138 (cover of Atlantic Macaroni Company booklet, 1905), 139 (c. 1940 illustration for Liebig stock cubes), 146, 147, front and back covers

THE NEWARK PUBLIC LIBRARY

13T, 16LR, 17B (by Brogi), 35T, 35B (painting by Alonzo Chappell), 79, 121TB (Rossini portrait after painting by Ary Scheffer, Verdi by H. Voltergio)

THE NEW YORK ACADEMY OF MEDICINE

11T (from 9th-century German hand copy of *De re coquinaria* by Apicius, in Rare Book Collection, 80 (from *Libro nuovo nel quale si insegna a far d'ogni sorta di vivande,* by Cristoforo di Messi Sbugo, published by G. DeBuglhat et A. H. Compagni, Ferrara, 1549), 81 (engraving by C. LaPlante after drawing by E. Ronjat), 119

From *The Royal Cookery Book,* by Jules Gouffé, Sampson, Low, Son, and Marston, London, 1868 (unless otherwise noted, engravings by C. LaPlante after drawings by E. Ronjat): 4 (*Paste,* woodcut after drawing by E. Ronjat), 29, 33, 68 (by E. Ronjat), 77 (by E. Ronjat), 84, 85, 88, 94, 104, 140, 142, 144, 152 (artist unknown)

THE NEW YORK PUBLIC LIBRARY

10 (bust of Horace by E. F. Burney, English, 1760–1845), 12 (from *Decisive Battles of the World,* vol. I, by Sir Edward Creasy, Colonial Press, New York, 1899), 43, 74 (from *The Nürnberg Chronicle, 1493*), 106, 150, (from *Ackermann's Repository of Arts,* vol. 4, plate 34, Strand, London, 1810

From *Come Posso Mangiar Bene?,* by Giulia Ferraris Tamburini, Milano, 1921: 76, 148

From *Il Cuoco Moderno,* by Antonio Barberis, Torino, 1910: 25T, 31B, 45T, 50T, 55, 65, 107, 140B

From *La Gastronomia Moderna,* by Carla Giuseppe Sorbiatti, Milano, 1911: 13B, 32, 125, 143

From *Le Livre de Patisserie,* by Jules Gouffé, Paris, 1873: 9 (engraving by C. LaPlante after drawing by E. Ronjat), 54 (engraving by Hildebrand after drawing by E. Ronjat), 58 (by E. Ronjat), 59T (by E. Ronjat), 62 (engraving by Hildebrand after drawing by E. Ronjat)

From *Practical Pastry,* by Fred T. Vine, London, 1907: 30B, 59B

From the Spencer Collection: 129 (from *Raccolta di Costumi Romani*), 132 (from *Raccolta di Costumi Romani*), 155

ADDITIONAL SOURCES

American Immigration Museum, National Park Service, Liberty Island, New York: 118B

Animal Art in the Public Domain, by Harold Hart, Hart Publications, New York, 1983: 136

Art Resource, New York: 25B, 118T

Armour company: 24

Joan Bard, San Francisco: 96 (artist unknown, 19th century)

Bertolli USA, Inc., Secaucus, New Jersey: 45B

Aldo Bozzi, Mezzaluna restaurant, New York: 67

Burndy Library, Norwalk Connecticut: 42T

Center for Immigration Studies of New York, Inc.: 8

Laura Cornell: 63, 71, 75, 82, 86, 100, 111, 113, 123, 124, 127, 151, 154

Houlgate Davenport: 101

Paolo Destefanis: 57TB

Edward Orme publishers, London: 30

Fini, Modena, Italy: 44

Food and Drink, A Nineteenth Century Pictoral Archive, edited by Jim Harter, Dover Publications, New York, 1980: 64, 69, 98, 103, 114, 128, 137, 153

Gebbie & Husson Co., Ltd., London, 1890: 140T

Gerardo di Nola, S.p.A., Castellammare di Stabia (Naples), Italy: 70, 87

Donna Guardino: 73

Maccaronee, by Merlin Cocai, 1521, via *Antichi Dolci di Casa,* Silvia Tocco Bonetti, Idea Libri, Milano, 1984: 91

Winifred McNeil: 92, 108

The Metropolitan Museum of Art, New York: 89

Meyer's Universum: Illustration and Description of the Most Seeworthy and Noteworthy Things of Nature and Art on the Entire Earth, published by Verlag von Bibliographischen Institut, Hildburghausen, Germany, 1850–52: 20 (detail)

San Vitale di Luppi, S.p.A.: 90

SAPIO, S.p.A., Bari, Italy: 149

Sardinia Export, Inc., New York: 135

Tableau des Principaux Champignons Comestibles, et Veneneux ("A Poster of the Principle Edible and Poisonous Mushrooms"), by various artists, published by Paul Dumée, Paris: 41

Taormina Company, Donna, Texas: 109

Index